Anonymous

An Act to Incorporate the Carpenters' Company of the City and

County of Philadelphia

By-laws, rules and regulations; together with reminiscences of the Hall, extracts

from the ancient minutes, and catalogue of books in the library

Anonymous

An Act to Incorporate the Carpenters' Company of the City and County of Philadelphia
By-laws, rules and regulations; together with reminiscences of the Hall, extracts from the ancient minutes, and catalogue of books in the library

ISBN/EAN: 9783337386641

Printed in Europe, USA, Canada, Australia, Japan

Cover: Foto ©Suzi / pixelio.de

More available books at **www.hansebooks.com**

AN ACT TO INCORPORATE

THE

CARPENTERS' COMPANY

OF THE

City and County of Philadelphia;

BY-LAWS,

RULES AND REGULATIONS;

TOGETHER WITH

REMINISCENCES OF THE HALL,

EXTRACTS FROM THE ANCIENT MINUTES,

AND

CATALOGUE OF BOOKS IN THE LIBRARY.

Published by Direction of the Company.

PHILADELPHIA:

H. C. COATES, PRINTER.

1873.

CONTENTS.

NOTE.

THE READER will find a repetition of some Facts in the following pages, arising from the articles being compiled at distant periods, and by different hands. It was thought best to republish, without attempting a condensation of them.

INTRODUCTION.

In no nation does the history of its early institutions possess more interest than those of our own country, where, while associating for "the mutual good," the germ of self-government was carefully guarded, and the embryo master-spirits fostered, who contributed finally to mould a nation's destinies.

One of the earliest Associations in Pennsylvania, and perhaps the oldest now existing, is The Carpenters' Company of the City and County of Philadelphia, maintaining an uninterrupted organization from the year 1724, about forty years after the settlement of the colonial government by William Penn. Among the early associators were many whose names are prominent in colonial history, and whose architectural tastes are impressed on the buildings that yet remain, memorials of that early day.

James Portius, whose name is second on the list of members, designed and executed Penn's mansion, on Second Street, above Walnut; and the lively interest he felt in the association with his fellows, induced him at his decease, in 1734, to bequeath his works on architecture to the Company.

Edmund Wooley, from plans by Robert Smith, (both members,) erected the "State House," on Chestnut between Fifth and Sixth Streets, assisted by the amateur labors of Dr. J. Kearsley.

The primary object of the Association was to "obtain instruction in the science of architecture; to assist such of its members, or the widows and children of members, as should be by accident in need of support;" and the adoption of such a system of measurement and prices "that every one concerned in building may have the value of his money, and every workman the worth of his labor." The difference between the plain, simple buildings erected in the province and those in the "mother country" was such, that it became necessary to examine the "method of measuring," as according to the "system practised in England," the prices were "set on the general and not on the particular parts of the work."

The price of admission (thirty shillings,) led, after the lapse of a few years, to the formation of a similar association, under the title of "The Second Carpenters' Company," but after a few years of separate existence, their efforts for a union with the first Company were successful, and they, according to their own declaration, "joined, and became members of the old Company." in 1752.

To build a hall for the use of the Company was an object of early interest, and the minutes show, by the appointment of committees to fix upon "a proper lot of ground," that it was never lost sight of. A determined effort was made in 1763, but it was not attained until 1768, when the present "lot on Chestnut Street" was purchased, at an annual ground rent of "176 Spanish milled pieces of eight." and conveyed to trustees appointed by the Company. Many schemes for its improvement were suggested. A proposition to unite with the Library Company of Philadelphia in erecting a "building that might accommodate both," was, among

others, seriously entertained, but· no feasible plan was
matured until 1770, when, "as the funds were not sufficient," it was agreed to open a subscription among the
members of the Company, in shares of four pounds each,
and when the sum subscribed shall amount to " three
hundred pounds," the Company, shall "appoint a number to begin to erect a building." Robert Smith prepared " a sketch of a building," and the subscription
paper having been filled in about one week to the required amount, a certificate was given to each subscriber,
entitling, "according to the sum advanced," to receive
a dividend " as often as rents of the building shall be
received by the Company's treasurer."

The fee of admission was raised in 1769 to four
pounds. This caused the formation of " The Friend-
·ship Carpenters' Company," whose admission fee was
·· five shillings." It was not long before overtures were
made to " their elder brethren " on the " different methods used in measuring and valuing carpenter work."
To this it was replied, that the mode of measuring and
valuing carpenter work pursued by their elder brethren was " more equitable, expressive, and satisfactory
than any method practised in the city before, and was
not inferior to the best method practised in any city in
the King's dominions."

The plan of building being adopted, it was commenced on the " 5th day of the second month, 1770."
The duties assigned the building committee were " dis-
charged with fidelity," and the building " so far completed that the annual meeting in 1771 " was held therein,
and during that year the Library Company of Philadelphia rented and removed " their library to the second
story of the new building," where it continued until
1782. Though the amount subscribed was more than
that proposed, yet it fell short of finishing the Hall;

hence the "outside finish of the doors and windows was deferred until the sums advanced by the several members were fully paid."

In 1775 the efforts of the Friendship Carpenters' Company to effect a union were renewed, and a committee of conference appointed; but it was not accomplished until 1785, when the members thereof, on " the payment of four pounds each to the treasurer, and signing the articles of association," were admitted into membership.

The Hall was freely used at the beginning of the Revolution. The committee appointed " at a general meeting of the inhabitants of the city and county " met therein on the second day of the sixth month, 1774, and "as Governor Penn had declined to convene the Assembly," they appointed three of their number to wait upon the speaker, and request "a positive answer whether he would call the Assembly together or not." They had the use of the Hall during their appointment.

On the 15th following, the " different county committees" met therein to consult the Philadelphia committee on " what was best to propose" to the General Assembly, which was to meet on the 18th inst. Their resolves "declaratory of the sense of the province," and the necessity for a " general congress of delegates from all the colonies," are matters of historical record. The regular quarterly meeting of the Company was not held, in order that these deliberations might not be interfered with.

AN ACT

TO INCORPORATE THE

CARPENTERS' COMPANY

OF THE

CITY AND COUNTY OF PHILADELPHIA.

WHEREAS, it appears to this Assembly that, in Preamble.
the year one thousand seven hundred and twenty-
four, a number of the House Carpenters of the
City and County of Philadelphia formed themselves into a Company, for the purpose of obtaining instruction in the science of architecture, and
assisting such of their members as should by accident be in need of support, or the widows and
minor children of members; and for the further-
ance of the said charitable and useful designs, did
for many years pay into the hands of the masters
of the said Company considerable sums of money;
a great part whereof was expended in the relief
of their unfortunate members, and the remainder
was appropriated, in the year one thousand seven
hundred and sixty-nine, to the obtaining a large
lot of ground, on which were several buildings
and other improvements, and towards the erecting
of the house known by the name of the CAR-
PENTERS' HALL in the said city: *And whereas,*
the members of the said Carpenters' Company
have prayed that they may be incorporated in
such manner as to secure the said estate to them
and to their successors, in order to further the
useful and charitable design of the institution;

2

And whereas, this Assembly is disposed to exercise the power vested in the legislature of the commonwealth for the encouragement of useful and charitable purposes : *Be it therefore enacted, and it is hereby enacted by the representatives of the Freemen of the Commonwealth of Pennsylvania in General Assembly met, and by the authority of the same,* That, for the purpose of promoting the useful and charitable objects before mentioned, the present members of the Carpenters' Company; that is to say, Isaac Zane, John Mifflin, Joseph Thornhill, Benjamin Loxley, James Worrell, Gunning Bedford, Thomas Nevell, James Armitage, Samuel Griscom, James Pearson, William Roberts, Richard Armitt, James Potter, George Wood, Joseph Rakestraw, Silas Engles, William Lownes, Samuel Powell, William Robinson, James Bringhurst, James Graisbury, Thomas Shoemaker, David Evans, William Colliday, William Ashton, Samuel Jervis, Samuel Wallis, Matthew McGlathery, Thomas Proctor, Adam Zantzinger, John Keen, John Lort, Joseph Govett, Joseph Ogelby, William Williams, Robert Allison, George Forepaugh, John Smith, Mathias Sadler, James Gibson, George Ingles, Frazer Kinsley, James Corking, Joseph Rakestraw, Junr., Joseph Thornhill, Junr., John King, Andrew Boyd, Conrad Bartling, William Garrigues, John Rugan, Mark Rhodes, Robert Evans, Joseph Wetherel, Hugh Roberts, Isaac Jones, Samuel Pancoast, Mathias Val Keen, Wm. Stevenson, Robert Morrel, Richard Mosley, John Reinhard, Samuel Pastorius, Josiah Matlack, John Piles, Joseph Clark, William Zane, Benjamin Mitchell, Thomas Savery, Nathan Allen Smith, Samuel Jones, John Hall, Joseph Howell, Junr., Israel Hallowell, John Harrison, Ebenezer Ferguson, John Cooper, William Linnard, Jonathan Evans, Joseph Worrell, James Boyer, be, and the same persons are hereby created

Members of the Carpenters' Company.

a body corporate and politic in deed and in name, Created a body by the name and style of " *The Carpenters' Company* corporate and politic. *of the City and County of Philadelphia,*" and by the same name they and their successors are hereby constituted and confirmed one body corporate and politic in law, to have perpetual succession, and to be able and capable to receive any sum or sums of money, or to receive, purchase, have, hold and enjoy any goods, chattels, lands, tenements, rents, hereditaments, gifts, devises and bequests, of what nature soever; either in fee simple, or any less estate or estates, or otherwise; and also to grant, alien, assign or let the same lands, tenements, rents, hereditaments, and premises, according to the tenures of the respective grants and bequests made to the said corporation, and of the estate of the corporation therein : *Provided*, That the clear yearly value of such real estate exceed not the value of one thousand pounds lawful money of this commonwealth.

Sect. 2. *And be it further enacted by the authority* Their powers, *aforesaid*, That the said corporation, by the name, &c. style and title aforesaid, be and shall be for ever hereafter, able and capable in law to sue and be sued, plead and be impleaded, answer and be answered unto, defend and be defended, in any court or courts, or other places, and before any judge or judges, justice or justices, or other persons whatsoever, within this commonwealth or elsewhere, in all and all manner of suits, actions, complaints, pleas, causes, matters and demands of whatsoever kind or nature they may be, in as full and effectual a manner as any other person or persons, bodies politic and corporate, may or can do.

Sect. 3. *And be it further enacted by the authority* Empowered to *aforesaid*, That the said corporation shall have make a seal. full power and authority to make, have and use one common seal, with such device and inscription as they shall judge proper, and the same to break, alter or renew at their pleasure.

General meetings, when to be held. SECT. 4. *And be it further enacted by the authority aforesaid,* That, for the well ordering of the affairs of the said corporation, there shall be a general meeting held of the members, on the third Monday or second day of the week in January, in every year hereafter, at the CARPENTERS' HALL, or such other place as they may direct, when a majority of those convened shall choose by ballot a president, a treasurer, and such and so many assistants, and such other officers or committees as they may judge necessary or useful; and shall have full power and authority to order quarterly and special meetings of said corporation, and do and transact all business and matters appertaining thereunto, agreeably to such rules, ordinances, regulations, and by-laws as may hereafter be made concerning the premises: *And* the corpora- The corporation to make by-laws, &c. tion at any of their said meetings shall have full power and authority to make and ordain such rules, ordinances, regulations and by-laws as a majority of the Company met shall from time to time judge necessary or convenient, and the same to put in execution, or to revoke, disannul, alter or amend at their pleasure: *Provided always,* That the said rules, ordinances, regulations and by-laws relate only to the useful and charitable purposes before mentioned, and be not repugnant to the laws of this commonwealth.

Officers to be regulated by by-laws, &c. SECT 5. *And be it further enacted by the authority aforesaid,* That the duties and the authorities of the officers, the times of meeting of the corporation, the admission of members, and the other concerns of the said corporation, shall be regulated by the by-laws and ordinances thereof: *Provided,* That no by-laws or ordinances of the said corporation shall be binding on the members or officers unless the same shall have been pro-

posed at one regular meeting of the corporation, and
received and enacted at another, after the interven-
tion of at least thirty days; and that no sale, aliena-
tion or lease for more than two years of any part of
the real estate of the said corporation shall be valid,
unless the terms or nature of such sale or lease be
proposed at a previous meeting of the corporation as
aforesaid.

SECT. 6. *And be it further enacted by the authority* No misnomer to
aforesaid, That no misnomer of the said corpora- or grant.
tion and their successors shall defeat or annul any
gift, grant, devise or bequest to the said corporation, if the intent of the donor shall sufficiently
appear by the tenor of the gift, testament or other
writing, whereby any estate or interest was intended to pass to the said corporation; nor shall
any non-user of the rights, liberties, privileges,
and authorities, or any of them hereby granted to
the said corporation, create or cause a forfeiture
thereof.

SECT. 7. *And be it further enacted by the authority* Duty of the Pre-
aforesaid, That, the president, assistants, wardens, other officers.
and committee appointed by the Company at their
meeting on the eighteenth day of January, one
thousand seven hundred and ninety, shall continue
to act in their several stations, and do and perform
the duties assigned them, for and during the remainder of the year, or unto the third Monday [or
second day of the week] in January, one thousand
seven hundred and ninety-one.

Signed by order of the House,
RICHARD PETERS,
Speaker.

Enacted into a law, in Philadelphia, on Friday, the
second day of April, in the year of our Lord one
thousand seven hundred and ninety.
(Signed) PETER ZACHARY LLOYD,
Clerk of the General Assembly.

Inrolled 7th June, 1790.

I, Mathew Irwin, Esquire, Master of Rolls, for the State of Pennsylvania, do hereby certify the preceding writing to be a true copy [or excmplification] of a certain law inrolled in my office.

In witness whereof, I have hereunto set my [L. S.]   hand and seal of office, this 26th day of July, Anno Domini, 1792.

(Signed)   MATHEW IRWIN, M. R.

BY-LAWS

OF

THE CARPENTERS' COMPANY

OF THE

CITY AND COUNTY OF PHILADELPHIA.

SECTION 1. The stated meetings of the Company Stated meetings. shall be held on the third Monday in January. April, July, and October, in each and every year. at the Hall, or such other place as the Company may, from time to time, direct. Twenty-five members shall form a quorum for the transaction of business.

SECT. 2. The Company shall, at their stated Elections, when meeting in January, elect, by ballot, a President, to be held. Vice-President, Secretary, and Treasurer, who shall be elected for one year; a Managing Committee, consisting of nine members, three of whom shall be elected annually, to serve for three years: and three Wardens, one of· whom shall be elected annually, to serve for three years; *Provided,* That no member shall be eligible to serve for more ·than three years in five, as President, Vice-President, or Secretary, nor for more than three years out of four as a member of the Managing Committee.

SECT. 3. If, from any cause, the Company shall Provision for be unable to elect their officers at the time pre- filling office in case of vacancy. scribed in these by-laws, the officers then in power shall continue to perform the duties of their respective offices until their successors be chosen;

and all vacancies occasioned by death, resignation, or otherwise, shall be supplied at the first stated meeting after such vacancies shall be known to exist, except in the office of Treasurer.

Duties of President and Vice-President. SECT. 4. The President, or in his absence the Vice-President, shall preside at all meetings of the Company, regulate the debates, and state the question when any matter is to be determined, also have the casting vote, and cause such entries to be made as shall be determined by the Company. And he shall affix the corporate seal of. the Company to powers of .attorney, to enable the Treasurer to satisfy or release mortgages whenever required by the Managing Committee. In the absence of the President and Vice-President, the members shall choose a President pro tem.

Special meetings. SECT. 5. The President, or in his absence the Vice-President, with the concurrence of three members of the Managing Committee, or upon the request of five members of the Company, shall have full power to call special meetings, by directing the Wardens, in writing, to notify the members.

Duty of the Secretary. SECT. 6. The Secretary's duty shall be to keep fair minutes of the proceedings of the Company, with marginal references; he shall furnish the Managing Committee regularly with a copy of such minutes as may, in any wise, relate to their duties; notify all committees of their appointment, and the duty assigned them: call the roll at each meeting precisely at the time adjourned to; he shall notify members of their election, and his books shall be left in charge of the Managing Committee, the first Wednesday after the Company's meeting.

Treasurer to give bonds—his duties. SECT. 7. The Treasurer shall give such security as may be required by the Managing Committee, in any sum not exceeding double the amount that may probably come into his hands, the bonds to be given within ten days from and after his election; he shall receive all moneys belonging to the Company, and deposit the same in the name of the Company in such bank, or other institution paying interest, as the Managing Committee may direct, and pay the orders of the Managing Committee, or as shall otherwise be ordered by the Company; he shall keep in his custody all the books, papers, and effects of the Company, not otherwise disposed of; he shall have full power and authority to receive the principal, and enter satisfaction on the Record To enter satisfaction. of any mortgage now held, or that may hereafter be held by the Company, whenever requested so to do by the Managing Committee; he shall report the condition of the treasury at each monthly meeting of the Committee, and in the week preceding the meeting in January, in every year, shall settle his accounts with the committee of three members, who Settle his accounts. shall be appointed by the President, or in his absence the Vice-President, at the meeting in October, for that purpose, and at the expiration of his term of office, shall pay the money, and deliver the books and effects in his hands, belonging to the Company, to his successor; and in case of the death, resignation, or Death or resignation. removal of any member chosen as Treasurer, the President, or in his absence the Vice-President, shall call a special meeting of the Company, within ten days after such death, resignation, or removal, and the Company, when met, shall proceed to elect, by ballot, some other member to serve as Treasurer, for the unexpired term.

SECT. 8. The Managing Committee shall hold Duties of the Managing Committee. stated meetings monthly, and on the Wednesday evening next succeeding the annual meeting of the Company, in each year, five of whom shall be a quorum for the transaction of business; they shall Rent the property. choose, by ballot, a Chairman and Secretary. The Chairman shall preside at the meetings of the Committee, and in his absence a Chairman pro tem. may be appointed; the Committee shall have power and authority to lease such portions of the estate of the Company, not reserved for their use, for any term not exceeding two years, for the best price that can reasonably be obtained, and take care that the property belonging to the Company be kept in repair; they shall have power

Invest funds.
to invest all surplus funds in loans of the United States, the State of Pennsylvania, the City of Philadelphia, or in first mortgages on real estate, well secured, taking security in the name of the Company; they shall settle all accounts and contingent expenses of the Company, and shall represent this Company at all meetings and elections of corporate bodies in which this Company own stock; they may delegate one of their number to vote in such manner as they may believe best for the interest of this Company, and for this purpose

May appoint proxies.
may execute a proxy, from time to time, under the corporate seal of the Company. They shall cause to be transcribed in a book provided for that purpose, all laws, alteration in by-laws, and resolutions of a permanent nature that may be passed by the Company, as soon after adoption as possible. They shall have prepared, and placed in a conspicuous

List of members.
place in the hall, a complete list of the members of the Company, together with the date of their joining, and of such as have deceased, the time of such decease, and provide for the continuance of the same hereafter. They shall, at the first meeting in every year, or at any subsequent meeting,

Appoint collectors.
when they may judge proper, appoint one or more of their number to collect all the rents and other income of the Company, and the collector or collectors so appointed shall give such security as may be required by the Committee, in any sum not exceeding double the amount that may come into his or their hands; the collectors shall keep a book, and enter therein all the moneys they shall

receive for the Company, and take receipts in the
same for all payments made to the Treasurer, and
shall make monthly reports to the Managing Committee of all the several sums received and paid
by them, as aforesaid, which the Committee shall
cause to be entered upon the minutes of their
transactions. They shall have discretionary power
to increase the quarterly allowance of members to
seventy dollars, and widows to thirty-seven and a
half dollars, and shall have power to grant inter-
mediate relief, not exceeding twenty-five dollars in
each quarter, to our widows and superannuated
members.

SECT. 9. It shall be the duty of the Wardens Duties of the
jointly, to notify the members of the meetings of Wardens.
the Company, at such time and place as may be
directed by the Company or President, or in his
absence the Vice-President, by written or printed
notices, left at their respective dwellings, within
the two days preceding the day appointed for
meeting, under a penalty of ten cents for each
member omitted; and at the quarterly meetings
are to collect the quarterages, penalties and fines Collect penal-
due to the Company: they shall also notify the ties, &c.
members of the funerals of deceased members.
On the death of any member residing in the city,
on due notice having been given them, they shall Provide car-
procure such number of carriages, as they shall riages.
think will be sufficient for the use of members attending such funeral; they shall report the death of Report death of
any member at the first meeting of the Company members.
thereafter, with the date of his decease, when the
same shall be entered on the minutes of the Company. They shall keep a book containing the
names of all the members, and enter in the same all
moneys they shall collect in their wardenship, and Pay to the col-
pay it to the collector immediately after each meet- lector.
ing, taking his receipt in said book; and in case of
the decease, removal or resignation of any officer

of the Company, they shall enter upon the notices
that another is to be elected in his place, and shall
also give notice when any person is to be balloted
for, and shall enter on the notices the quarterages
and fines due. They shall notify all members who
are two-years or upwards in arrears, to "come
forward and pay their arrearages or show cause
why the same is not paid, or otherwise the 18th
section of the By-Laws will be enforced against
them:" (the seal of the Company shall be attached
to such notices with the signatures of the President and Secretary,) and make report thereof to
the Company at their next meeting.

SECT. 10. There shall be a Committee on the
Book of Prices, consisting of five members, one
of whom shall be elected annually by ballot, at
the stated meeting in January, to serve for five
years, whose duty it shall be to fix a price on all
new-fashioned Carpenter work, that may be in-
troduced from time to time; and further to equal-
ize such of the prices as may be requisite, and to
enter the same in the manuscript book to be kept
by them in the Hall for that purpose, for the use
of the members of the Company. At all times a
majority of the committee shall constitute a quorum for the transaction of business. It shall be
the duty of the said committee to settle any differences that may arise in the measurement and
valuation of Carpenters' work, between Carpenters and their employers, or between members of
the Company measuring work together, and their
decision shall be binding on the parties as respects
the prices of said work. It shall also be the duty of
said Committee to meet on the first Wednesday
of each month, or at such other time as they may
agree upon, and in case of a vacancy by death,
resignation, or otherwise, such vacancy shall be
filled at the next quarterly meeting of the Company.

SECT. 11. Every member of this Company that is disposed to measure Carpenter work hereafter, provided he shall have been a member at least five years, shall apply to the Managing Committee for a certificate to that effect, and on approval thereof, they shall give such certificate, under the seal of this Company, to be signed by the President and Secretary: *Provided always*, That such applicant, before he receives his certificate, shall make oath or affirmation, before an Alderman or Justice of the Peace, that he will well and truly measure and value Carpenter work. agreeably to the standard Book of Prices of this Company, to the best of his judgment and ability. always having special regard to the quality of the work. If any member of this Company shall measure or value Carpenter work not having been qualified, and received a certificate agreeably to the by-laws regulating measures. such member shall, on sufficient proof thereof, be fined the sum of ten dollars for the first offense. and for the second shall be liable to expulsion, provided that this shall not be so construed as to affect the right of members to measure and value their own work. *(Measurers of Carpenters' Work. Make oath or affirmation. Penalty.)*

SECT. 12. At the stated meeting in January, the Company shall elect by ballot, a Committee on Vice and Immorality. It shall consist of three members, one of whom shall be elected annually, to serve three years, whose duty it shall be to admonish such members, if any there be, who to their knowledge, shall be in the practice of any immoral conduct; and, if their efforts to reclaim them should prove ineffectual, it thall be their duty to report such members to the Company, who shall take such order thereon as to them may appear just and proper. *(Committee on Vice and Immorality.)*

SECT. 13. Any person chosen to any office, and refusing to serve, shall pay ten dollars, unless he has already served in that office; and if any *(Penalty for refusing to accept of office.)*

member shall be absent at roll-call, on due notice of the time and place appointed for quarterly or **Fines.** special meetings, he shall pay a fine of twenty-five **Quarterages.** cents; and every member at each quarterly meeting shall pay fifteen cents into the stock, for the use of the Company.

Relief—to whom granted. SECT. 14. Any member, widow or minor children of a member, being by sickness or accident, in reduced circumstances, making application to the Managing Committee, they may relieve him, her or them, at their discretion, in any sum not exceeding forty dollars, until the next quarterly or special meeting: and if further aid be deemed necessary, shall lay a statement of their circumstances before the Company, who shall determine what may be further necessary to be done. Such widows during their widowhood, shall be entitled **Quarterly allowance.** to receive from the Company the sum of one hundred dollars per annum, payable quarterly, provided such widow shall certify to the Managing Committee her willingness to receive the same.

Election of members. SECT. 15. Any master Carpenter following the business, making application to be admitted a member of this Company, shall be proposed at one meeting, and balloted for at the next, or some subsequent meeting; such person, being approved of by two-thirds of the Company met, on paying **Entrance fee.** one hundred dollars admission money, and signing the Constitution, shall be a member. If any person so chosen, having proper notice thereof, and neglecting to attend at the next stated meeting of the Company, after his election and pay as aforesaid (unless sickness or some other sufficient reason be given), shall not be a member unless re-elected. Provided that no person having one or more partners, shall be elected unless all the members of the firm apply, and the ballot shall be taken at the same time upon all, and no member of a firm thus elected shall be deemed a member, unless they all appear together, sign the Constitution, and pay the entrance fee as aforesaid.

SECT. 16. After the decease of a member of this Company, leaving sons, being master Carpenters following the business, the eldest of whom having been proposed and balloted for as aforesaid, and of good character, may be admitted without paying any admission-money. Eldest son of deceased member may be admitted without fee.

SECT. 17. If any difference arise between members, relating to the trade, the person who thinks himself aggrieved may apply to the President, or in his absence the Vice-President. who, with the Committee on the Book of Prices, shall endeavor to accommodate the affair; but if their efforts prove ineffectual, the parties are at liberty, each of them, to choose two members, the President or the Vice-President and Committee to choose another member, in addition to the four so chosen; and those persons, or any three of them, are to determine the matter, and report their proceedings to the President, or in his absence the Vice-President, for the information of the parties, who are required to acquiesce in the determination of the said referees. But if either of the parties shall refuse to abide by the decision of the referees, the President, or in his absence the Vice-President, shall lay the case before the Company at their next meeting, who shall take such action thereon as may appear necessary. Disputes between members—how settled. Choose referees.

SECT. 18. If any member neglects or refuses to pay the fines or quarterages due to the Company, for two or more years, unless exonerated therefrom, or otherwise disregard the laws or determinations of the Company at their meetings, such person shall no longer be a member of this corporation, and his name shall be erased from the list of members: *Provided, nevertheless,* that this Arrearages. Name to b erased.

section, so far as respects fines for non-attendance, is not intended to extend to those members who reside five or more miles from the place of meeting, or to those who are sixty-five years of age.

Proceedings to be kept secret. SECT. 19. If any member shall communicate the sentiments of any of the members, when discussing a question in debate, to any person not a member, he shall pay ten dollars; and in case of a second offense, shall be expelled from the Company.

Expulsion for immoral conduct. SECT. 20. If any member by such immoral conduct as, in the judgment of this Company, is disgraceful, or shall abscond with a view of defrauding his creditors, and satisfactory proof thereof being made to the Company, he shall no longer be a member: *Provided, nevertheless*, that should it appear to the Company that the widow or minor children of a member who has so transgressed do conduct themselves in an orderly manner, they shall be attended to by the Company, as to them may appear proper.

Book of Prices not to be shown. SECT. 21. If any member show the Book of Prices to any person not a member, he shall pay for the first offence, five dollars, for the second offense, the further sum of ten dollars: for the third offence, or showing the Book of Prices, as aforesaid, so that a copy be taken therefrom, such member shall be expelled.

Measurement of work. SECT. 22. If any Member of this Company shall measure or value Carpenter work, or be concerned in measuring with a measurer of any other company, on proof thereof, at their meeting, shall be expelled.

Committee on Library. SECT. 23. The Committee on the Library shall consist of three members, one of whom shall be elected at each stated meeting in January, to serve three years, whose duties shall be to have the care of the Library, and attend to the enforcement of all rules for its government that may be approved of by this Company; and they may purchase such books on Architecture, History, or the Arts and Sciences, as a majority of them may deem expedient, and for that purpose, the sum of one hundred dollars is hereby annually appropriated, and the Managing Committee are directed to pay all bills approved by said Committee not exceeding the amount hereby appropriated or accumulated. Any member borrowing books, must conform to the rules laid down for the regulation of the Library.

Annual appropriation to Library.

SECT. 24. All rules and regulations that are hereby altered and supplied, be, and they are hereby repealed.

RULES AND REGULATIONS

PRESERVATION OF ORDER AT THE TIMES OF MEETING.

RULE I. The President to take the chair at the time adjourned to, when the members shall take their seats, and the business proceed in the following order :

1. The roll shall be called, and absentees noted.

2. The absentees called, and any member, not answering to to his name, fined.

3. The rules for the preservation of order, and the 19th and 22d Sections of the By-Laws shall be read.

4. The minutes of the Company shall be read.

5. The minutes of the Managing Committee shall be read.

6. Unfinished business.

7. New business.

8. Balloting for members.

9. Elections.

RULE II. No member shall introduce any subject of conversation foreign to the intention of the meeting : and all resolutions and propositions offered shall be in writing, signed by the member offering.

RULE III. Only one person shall speak at a time, he standing up and addressing the President ; and no member shall speak more than twice to one question without leave.

RULE IV. The yeas and nays shall be taken upon any question when requested by five members, and recorded upon the minutes.

RULE V. If two members rise to speak at the same time, the President is to decide who shall be first heard.

RULE VI. No member shall leave the Company when met, without permission from the President.

RULE VII. Any member transgressing the preceding Rules, shall be called to order by the President ; he not complying, shall be personally named ; when on refusal, he shall be subject to such penalty as may be directed by the Company.

STANDING RESOLUTIONS.

Resolved, That no Measurer of the Company shall re-measure work until the first Measurers have been paid, and sufficient security be given that re-measuring will be paid, or that it has been paid in advance; and that any member transgressing the above shall be fined in the sum of twenty dollars.

Resolved, That hereafter, at the annual election of officers and committees of the Company, they shall all be voted for upon one ticket, and tellers appointed by the President, who shall receive the ballots and report the result to the Company.

Resolved, That at each stated meeting in October, nominations shall be made of suitable members of this Company to serve as officers thereof, to be elected at the ensuing stated meeting in January, and the Secretary shall furnish a list of such persons to the Managing Committee, who shall obtain for the use of members a sufficient number of tickets with all the names so nominated thereon, and in the exact order in which they were named, with notice on the margin or bottom of the number to be elected to each office. The notices served on the members in October, shall have the words "nominations will be made at this meeting for officers to be elected at the stated meeting in January" upon them.

Resolved, That for the future, the Wardens be, and they are hereby directed to make no provision at our anniversary suppers, other than such as may be required for the accommodation of the members, on the days upon which our anniversary meetings are held.

Resolved, That the Wardens and Managing Committee be, and they are hereby instructed, not to purchase any spirituous liquors, to be used at the next, or any subsequent anniversary supper of the Company, and that hereafter, no bill shall be paid by the Treasurer for that article, that may be for the use of the Company, or any of its committees.

Resolved, That the Committee on the Book of Prices report, at each stated meeting of the Company, all the alterations made in the Book of Prices, if any there should be.

Resolved, That the illumination decorations be put in place, and lighted on each succeeding celebration of the anniversary of American Independence.

Resolved, That the meeting of any association or society in this Building be strictly forbidden, provided that this resolution shall not apply to the "Captains' Society of the City and County of Philadelphia."

CARPENTERS' HALL.

In a country so new as this, there can be but little, yet, of the interest which springs from the memories of the past,—from the storied recollections which cling to old places and things, and which now give to so many scenes in the old world, their never-dying interest, and even of that little here, the unsparing hand of what we call Progress, which too often tears down and destroys, only because its object has grown gray and venerable, deprives us of the lessons which these mute walls would give us, of the men who have figured, and the acts which have been done within them—lessons fraught with profitable instruction, with wisdom and patriotic impulses.

There are probably few associations in this country which can now trace an unbroken existence as far back as "The Carpenters' Company of the City and County of Philadelphia," nor are there many buildings which have so well stood the test of time, and been connected with so many stirring incidents of our Revolutionary history, as the old Hall which still belongs to it. Reverence for the memory of those who have gone before them, attachment for the old building which has been so intimately connected with the history of their country and city, and a belief that its story is instructive and valuable, has induced its present members to withdraw the Hall from the purpose of trade and commerce for which it has been recently used, and to devote it hereafter to the objects of the Company, and the recollections of the past.

On the occasion of taking formal possession of the Hall on the 5th of September, 1857, the Managing Committee, in reporting their proceedings to the Company, took occasion to accompany their report with various extracts from the minutes of the Company, and with the names of the officers of the Company from its date to the present time, as far as practicable.

The Company having directed that such portions of this report should be printed for the use of the members as might be deemed proper by the Managing Committee, the present brief summary of the History of the Association and its Hall, has been prepared in obedience thereto.

It was as early as the year 1724, about forty years after William Penn first landed on these shores, that the Master Carpenters of the City and County of Philadelphia organized an Association called the " Carpenters' Company."

The object of this Association, as expressed in the subsequent act of incorporation, was to obtain instruction in the science of Architecture, and to assist such of their members as should by accident be in need of support, and of the widows and minor children of such members.

Among the first results of this Association, was the fixing of a uniform scale of prices upon their work, so that the workman should receive a fair compensation for his labor, and the employer obtain a fair value for his money.

From this early beginning has come down the present "Book of Prices," by which all carpenter's work in the City of Philadelphia is regulated, and which is believed to be as just and equitable as it is possible to attain.

Some time after the parent Company was organized, another society was formed, having the same objects in view, but, in 1752, it united with the original body. Again in 1769, still another similar association was organized, which continued an independent existence until the year 1785, when, after negotiations through committees of each body, the last Company, called the "Friendship Carpenters' Company," was admitted into membership, and became part of the original association.

The minutes of the Company from 1724 to 1763, have unfortunately been lost, but sufficient data still remain to trace its continued existence by history.

In the year 1763 the attention of the Company seems to have

been first attracted to the construction of a hall, and a committee was appointed to select a suitable site for the purpose. It was not, however, until February 3, 1768, that the ground upon which the Hall now stands was procured. The original lot, 66 feet on Chestnut Street by 255 feet in depth, was purchased at an annual ground rent of 176 Spanish milled pieces of eight, of fine silver. A portion of this ground on its eastern side was subsequently sold, leaving at present an entrance to the Hall on Chestnut Street, by what is known as Carpenters' Court. The funds of the Company not being sufficient to erect the building, the necessary amount was raised by loan, principally among the members, and among its most valued relics, is still preserved in a glass case, the original paper of subscription.

A plan being adopted, the building was commenced on the 5th day of February, 1770. It was soon found, however, that the amount raised was not sufficient to entirely complete the building; but the members being averse to incurring any considerable debt, it was resolved that the Company would occupy it in its unfinished condition, and accordingly, the first meeting was held in the Hall January 21st, 1771. The building was not entirely completed until 1792.

On the 5th of September, 1774, the first Continental Congress met in the Hall, and commenced that series of deliberations which ultimated, on the 4th of July, 1776, in declaring the Colonies " Free and Independent."

When Congress met, Mr. Cushing made a motion that it be opened by prayer. Accordingly, on the following day, the morning after news had been received of the cannonade of Boston, the Rev. Jacob Duché, then Pastor of Christ Church, opened the proceedings with solemn prayer. " Washington was kneeling there, and Henry, and Randolph, and Rutledge, and Lee, and Jay, and by their side stood, bowed in reverence, the Puritan Patriots of New England, who, at that time, had reason to believe that an armed soldiery were wasting their humble households. They prayed fervently for America, for the Congress, for the province of Massachusetts Bay, and especially for the town of Boston." " I saw the tears," said Mr. Adams, "gush from the eyes of the old pacific Quakers of Philadelphia."

On the 26th of October, Congress, having concluded its business, dissolved itself, but was called together again on the 10th of May, 1775, at the State House, where it afterwards continued to hold its sessions.

The Provincial Assembly also occupied the Hall for its deliberations, during this and the following year. Christopher Marshall, in his diary, under date of October 24th, 1775, says: "Past two, went and met part of Committee at Coffee House, and from thence went in a body to Carpenters' Hall, in order to attend the funeral of Peyton Randolph, (the first President of the first Continental Congress,) who had departed suddenly after dinner last first day, at the country house of Richard Hill; then proceeded to Christ Church, where a sermon was preached by Jacob Duché; then to Christ Church burial-ground."

When the British took possession, in 1777, of the city of Philadelphia, a portion of their army were quartered in the Hall, and continued there during the time they occupied the city. The soldiers made a target of the vane on the cupola, and several holes were drilled through it by their bullets.

In 1787, the United States Commissary General of Military Stores occupied the Hall, and from 1773 to 1790 the books of the Philadelphia Library, then the nucleus only of the magnificent collection which now exists, were also deposited there. It is here worthy of remark, that during the time the British occupied the Hall, no loss was sustained by the Library Company, who, at the same time, occupied the second story; the officers, without exception, left deposits and paid hire for the books borrowed by them.

In 1777, the library room was occupied by the sick soldiery.

In 1791, the Society quit meeting in the Hall, and from that time to 1797, the building was occupied by the first Bank of the United States, as a banking house. The Bank of Pennsylvania also transacted its business therein during 1798, 1799, and 1800.

In 1797 and 1798, the United States used it as a Land Office, and from 1802 to 1817, the Government occupied it as a

Custom House, at which latter time, the Second Bank of the United States took possession, and continued there until 1821. In 1822, the Musical Fund Society held its meetings within the Hall, followed in 1825 by the Franklin Institute, who occupied it for its sessions, and in 1827, the Society of Friends used it as a meeting-house.

During the Revolutionary period, the Carpenters' Hall was also used for the sessions of various temporary organizations intimately connected with the stirring events of that time. Thus, for instance, the various city and county committees convened for mutual council and defence, as well as meetings for the establishment of American manufactures of wool, cotton, flax, &c., was held within it.

Many of the members of the Company have, at different times, occupied prominent positions in the social, political, and Revolutionary history of Philadelphia, and the names of the progenitors of many of our best-known citizens will be found recorded on its rolls. Few, especially of the older public buildings, were constructed without the aid of its associates, and even down to the present day, most of the important public improvements have had the benefit of the practical skill and knowledge of its members.

The State House, commenced in 1729, and finished in 1734, was built by Edmund Wooley, a member, from the plan of Robert Smith, as architect, also a member, assisted by the amateur labors of the Rev. J. Kearsley, who had considerable skill and taste in architectural matters. Penn's Mansion, still existing in Second Street, above Walnut, and one of the oldest memorials of the past yet left to us, was constructed by Jos. Portius, another member, who, upon his death, which occurred in 1734, bequeathed to the Company all his books on architecture.

The contributions of its members, and the increase in the value of its property, has enabled the Carpenters' Company to accomplish much good, and to extend efficient assistance to necessitous members, and especially to their widows and orphans. Among the proudest testimonies to the Society, is the fact that several well-known men in this community, who are recognized as useful citizens and successful busi-

ness men, owe their advantages in life to the education which
the Company provided them under the obligation of their
charter.

The Company are in possession of a well-selected library.
numbering about 2,500 volumes, which was commenced in
1736, and now embraces many of the standard works in all
departments of knowledge, especially in those connected
with the objects of the Association, which books are accessible, not only to each member, but also to all the inmates
of his family.

In restoring their ancient Hall, the Carpenters' Company
have adhered as closely as possible to the original plan of the
building.

The first story, in which the Continental Congress assembled, has been carefully renovated, and various articles of furniture placed therein which tradition says were in use in 1774,
as well as other articles made to conform as far as possible to
their style and appearance. Prominent among these. on either
side of the platform, are two old-fashioned chairs, which it is
believed were used by the officers of that Congress, and which
are labelled " Continental Congress, 1774." The upper rooms
have been fitted up for the library. and the accommodation of
the Superintendent.

In the future, it is the intention of the Company that this
old memorial of the past shall be devoted to its original
purpose, and aid in keeping alive the interesting memories
which attach to it, and with this view, strangers and citizens
will be afforded an opportunity of visiting and inspecting
this relic of the most interesting periods of the city's
history.

REMINISCENCES.

AT a meeting of the Carpenters' Company of the City and County of Philadelphia, held April 28th, 1856,* the following resolutions were unanimously adopted :

" 1. *Resolved,* That it is expedient for the Company to remove as soon as possible to the old Hall.

"2. *Resolved,* That the Managing Committee immediately take the necessary measures for obtaining possession, and fit up for the meetings of the Company, and for the accommodation of the Superintendent, the building on the south end of Carpenters' Court, known as Carpenters' Hall, and that in such fitting up especial care be taken to preserve, as much as possible, every feature in said Hall as it now exists indicative of its original finish."

Agreeably to the foregoing resolutions, the Managing Committee, having obtained possession on the 23d day of May, 1857, proceeded to prepare the building for the use of the Company, and having completed the duty assigned them, agreed to notify the Company to meet this day, September 5th, 1857, being the eighty-third anniversary of the meeting of the first Congress in this Hall.

* This meeting was held in the usual place, second story of building, west side of court.

To the Carpenters' Company
of the City and County of Philadelphia.

Report of Managing Committee.

The Managing Committee, who were charged with the duty of fitting up the old Hall, report the same completed and now ready for occupation by the Company.

On the 4th ult., the second story being nearly completed, the family moved in, and on the 15th ult. the Committee met for the first time in their room. This was done in order the sooner to let the building lately occupied by the Company.

The Committee present to the Company the following statement (being extracts from our minutes), as matter worthy of record, and as a means in future of easy and useful reference.

> JAMES HUTCHINSON,
> MICHAEL SHAFFER,
> RICHARD K. BETTS,
> CHARLES CONARD,
> THOMAS T. SHUSTER,
> SAMUEL WILLIAMSON,
> MICHAEL ERRICKSON,
> D. R. KNIGHT,
> JOHN WILLIAMS,
> Managing Committee.

PHILADELPHIA, September 5, 1857.

Extracts from Ancient Minutes.

1763.

AT this meeting the following members were appointed a committee to set prices to various sorts of carpenter's work, which is to be laid before the whole Company for their approbation at our next meeting, viz.: Robert Smith, John Thornhill, Joseph Thornhill, Gunning Bedford, Thomas Nevell, Benjamin Loxley, Abraham Carlile, James Worrell, William Dilworth, John Goodwin, James Pearson, Joseph Rush.

Committee on pricing work.

APRIL 18th, 1763.

At a general meeting of the Carpenters' Company, agreed to continue the former committee to finish their proceedings about regulating the prices of all kinds of carpenter's work, which is to be laid before the Company at the next meeting of third Monday in July, which will be the 18th day. Likewise the following members were appointed: Joseph Fox, John Thornhill, John Goodwin, Benjamin Loxley, and Gunning Bedford, to fix upon a proper lot of ground to build a hall for the use of the said Company, when their proceedings are to be laid before the Company. Likewise there was eight new members entered, and paid their entrance-money and quarterages, and their proportionable part of the expenses of the committee.

Committee on lot.

New members.

1763.   JULY 18th, 1763.

Inquiries for a   At this meeting it was desired that the com-
lot.   mittee should continue their inquiries after a
proper lot of ground to accommodate the Com-
pany for building a hall, and to make report. It
was likewise desired, as our Master Fox had informed the Company at our last meeting of a lot
of ground in the possession of John Ross, Esq.,
which was approved of by the Company met, and
our Master was desired to treat about the lowest
price, and make report.

Committee on pricing work and on lot continued.

There does not appear anything in the minutes
in relation to a lot for building since the above
1768.   until 1768, when the lot now owned by the Company, upon which this Hall and the building in
front now stand, together with the lot on the east
Purchase of lot. side of court (since sold) was purchased by the
Size.   Company February 3d, 1768, being 66 feet front on
Price.   Chestnut Street by 255 feet deep; the price was
an annual ground rent of 176 Spanish milled
pieces of eight, of fine silver, each 17 penny-
weights and 6 grains. It was first conveyed by
George Emlen and wife to Benjamin Loxley,
Thomas Nevel, and Robert Smith, and on the
15th of January, 1770, conveyed to the following
Trustees.   members, who had been elected Trustees, viz.:
Gunning Bedford, John Goodwin, James Pear-
son, Joseph Rakestraw, Abraham Carlile, Thomas
Shoemaker, and James Bringhurst. (A deed of trust
executed January 16th, 1770.)

APRIL 18th, 1768.

Sketch of build-   At this meeting, the Company taking into con-
ing presented. sideration the improvement of their lot, Robert
Smith exhibited a sketch for a building to be
thereon erected, and the members were desired
to consider when will be a proper time to begin the
building, &c.

FEBRUARY 1st, 1769.

1769.

At this meeting present 28 members. Entrance fee at this time, four pounds.

APRIL 17th, 1769.

At this meeting, the former committee were appointed to treat with the Library Company of Philadelphia, respecting their joining with this Company in a building suitable for a Carpenters' Hall and for a Library, and, if necessary, to call our Company together to lay the matter before them.

OCTOBER 23d, 1769.

At this meeting, the copy of deed to the trustees, and declaration of trust from them to the Company, were again read, and there appearing no proper provisions in the said declaration to indemnify the said trustees or their heirs from the bond given to George Emlen, it was concluded by the Company that there should be a clause inserted in the declaration of trust to indemnify the said trustees.

Resolutions to indemnify Trustees.

JANUARY 16th, 1770.

1770.

At this meeting, it was proposed that the members present should think of some method or scheme to get a hall erected, if possible, next summer.

To think of some method for building Hall.

JANUARY 19th, 1770.

At this meeting, Gunning Bedford and James Bringhurst were appointed to endeavor to let part of the lot, viz., 26 feet front by 140 feet deep, east of the 14 feet alley.

Committee to let part of lot.

JANUARY 30th, 1770.

At this meeting, a motion was made that a convenient building should be erected on their lot on Chest-

Proposition to build.

nut Street, to meet in as occasion may require, to
transact the business of the Company, and to calcu-
late and settle their private accounts of measuring
and valuing carpenters' work ; and as the funds are
not sufficient, it was agreed to open a subscription amongst the members of the Company, which
shall be divided into shares of four pounds each, and
when the sum subscribed shall amount to £300, the
Company shall appoint a number to begin to erect
the building, the plan and dimensions of which shall
be fixed by a majority of the Company, and as soon
as the foundation is laid, the sums subscribed shall be
due, and when paid into the hands of the Company's
treasurer, he shall be empowered to give to each, on
the payment of the subscription, a certificate for the
receipt of so much, which certificate shall entitle every
member, according to the sum he has advanced, to receive a dividend as often as the rents of the building
shall be received by the Company's treasurer, till the
whole is repaid that has been advanced by the several
members.   And as every member of the Company
will have an equal property and advantage in the
building, it will be necessary for them to set a rent
on said building, which shall in part be paid from the
Company's money or stock, in order to repay those
members that do advance, till the whole of the subscriptions are repaid ; and at the death of any one of
the members, if any part of his subscription should
not be repaid, that part shall be due to his heirs, &c.,
as part of his personal estate, and paid, agreeable to
the tenor of his certificate.

The Company have appointed the following persons
to take subscriptions of the members for the uses above
mentioned, viz.: Robert Smith, Abraham Carlile,
Thomas Shoemaker, Benjamin Loxley, John Thornhill, and John Goodwin.

FORM OF SUBSCRIPTION.

Now we, the subscribers, having considered the
above proposal, do promise to pay to the treasurer

Loan.

When to be re-
paid.

Plan to repay
loan.

Heirs of deceas'd
member to be
paid.

Committee to re-
ceive subscrip-
tions.

Form of sub-
scription.

appointed by the Carpenters' Company the several 1770.
sums that stand against our names, as soon as £300
is subscribed and the foundation of the building is
laid. Witness our hands, &c.

The above copy of subscription paper having Committee to procure sub-
been several times read, was agreed to, and then scribers.
the members present proceeded in signing it, and
the persons before named were appointed to apply
to the rest of the members and others, to endeavor
to get what they could added to the subscription
already begun, and when they have got £300 subscribed, the Company are to be called together in
order to nominate persons to undertake the care and
oversight of erecting the Hall.

FEBRUARY 5th, 1770.

The subscription paper being nearly filled up to the
sum required, the Company were warned, and met at
their own house (on this day) in order to consider of Plan and size for
a plan and dimensions for a Hall. It was proposed Hall.
in the first place to fix on the dimensions, which after
being considered was agreed should be 40 by 50 feet,
or not to vary more than a foot more or less, that to
be left with the committee who shall be appointed to
see it carried out. The following twelve members
were appointed as a Building Committee, viz.: Robert Building Com-
Smith, Benjamin Loxley, Abraham Carlile, James mittee.
Pearson, John Goodwin, James Bringhurst, Gunning Bedford, Joseph Rakestraw, Thomas Nevell,
James Worrell, John Thornhill, and Thomas Shoemaker.

APRIL 16th, 1770.

A meeting was held this day on our own lot.

APRIL 18th, 1770.

At this meeting James Worrell mentioned that
Evan Peters told him he would give £4 towards the
Hall; he is therefore requested to speak to Evan

4

1770.

Pump.

Peters to make a pump to have an iron chamber in it, and fix in the old well on the lot, and to agree with him to wait as long as he can for the remainder of the money.

JULY 16th, 1770.

Committee from Friendship Co.

At this meeting Hezekiah Herbert, Samuel Clark, and Richard Jones, came with a letter from Friendship Carpenters' Company, which being read and considered, it was thought necessary to be reconsider- at a meeting to be called on other business the 23d inst.,* at 6 o'clock, at this place.

DECEMBER 20th, 1770.

Ball and vane.

At this meeting Benjamin Harbeson was paid £7 for ball and vane.

1771.

January 21st, 1771, Hall first occupied by the Company.

1772.

JANUARY 20th, 1772.

Library Company.

At this meeting it was agreed that the Library Company might be accommodated in the new Hall, and a committee was appointed to confer with said Library Company in reference to their application.

1773.

JANUARY 18th, 1773.

£300 borrowed.

The Company borrowed of Joseph Fox £300 for the purpose of finishing the building and to pay debts.

1774.

JANUARY 17th, 1774.

Chairs and tables.

At this meeting, James Graisbury agreed to give 15 shillings towards the chairs, and Joseph Ogilby and Joseph Govett agreed to make four tables, Matthew McGlathery two, and Ezekiel Worrell two, for the use of the Hall, and the Committee is desired to give directions for the size and mode of making them.

* There does not appear any minutes of a meeting on the 23d of July, as referred to above.

APRIL 25th, 1774.   1774.

The Committee on Prices of Work produced a book Book of Prices.
this evening, which was read.

APRIL 26th, 1774.

At this meeting, it was thought advisable to choose Person to have
by ballot a proper person to take care and keep our charge of Hall.
Hall and furniture in order, to make fires, to put
out the same, when the different companies meet,
in order to prevent, if possible, any danger that
might happen through neglect, for the want of such a
person.

When Mr. —— (Here the minute ends.)

By determination of a ballot in general this even- Book of Prices.
ing, that the Book of Prices, which hath been lately
revised by a committee chosen for that purpose, and
laid before the Company at a meeting the 18th inst.,
which received their sanction, being audibly read by
the Moderator.

And further agreed, that every member choosing a
copy of the prices, must write them in the Hall, as
the book is to be lodged with the Committee only.

NOTE.—The stated meeting of July 18th, 1774, Provincial Com-
was not held, in consequence of the Provincial Com- mittee.
mittee meeting in the Hall.

AUGUST 1st, 1774.

The Company taking into consideration the state Pump.
of our pump, it being used in general by the neighborhood, think it advisable that every family who are
able, shall pay at the rate of six shillings per year;
and we further direct Isaac Lafever to collect the
same for the benefit of the Company, commencing the
1st of August, 1773, being one year's water-money
due this day.

1774.   SEPTEMBER 5th, 1774.

Congress.   The Delegates to the First Congress met in the Hall this day, and continued to meet therein until the 26th of October inclusive.

Total number of members, 55.

For history of their proceedings, see book in our Library, No. 1301, commencing page 7.

NOTE.—No minutes from August 1st, 1774, to January 17th, 1775. January 16th, 1775, part of lot, 26 feet on Chestnut Street, by 140 feet deep, sold to Joseph Pemberton.

1775.   JANUARY 17th, 1775.

Provincial Convention.   At this meeting, it was agreed that the Provincial Convention might meet in the Hall; to pay ten shillings per day.

APRIL 20th, 1775.

No more to be expended, &c.   At this meeting, it was agreed, that as the Hall is so far finished as to accommodate the Company, that no more money be expended on the premises, until the sums advanced by the several members be fully paid, except it be necessary for repairs, or by voluntary subscriptions hereafter for that purpose; and it is

Accounts to be adjusted. further agreed that all the accounts relative to the building of the Hall, &c., be brought in as soon as possible, and adjusted by the Committee, and a certificate be given by the Master and assistants, for the time being, for the balance that shall be found due on said account.

Friendship Company.   James Pearson and Thomas Nevell informed the Company that, on conversing with several members of the Friendship Company of Carpenters, it appears that there is a desire of the majority of the members of said Company to join with us, and as many inconveniencies do frequently arise by continuing in a separate state, the members now met in order to

remove such inconvenience and facilitate a union of   1775.
the respectable master carpenters; we do appoint
Joseph Fox, Gunning Bedford, Thomas Nevell, Abraham Carlile, James Worrell, and James Pearson, a
committee to confer with a committee that is or may
be appointed by the other Company, respecting said
union, and report their proceedings to the next meeting of this Company.

JANUARY 26th 1776.   1776.

At this meeting a standing Committee on Pricing Committee on
Work was chosen, consisting of twelve members.   Prices.

The Company taking into consideration the trouble Taking care of
Mrs Lafever has in taking care of the Hall, have Hall.
agreed to allow her ten pounds per year.

NOTE.—There appears to be no minutes between a
special meeting held April 26th, 1776, and October
23d, 1778, which appear next in the book.

The British troops had possession of the Company's
property from September 26th, 1777, to June 18th,
1778,—8 months and 23 days.

OCTOBER 23d, 1778.   1778.

At this meeting James Pearson reported that he Occupants
had suddenly been called upon by the Barrack-master-
General, and having no opportunity to consult with
members, did set the rent of the lower story and
cellar of the Hall, at £110 per annum, to the U. S.
Col. Flower, Commissary-General of military stores
department. Although the price was considered low
by the Company, yet under the circumstances, it was
sanctioned. The rent of the said part of the Hall,
for the time it was occupied as a store, office, &c., for
the use of the United States, previous to the English
troops taking possession of the city, was fixed at the
rate of £60 per annum.

It was agreed that John Hanlan's rent, for one Rent.
year two months and sixteen days, ending the 10th of
August, 1778, amounting to 32l. 2s. 6d., in consider-

1778. ation of the house, or a great part of it, being occupied
by the British troops while in this city, shall be £20
in full of said rent.

NOVEMBER 9th, 1778.

A special meeting of the Company was held at the
house of Thomas Nevell.

DECEMBER 14th, 1778.

Company met at Thomas Nevell's.

At this meeting it was agreed to meet at the Hall
at the annual meeting, and George Wood and John
Keen, wardens, are appointed to give notice to the
Company, and to provide some refreshments at said
meeting.

1779.   JANUARY 18th, 1779.

First meeting in   Annual meeting held in the Hall. At this meeting
Hall after the
British left. it was unanimously agreed that no fines be required
No fines, &c. of the members of the Company since the 17th of Jan-
uary, 1774, until this meeting. At this meeting the
Rent. rent of first story and cellar, occupied by Commissary-
General, was raised to £180, from January 1st, 1779.

Brand. Joseph Rakestraw was appointed to have a brand
made with the words thereon, "Carpenters' Company," and to brand the chairs and other articles belonging to the Company.

APRIL 19th, 1779.

Joseph Rakestraw reports that he has provided a
brand, which cost £9 15s.*

At this meeting a part of the lot was rented to
the Commissary-General on behalf of the United
Brassfounder States, for the purpose of building a brass-founder
and file-cutter and file-cutter shop, at an annual rent of £25; the
shop. rent to commence April 1st, 1779.

* We suppose this to be Continental money.

JULY 19th, 1779.

1779.

At this meeting it was thought that the Library Company ought to pay at least four times the usual annual rent, in lieu of the sum of £30 payable from said Library.

NOTE.—The proposition last stated was agreed to and paid by the Library Company, and the ground rent of lot was paid at the same rate.

OCTOBER 16th, 1780.

1780.

At a quarterly meeting of the Company held at the house of William Jones, but few members attending, it was judged proper to adjourn the meeting to Wednesday, the 18th inst., at 5 o'clock in the evening, when the Wardens are to give the following notice, viz.:

October 18th, 1870.

You are earnestly requested to attend a special Copy of notice. meeting of the Carpenters' Company, at the front house on their lot, at 5 o'clock this evening, to take in consideration matters of the utmost importance to the Company, when a rule is to be proposed for paying quarterages and fines in some proportion to the depreciation of money.

OCTOBER 18th, 1780.

At this meeting the Committee appointed on the In relation to 5th of January last, were directed to take such fur- taxes. ther steps as they shall judge most proper to have the Hall and estate belonging to the Company exempted from the payment of taxes, and if such exemption cannot be obtained, to use their utmost endeavors to collect the rents and pay the taxes.

The consideration of fines, &c., was postponed un- Fines, &c. til the annual meeting in January, 1781.

Quarterages and
fines to be paid
in specie, &c.

The Company taking into consideration the quarterages and fines, have agreed that all quarterages and fines after this evening shall be paid in specie, or the value thereof in current money.

APRIL 30th, 1781.

Certificate.

At this meeting Thomas Nevell reported that he had procured one hundred and thirty blank Certificates of Membership, printed on parchment, and that he paid 30 shillings, State money, for the parchment used for that purpose, and that Mr. Francis Bailey generously gave the printing to the Company.

At this meeting thirty-nine of the certificates above mentioned were signed and sealed, and delivered by Mr. Rhoads to the Committee on Accounts, to be delivered to the members, on their complying with the terms of admission.

JULY 16th, 1781.

Smith's forge.

At this meeting application was made by the Commissary-General for permission to erect a smith's forge on the Company's lot, in front of the Hall; when, on being put to vote, it was unanimously determined that none should be erected nor any part of the yard incommoded. The Committee on Rents, &c., are directed to pay proper attention to these directions.

1782.   JULY 22nd, 1782.

Library Company.

The Library Company having, at the meeting 15th of July last, made application to know upon what terms they may be permitted to occupy the second story of the Hall, after the expiration of their lease, it was now agreed that the said Library Company can have the second story at £80 per annum.

OCTOBER 21st, 1782.

Admission fees.

At this meeting, it was agreed that, in future, any member that may hereafter be admitted, do pay such entrance as may be agreed on by the Company at the time of their admittance.

JULY 21st, 1783.

At this meeting, George Forepaugh, Thomas Nevell, James Pearson, George Engles, and Robert Allison, were appointed a committee to act with other committees of manufacturers and mechanics, in considering the propriety of preparing and presenting a memorial to the honorable Assembly of this Commonwealth, to lay such duties or imposts on foreign manufactures imported into this State, as on mature consideration may be judged useful and necessary.

Committee on manufactures, &c.

It was agreed to adjourn to the 28th instant; and it was the unanimous opinion, that at the adjourned meeting the first business entered upon shall be to appoint a committee to make application to the Legislature for an act to incorporate the Carpenters' Company.

Act to incorporate.

It was also proposed that William Moulder, Thomas Pryor, and Jacob Graff, be requested to survey and regulate the Carpenters' Company's lot, and make out the bounds thereof.

Survey of lot.

JULY 28th, 1783.

This was a special meeting, called as stated in the last minute. " The Company not meeting generally, the members that met thought proper to postpone the meeting until some other opportunity, when each member will expect to get notice." Ten members only were present.

JANUARY 17th, 1784.

In consequence of the inclemency of the weather, and several other causes, there was no meeting of the Company at this time.

The election for officers, and other business belonging to the annual meeting, (omitted as above,) was attended to at a meeting held April 12th, 1784.

APRIL 19th, 1784.

Chest.   At this meeting, "the Company considering the frequent disappointments to the Company, owing to the want of their books being lodged in a convenient place, do authorize the Committee of Rents, &c., to procure a proper chest, and lodge it in their Hall, to contain the papers, &c., belonging to them; and Matthew McGlathery was requested by the Committee of Rents, &c., to make a chest for the use of the Carpenters' Company, 3 feet 10 inches long, 20 inches wide out to out, and 13 inches deep, besides two drawers beneath, of 5 inches deep; a till at the right end, and divisions for three bottles, &c., at the other end; a good lock with two keys to the upper part, and a lock and two keys to each drawer, and handles at each end, and painted chocolate color."

JULY 19th, 1784.

Committee on Book of Prices.   At this meeting, the Committee on Book of Prices reported progress, and were continued.

OCTOBER 18th, 1784.

Entrance fee.   At this meeting the admission-money was fixed at £6.

DECEMBER 27th, 1784.

Committee from Friendship Company   At this meeting (held at James Patton's) a Committee from the Friendship Carpenters' Company attended, and informed they were appointed by their Company to confer with a Committee appointed by our Company, on such topics as would be useful to the carpenters in general.

After some conversation, the finishing of the business was referred to Joseph Rakestraw, James Pearson, and George Engles.

JANUARY 17th, 1785. 1785.

At this meeting it was agreed that the Committee on Accounts (consisting of 13), should be continued for one year, and to be a standing Committee, to transact all business relating to the Company, and report thereon.

Committee on Accounts.

MARCH 1st, 1785.

Special meeting. "The Committee report that they have had several conferences with the Committee of the Friendship Carpenters' Company, respecting sundry matters relative to the reputation and benefit of the trade, and generally agree, that a union of the two Companies would best promote the above design."

Friendship Company.

The Company proceeded to consider the propriety or utility of the aforementioned union. The question being put, Shall the Friendship Carpenters' Company be received into union with this Company? Which was carried in the affirmative.

A second question being put: On what terms shall the Friendship Carpenters' Campany be received into union with this Company? And it was unanimously agreed that the said union should take place upon each member of the Friendship Carpenters' Company paying into the stock of this Company the sum of four pounds, and signing our articles.

NOTE.—First meeting of carpenters for the purpose of forming the "Friendship Carpenters' Company," was held at the late "Union Library," November 18th, 1769.

Articles reported and agreed to at a meeting held November 23, 1769. (Does not say where.)

This Company joined the "Carpenters' Company of the City and County of Philadelphia," March 1st, 1786.

1785.   JULY 18th, 1785.

Friendship Company.   At this meeting George Engles, warden, was requested to serve the Friendship Carpenters' Company with a certified copy of the minutes made the 1st day of March last, respecting the union.

OCTOBER 17th. 1785.

Friendship Company.   The committee appointed for that purpose, report that they had delivered a copy of the minutes of March last to the Friendship Carpenters' Company.

Joseph Rakestraw, Joseph Ogilby and George Engles were appointed to inform the Friendship Carpenters' Company, that whenever they judge it proper, we are ready to call the Company together to admit them.

1787.   JANUARY 15, 1787.

Assessment of members.   At this meeting an assessment of two dollars was made upon each member, towards defraying some necessary expenses of the Company, incurred in the course of last year.

1788.   JANUARY 21st, 1788.

Fire buckets,&c.   At this meeting it was agreed that there be twelve fire buckets and one ladder; and the Committee are desired to get them; likewise, examine our fire engine, and report its state at our next meeting.

1790.   JANUARY 18th, 1790.

Act to incorporate.   On motion of Thomas Nevell, seconded by Samuel Jones, to take the sense of the Company on making application to the General Assembly for a bill to incorporate this Company, which was agreed to, and a Committee of thirteen members was appointed.

MARCH 8th, 1790.   1790.

The business of this meeting being to consider Act, &c., agreed
a bill for incorporating this Company, which, to.
being several times read, was, with some alterations,
agreed to.

APRIL 19th, 1790.

James Pearson, on behalf of the Committee on Act, &c.
the bill for incorporating this Company, reports
that they have obtained a bill, which has passed
the House, and is signed by the Speaker, and sent
to the printers. He also informed the Company
that Peter L. Loyd, Clerk of the House of Assembly,
presents this Company with his fees accruing from
the bill of incorporation.

Joseph Rakestraw and James Pearson are desired Thanks.
to present the thanks of this Company for his attention to that business; they are also desired to
get the said bill recorded.

A Committee of ten members were appointed Rules.
to draw up rules and regulations corresponding
thereunto.

JULY 19th, 1790.

The Committee appointed for that purpose, Thanks and re-
report, that they have returned the thanks of this cord.
Company to Peter L. Loyd, for his services and
attention to the business of the bill; they also
report that they have put the same in the way to
be recorded.

James Pearson, George Engles, and Samuel Materials for
Pancoast, are appointed a Committee to collect steps, &c.
materials for the steps, frontispiece, and windows
of Hall.

DECEMBER 27th, 1790.

The Company proceeded to consider the pro- Rules, &c.
posed laws for the well regulating this corporation,
when, after some alterations, the Committee are

1790. desired to get one hundred copies printed, in order that each member may be supplied, and be prepared to adopt the same, if agreeable, in the first month, agreeably to the constitution.

1791.   JANUARY 17th, 1791.

First election, &c. At this meeting the first election for officers took place, under the laws passed agreeably to the act of incorporation.

      JANUARY 20th, 1791.

Columns. Samuel Fletcher was paid £2 0s. 3d., for turning columns for frontispiece.

      JANUARY 31st, 1791.

Rules. The Committee on Rules laid before the Company the proposed rules. After being debated by sections, and sundry alterations made, were agreed to; and it was agreed that they should be entered by the Standing Committee on the record of the Company.

      MARCH 27th, 1791.

Frontispiece. At this meeting the frontispiece was put up.

1791.   APRIL 7th, 1791.

Bill of painters. John Stock was paid £12 6s. 1d., for painting two rooms in the lower part of the Hall, priming the frontispiece and five windows.

      MAY 5th, 1791.

Cedar posts. Simmons & Robinson were paid £5 9s. 10d., for a quantity of cedar posts for platform of steps leading to the Hall.

      SEPTEMBER 7th, 1791.

National Bank. James Pearson informed the Company that the Committee to whom the matter had been referred,

had let the Hall to the National Bank for two years, 1791.
at £350 per annum.

At this meeting the Company agreed to build a Building west
brick building on west side of lot, for the accommoda- side of lot.
tion of the Company, 18 feet by 60 feet in the clear,
two stories high, and the Committee are authorized to
see it completed as soon as possible.

JANUARY 16th, 1792.* 1792.

At this meeting it was agreed to have a Secretary, First Secretary.
and Joseph Ogilby was elected (being the first Secretary), the duties of Secretary having up to this time
been performed by the Warden.

APRIL 17th, 1792.

At this meeting it was resolved to pay the Salary of Secre-
Secretary for his services, £6 for the ensuing tary.
year.

Resolved, That the Committee be authorized to Relief of a mem-
pay the sum of £15, being the ground rent now ber.
due on the house in possession of a member of
this Company (late the estate of Widow Weed), in
order to extricate his goods from the demands of
the ground landlord; and also to take the goods
of the said member as security for the sum advanced, and place him at board, where he may
be well accommodated; the goods to be sent with
him.

NOVEMBER 14th, 1792.

At this meeting William Linnard was desired to South frontis-
get the frontispiece to the south front of the Hall piece.
finished, as soon as materials suitable can be
obtained.

NOTE.—The first Secretary and Treasurer
elected this year (1792), the Wardens heretofore
having kept the minutes, and the Master acting as
Treasurer.

* This was the first meeting in long room west side of court.

1793.   JULY 15th, 1793.

U. S. Bank.   Samuel Jones reported that the Directors of the United States Bank applied to him in order to be informed if they could have a lease of the Hall for a term of three years, after the expiration of the present lease. The Company agreed that they might, and authorized the Committee to settle the rent.

OCTOBER 21st, 1793.

Fever.   Only seven members appeared, on account of a malignant fever prevalent in the city.

NOVEMBER 27th, 1793.

South frontis-piece.   William Linnard was paid this evening, £12 2s. 10d., in full for his account for work done to south frontispiece of Hall.

1794.   JANUARY 20th, 1794.

U. S. Bank.   The Committee reported that they had leased the Hall to the United States Bank for three years, at $1000 per annum.

MAY 17th, 1794.

Architecture.   William Garrigues was desired to subscribe for three sets of Joseph Clark's intended publication on architecture, advertised in Maryland.

OCTOBER 20th, 1794.

Architecture.   The Committee was ordered to purchase such books of architecture as will be most useful to the Company, and that a sum not exceeding $200 be at the disposition of the Committee for that purpose.

1795.   JULY 20th, 1795.

Entrance fee.   At this meeting the admission-money was raised to $30.

OCTOBER 19th, 1795.

1795.

Lien Law.

At this meeting the Committee of Seven were directed to prepare a petition to the Legislature, in favor of workmen and other citizens, in order to secure their property in buildings.

JANUARY 18th, 1796.

1796.

Relief of a member.

By information received this evening, it appears that one of our members, whom we much esteem, has met with a considerable loss by fire; the Company, considering the circumstances, appoint William Robert, Edward Garrigues, and Conrad Bartling, as a committee to hand him such sum of money as they may think necessary, for which they have the authority of the Company to draw upon the Treasurer.

OCTOBER, 1797.

1797.

Epidemic.

The stated meeting of this month was not held, in consequence of the prevalence of an epidemic fever with which our city has been visited.

NOVEMBER 20th, 1797.

At this meeting the following communication was received:

Letter of Robert Wharton.

SIR: The Board of Commissioners have directed me to present their thanks through you to the Corporation of Carpenters of Philadelphia, for the friendly and polite offer of the use of their Hall, as tendered by their Committee, and to assure them of the perfect convenience and accommodation which they experienced while meeting there; but considering that the local engagements of the Corporation might be impeded by a further stay, and the County Commissioners offering an unoccupied apartment in the old Court-house, it was judged advisable to accept of it. Be pleased to communicate the foregoing to the respectable

5

1797.

Society of which you are President, and believe me to be your sincere friend,

ROBERT WHARTON,

Chairman.

To the President of
 the Incorporated Society of Carpenters.

NOTE.—The Library was moved this year from the President's dwelling to the Hall.

1798.   OCTOBER 15th, 1798.

Epidemic.

But few members attending this evening, in consequence of the prevalence of an epidemic fever, it was agreed to adjourn to the 19th of next month.

NOVEMBER 19th, 1798.

Sum granted to a widow.

The following resolution was adopted:

Resolved, That the Committee of Seven be authorized to grant any sum, not exceeding $100, to the widow of a late deceased member, to enable her to commence business for the support of her family.

1799   OCTOBER 21st, 1799.

But few members attending this evening, in consequence of the prevalence of an epidemic fever, it was agreed to adjourn to the 10th of next month.

BRIEF OF TITLE

TO LOT ON WHICH THE HALL IS BUILT.

May 6th, 1688.—Patent to David Breintnall, for 54½ feet by 255 feet deep. 1688.
Patent.

David Breintnall to John Lancaster, October 31, 1720, for 28 feet, part of the above 54½ feet. 1720.
Deed.

July 28, 1731.—John Lancaster to George Emlen, for 28 feet last described. 1731.
Deed.

May 6, 1688.—Patent to David Breintnall, for 35 feet in breadth, by 255 feet deep, adjoining the above. 1688.
Patent.

October 31, 1720.—David Breintnall to Joseph Breintnall, for 83 feet—26½ feet being the remaining part of the above 54½ feet lot, and the remainder, 11½ feet, being part of the 35 feet lot. 1720.
Deed.

September 10, 1745.—Joseph Breintnall to George Emlen, for 38 feet in width. 1745.
Deed.

February 7, 1749.—George Emlen devised the 38 feet lot, and the 28 feet lot to his son, George. 1749.
Will.

February 3, 1768.—George Emlen and wife to Benjamin Loxley, Thomas Nevell, and Robert Smith, for said lot, being 66 by 255 feet. 1768.
Deed.

January 15, 1770.—Benjamin Loxley, et al., to Gunning Bedford and others, trustees for Carpenters' Company. 1770.
Deed.

Gunning Bedford et al., to Joseph Pemberton, ground east side of court, 26 feet by 140 feet. 1775.
Deed.

Deed, January 16, 1775.

SUBSCRIBERS TO STOCK

FOR THE

ERECTION OF CARPENTERS' HALL.

	SHARES.		SHARES.
Robert Smith,	20	Thomas Nevell,	12
John Goodwin,	16	Silas Engles,	6
Abraham Carlile,	12	William Colladay,	6
Patrick Craghead,	4	James Worrell,	20
William Robinson,	12	Joseph Rakestraw,	6
Gunning Bedford,	12	William Roberts,	4
James Pearson,	16	James Davis,	10
Benjamin Loxley,	20	Isaac Lafever,	6
Levi Budd, :	5	Joseph Rhoads,	12
Richard Armitt,'.	12	Robert Cannon,	4
James Bringhurst,	6	Samuel Griscom,	8
William Lownes,.	12	Henry Potter,	6
Thomas Shoemaker,	10	Ezekiel Worrell,	4
George Wood,	4	Joseph Govett,	6
Joseph Fox,	20	James Coats,	4
Samuel Powell,	4	James Graisbury,	4
John Keen,	8	Matthew McGlathery,	4
John Thornhill,	12	Joseph Rush,	4
John Hitchcock,	5	James Armitage,	6

STATISTICS.

1724. The Carpenter's Company of the City and County of Philadelphia, founded under the title of the First Carpenters' Company of Philadelphia.

1724. Entrance fee one pound ten shillings, $6.67.

1734. James Porteus bequeathed his collection of books on architecture to the Company.

1736. First book purchased, the beginning of the Library.

1752. The Second Carpenters' Company admitted into membership.

1763. Entrance fee two pounds, $8.89.

1763. Committee of twelve on Book of Prices appointed.

1763. Committee appointed to procure a lot for the erection of a Hall.

1768. Purchase of the site on which the Hall now stands.

1769. Entrance fee four pounds, $17.75.

1770. Friendship Carpenters' Company ask to be united.

1771. Meetings first held in the Hall.

1772. The Philadelphia Library located in the Hall.

1774. Superintendent of Hall appointed, salary ten pounds.

1774. July 18th. Hall occupied by the Provincial Assembly.

1774. Sept. 5th. First American Congress assembled in the Hall, and continued throughout its entire session, deliberately avowing, that to the oppressive acts of the mother country, "Americans cannot submit," and the patriotic determination to "sell their liberty only with their lives."

1774. Sept. 7th. First prayer in Congress.

1775. Hall occupied again by Provincial Assembly.

1775. Hall occupied by those interested in "The American Manufactory for making Woolens, Linens, and Cottons," for the election of officers, and their meetings. The factory was located at Ninth and Market Streets.

1776. The Provincial Committee occupied the Hall. Among their resolves was, "the calling a convention for the express purpose of forming a new Government in the Province, which shall derive all its authority from the people only."

1777. The Hall and Company's property seized by the British troops.

1778. The Company again meet in the Hall, having been debarred that privilege during the occupancy of the city by the British; the fines of all members remitted, and an abatement made to the tenants for rent collected by British officials.

1778. Part of the building occupied by the United States Barrack-master.

1779. Hall occupied by the United States Commissary-General, who was allowed to erect a brass foundry and file-cutting shop on part of the lot.

1781. Committee on Book of Prices authorized to receive rents and settle accounts.

1782. Committee on Book of Prices reduced to five, and called Committee on Rents and Book of Prices.

1784. Six members added, and the Committee authorized to transact all business relating to the Company.

1786. Friendship Carpenters' Company admitted into membership, after sixteen years' efforts tending thereto, by paying four pounds each to the Treasurer.

1787. Hall occupied by the Convention to frame the Constitution; they deliberated with closed doors, and at the end of four months, agreed upon a Constitution for the United States of America.

1787. Part of the building occupied by the United States Commissary-General of Military Stores.

1787. Entrance fee six pounds, $26.67.

1787. Committee on Rents and Book of Prices separated into two Committees, seven on the former, and thirteen on the latter. This arrangement discontinued the next year.

1791. Notices first printed for use of the Wardens.

1791. Hall occupied by the Bank of the United States, where it commenced business and continued until 1797.

1791. Meetings of the Company ceased to be held in the Hall, being removed to the new building of the Company, on west side of the court, continuing there sixty-five years.

1792. The Company incorporated by the State of Pennsylvania, under the title of The Carpenters' Company of the City and County of Philadelphia.

1792. Duties of officers separated. Treasurer first appointed, the duty having been performed by the Master.

1792. Title of presiding officer changed from Master to President.

1792. Secretary first appointed, that duty having been attended to by the Wardens.

1794. Special appropriation to the Library of two hundred dollars.

1795. Entrance fee changed from sterling to Federal money, and made thirty dollars.

1797. Hall occupied by the Bank of Pennsylvania until 1799.

1797. Library removed from the President's house to the new meeting room of the Company.

1798. Hall used by the United States for a Land Office.

1798. Appropriation of one hundred and fifty dollars to the Library.

1799. Appropriation of four hundred dollars to the Library.

1800. Vice-President first appointed.

1802. Hall used by the United States for a Custom-House until 1817.

1804. Secretary's minutes separated from the Wardens' accounts.

1805. Entrance fee forty dollars.

1806. Refreshments at the quarterly meetings discontinued.

1812. Committee on Rents increased to nine, and name changed to the Managing Committee.

1817. Hall occupied by the (second) Bank of the United States.

1821. Apprentices Library located in the second story of the Hall.

1821. Hall rented to the Musical Fund Society.

1822. The Fuel Saving Society held their meeting in the Hall.

1822. Committee on Book of Prices reduced to seven members.

1822. Hall used as a school room by the Society for the Education of Female Children.

1823. A part of the building occupied as a school-room by John Willets, continuing for eight years.

1825. Hall used by Franklin Institute of the State of Pennsylvania.

1826. By-law enacted, making an annual appropriation of one hundred dollars to the Library.

1827. Committee on Book of Prices elected by ballot.

1827. First story of Hall used by the Society of Friends as a place of worship.

1828. Part of the building rented for an auction-room.

1829. Entrance fee sixty dollars.

1833. Hall used for sittings of the Supreme Court.

1838. Entire building rented for an auction store.

1852. Entrance fee eighty dollars.

1857. Hall reoccupied by the Company for their meetings and directed to be open to the visits of citizens and strangers, who may wish to visit the spot where Henry, Hancock and Adams inspired the delegates of the Colonies with nerve and the sinew for the toils of war. A body of greater men never convened together, or crowned a nation's annals.

1857. Entrance fee one hundred dollars.

1859. City Councils propose to purchase the Hall because of its historical interest and associations with the early events of our national existence. The proposition was respectfully declined.

The following appeared in the North American and United States Gazette in June, 1859, in relation to this subject:

CARPENTERS' HALL.·

Of the cherished objects yet amomg us, mementoes of the "early times," that are regarded with veneration and held sacred from the hand of "modern improvement" and "progression," none possess more thrilling interest, or were the theatre of more anxious deliberations, than the "Hall" of the Carpenters' Company of the City and County of Philadelphia. We may venerate, but cannot enter into the patriotic devotion that offered its use to the popular cause, whilst the Royalist pointed to its certain confiscation and the ruin of the Company.

It is a source of just pride that it is accessible to the public, whether citizens or strangers, and is visited even by subjects of the monarchies of Europe, being freely shown by the attentive Superintendent having it in charge. It was here that the delegates of the "town meeting" met in June, 1774, to request Governor Penn to convene the Assembly, and on his refusal appointed three of their number to wait upon the Speaker, and request a positive answer whether he would do it or not. Here the representatives of the different County Committees met to confer with the Philadelphia Committee, and prepare their resolves as the sense of the Province on the then existing state of affairs, and the necessity of a general Congress of Delegates from all the Colonies.

Within its sacred inclosures, when our own State House was closed against them, met the band of patriots who composed the First American Congress, who, conscious of the impending perils of the movement, resolved that all their transactions, except such as they should resolve to publish, should be kept inviolably secret.

Here Henry, Hancock and Adams inspired those delegates with nerve and sinew for the toils of war. Here, with the news of the cannonade of Boston bursting upon them, arose the first prayer in Congress. "Washington was kneeling here, and Henry, and Randolph, and Rutledge, and Lee, and Jay, and by their side stood, bowed in reverence, the Puritan patriots of New England, who at that time had reason to believe that an armed soldiery were wasting their humble households. They prayed fervently for America, for the Congress, for the Province of Massachusetts Bay, and especially for the town of Boston. I saw the tears," said the venerable John Adams, "gush from the eyes of the old pacific Quakers of Philadelphia." Here they deliberately avowed that to the oppressive acts of the mother country Americans cannot submit.

Here the Provincial Conference held their sittings; here they resolved to call a Convention to form a new Government for the Province, that should derive all its authority from the people only. I should not have troubled you, Mr. Editor, by thus referring to Carpenters' Hall, but for the passage of a resolution by our City Councils having reference to its purchase, which may induce some of our fellow citizens to suppose such a thing possible. To such I would say, that the Carpenters' Company is one of the oldest in the United States, having been instituted in 1724; that they built the Hall for their own, use it as such for their accommodation, and that they have no idea of parting with it; and to Councils, as Henry Pratt said to Joseph Bonaparte on a like occasion, that they "have not money enough to buy it."

1860. The Convention for the Erection of a Monument to the Signers of the Declaration of Independence, assembled and held their meetings in the Hall.

OCCUPANTS OF OLD HALL,

FROM ITS FIRST BUILDING UNTIL MAY 23, 1857, WHEN THE COMPANY, AFTER
FITTING IT UP, REOCCUPIED IT, SEPTEMBER 5, 1857.

———————

The lot was purchased February 3d, 1768; building commenced February 5th, 1770, and first occupied by the Company January 21st, 1771, in which they continued to meet until the British took possession, in 1777; and after they left, the first meeting of the Company in the Hall was January 18th, 1779, in which they continued to meet until the beginning of 1792. They then removed to the new building on the west side of court, second story, where they continued to meet until September 5th, 1857, when they reoccupied the old Hall.

1773 to December 30th, 1790, included, the Library Company occupied the second story.

July 18th, 1774. Provincial Committee.

September 5th, 1774, up to October 26th. 1774, inclusive. First Colonial Congress.

1775. The Provincial Convention.

1775. Committee on American Manufactures.

1776. Provincial Congress.

Up to the time the British took possession, the cellar and part of first story, United States, as storehouse and office.

September 26th, 1777, to June 18th, 1778, by the British.

1778. United States Barrack-master.

1779 to January 1st, 1792. First story and cellar, General Knox, Commissary-General.

February 22d, 1792. George Eddy, part lately occupied by Commissary-General, and, by arrangement, given up to National Bank.

September 7th, 1791. Leased to National Bank for two years.

January 20th, 1794, to August 17th. 1797, to United States Bank.

October 3d, 1797, to April 3d, 1798. Land Office.

1798 to 1801, three years. Bank of Pennsylvania.

April 1st, 1802, to January 1st, 1811, and from April 1st, 1811, to January 1st, 1817. Custom-House, fourteen years, three months, and nineteen days.

October 1st, 1816, to February 9th, 1821. Second Bank of the United States, four years, four months, and eight days.

March 12th, 1821, to December 12th, 1824. First story, Musical Society, three years and nine months.

March 12th, 1821, to September 12th, 1828. Second story, Apprentices' Library Company, seven years and six months.

March 12th, 1821, to December 12th, 1822. Second story, Society for Education of Female Children, one year and nine months.

December 26th, 1822, to December 16th, 1824, and a second time, March 16th, 1826, to December 31st, 1832. Second story, John Willets, for school, eight years, nine months and six days.

November 15th, 1824, to February 15th, 1826. Cellar, Jedediah Allen, one year and three months.

December 12th, 1824, to April 12th, 1826. First story, Franklin Institute, one year and four months.

November 9th, 1826, to August 9th, 1828. Cellar, Gillen & Hill, one year and nine months.

June 1st, 1827, to March 1st, 1828. First story, Society of Friends, eight months.

August 4th, 1828, to May 23d, 1857. C. J. Wolbert, auction-room; part of this time, first story only, part first story and cellar, and part the whole building, twenty-eight years, nine months, and twenty-seven days.

OFFICERS OF THE COMPANY,

AS FAR AS CAN BE OBTAINED FROM THE MINUTES.

YEAR.	MASTER.	ASSISTANT.	TREASURER.	SECRETARY.
1762		John Thornhill,		
1763	Joseph Fox,	Benj. Loxley,		
1764	"	John Thornhill,		
1765	"	James Worrell,		
1766	"	Gun. Bedford,		
1767	"	James Davis,	During this time the Master acted as Treasurer.	Warden acting as Secretary.
1768	"			
1769	"			
1770	"	James Pearson,		
1771	"	Ab'm Carlile,		
1772	"	Th. Shoemaker,		
1773	"	Joseph Rush,		
1774	"	Jos. Rakestraw,		
1775	"	James Worrell,		
1776	"	John Thornhill,		
1777				
1778				
1779	"	Joseph Rush,		
1780	Samuel Rhoads,	Levi Budd,		
1781	"	Robert Allison,		
1782	"	Joseph Ogilby,		
1783	"			
1784	Th. Shoemaker,	Silas Engles,		
1785	"	James Pearson,		
1786	"	George Engles,		
1787	"	Gun. Bedford,		
1788	"	Jos. Rakestraw,		
1789	"	S. Pancoast,		
1790	"	Samuel Jones.		

INCORPORATED 1790.

YEAR.	PRESIDENT.	VICE-PRESID'T.	TREASURER.	SECRETARY.
1791	Gun. Bedford,		Th. Shoemaker,	
1792	"		"	Joseph Ogilby.
1793	"		"	"
1794	"		"	Wm. Garrigues.
1795	George Engles,		"	"
1796	"		"	"
1797	"		Jos. Wetherill,	Wm. Powell.
1798	"		"	Ed. Garrigues.
1799	"		"	Wm. Garrigues.
1800	"	Wm. Garrigues,	"	Ed. Garrigues.
1801	"	John Keen,	"	Joseph Worrell.
1802	"	Wm. Garrigues,	"	"
1803	"	"	"	"
1804	"	"	"	J. Smith, Jr.
1805	"	"	"	"
1806	"	Wm. Linnard,	Wm. Powell,	Philip Justus.
1807	"	"	"	F. Forepaugh.
1808	"	"	"	"
1809	"	"	"	"
1810	"	"	"	John D. Smith.
1811	"	"	"	"
1812	"	"	"	"
1813	"	"	"	"

YEAR.	PRESIDENT.	VICE-PRESIDENT.	TREASURER.	SECRETARY.
1814	Joseph Morris,	Wm. Garrigues,	Wm. Powell,	John D. Smith.
1815	"	"	Jacob Lybrand,	Geo. Summers.
1816	"	Wm. Stevenson,	"	"
1817	Wm. Stevenson,	Jona. Roberts,	"	"
1818	Jona. Roberts,	Joseph Worrell,	Michael Baker,	Cor. Stevenson.
1819	"	"	"	"
1820	"	"	"	"
1821	Joseph Worrell,	Joseph Morris,	Wm. Wagner,	John O'Neill.
1822	"	"	"	"
1823	"	"	"	"
1824	Joseph Morris,	J. Williamson,	"	Wm. Randolph.
1825	"	Cor. Stevenson,	"	"
1826	"	"	"	"
1827	Joseph Worrell,	"	Michael Baker,	John Gilder.
1828	"	Wm. Wagner,	"	"
1829	"	"	"	"
1830	Wm. Wagner,	John Gilder,	"	James Weer.
1831	"	"	"	"
1832	"	"	"	Jas. Hutchinson
1833	John Gilder,	John O'Neill,	"	"
1834	"	"	"	"
1835	"	"	"	D. H. Flickwir.
1836	Michael Baker,	John M. Ogden,	James Mitchell,	"
1837	"	"	"	"
1838	"	"	"	"
1839	John M. Ogden,	Jas. Hutchinson	"	Danl. R. Knight.
1840	"	"	"	"
1841	"	"	"	John Lindsay.
1842	Jas. Hutchinson,	Daniel Smith,	"	"
1843	"	"	George Linck,	Saml. Copeland.
1844	"	"	"	"
1845	Daniel Smith,	John Lindsay,	"	Joseph Moore.
1846	"	"	"	"
1847	"	"	"	"
1848	John Lindsay,	Robert O'Neill,	"	Jos. Hutchinson
1849	"	"	"	"
1850	"	"	"	"
1851	Robert O'Neill,	D. H. Flickwir,	"	Peter Weyant.
1852	"	"	"	Wm. T. Forsyth.
1853	"	"	"	"
1854	D. H. Flickwir,	Joseph Moore,	"	J. A. Campbell.
1855	"	"	"	"
1856	"	"	"	"
1857	Joseph Moore,	J. A. Campbell,	"	Wm. T. Forsyth.
1858	"	"	Jas. Hutchinson,	"
1859	"	"	"	"
1860	J. A. Campbell,	W. T. Forsyth,	"	John Williams.
1861	"	"	"	"
1862	"	M. Errickson,	"	"
1863	M. Errickson,	John Williams,	"	Chas. Conard.
1864	"	"	"	"
1865	"	"	"	"
1866	John Williams,	Chas. Conard,	"	Samuel Rain.
1867	"	"	"	"
1868	"	"	"	"
1869	Chas. Conard,	Samuel Rain,	"	Tho. F. Shuster.
1870	"	"	"	"
1871	"	"	"	"
1872	Samuel Rain,	Thos. F. Shuster,	"	Wm. T. Forsyth.
1873	"	"	"	"

WARDENS.

1762. James Worrell.	1777.
1763. Gunning Bedford.	1778.
1764. James Pearson.	1779. Silas Engles.
1765. Thomas Nevell.	1780. George Forepaugh.
1766. Joseph Rush.	1781. Samuel McClure.
1767. Abraham Carlile.	1782.
1768. Joseph Rakestraw.	1783.
1769. James Bringhurst.	1784. George Engles.
1770. James Armitage.	1785. William Williams.
1771. Samuel Powell.	1786. Matthias Saddler.
1772. William Lownes.	1787. { Samuel Jones and
1773. William Robinson.	{ William Linnard.
1774. Thomas Proctor.	1788. William Garrigues
1775. Joseph Ogilby.	1789. William Stevenson.
1776. George Wood.	1790. Thomas Savory.

INCORPORATED 1790.

1791.
Joseph Rakestraw,
John Hall,
Conrad Bartling.

1792.
Nathan A. Smith,
John Hall,
Conrad Bartling.

1793.
Conrad Bartling,
Nathan A. Smith,
John Wilson.

1794.
Nathan A. Smith,
Ebenezer Ferguson,
In place of J. Wilson,
Joseph Morris.

1795.
Ebenezer Ferguson,
Joseph Morris,
Jacob Colladay.

1796.
Same as 1795.

1797.
Joseph Morris,
Jacob Colladay,
Daniel Knight.

1798.
Jacob Colladay,
Daniel Knight,
Samuel Wayne.

1799.
Daniel Knight,
Samuel Wayne,
George Summers.

1800.
Samuel Wayne,
George Summers,
Jacob Lybrand.

1801.
George Summers,
Jacob Lybrand,
Jonathan Roberts.

1802.
Jacob Lybrand.

Jonathan Roberts,
A. C. Ireland.

1803.
Jonathan Roberts,
A. C. Ireland,
John How.

1804.
A. C. Ireland,
John How,
Frederick Forepaugh.

1805.
John How,
Frederick Forepaugh,
David Flickwir.

1806.
Frederick Forepaugh,
David Flickwir,
William Palmer.

1807.
David Flickwir,
William Palmer,
Philip Justus.

1808.
William Palmer,
Philip Justus,
Jesse Williamson.

1809.
Philip Justus,
Jesse Williamson,
Michael Baker.·

1810.
Jesse Williamson,
Michael Baker,
Richard Chamberlain.

1811.
Michael Baker,
Richard Chamberlain,
Cornelius Stevenson.

1812.
Richard Chamberlain,
Cornelius Stevenson,
Isaac Forsyth.

1813.
Cornelius Stevenson,
Isaac Forsyth,
John Adolph.

1814.
Isaac Forsyth,
John Adolph,
John O'Neill.

1815.
John Adolph,
John O'Neill,
William Hause.

1816.
John O'Neill,
William Hause,
Joseph Eberth.

1817.
William Hause,
Joseph Eberth,
John Warner.

1818.
Joseph Eberth,
John Warner,
Samuel Baker.

1819.
John Warner,
Samuel Baker,
John M. Ogden.

1820.
Samuel Baker,
John M. Ogden,
James Hall, resigned.

1821.
John M. Ogden,
Joseph Strahan,
William P. Paxson.

1822.
Joseph Strahan,
William P. Paxson, Dec'd.
George Linck.

1823.
James Clark,
George Linck,
Finnix Stretcher.

1824.
George Linck,
Finnix Stretcher,
James Weer.

1825.
Finnix Stretcher,
James Weer,
Jacob Kenderdine.

1826.
James Weer,
Jacob Kenderdine,
James Hutchinson.

1827.
Jacob Kenderdine,
James Hutchinson,
Ralph H. Smith.

1828.
James Hutchinson,
Ralph H. Smith,
Henry L. Coryell.

1829.
Ralph H. Smith,
Henry L. Coryell,
D. Henry Flickwir.

1830.
Henry L. Coryell,
D. Henry Flickwir,
James R. Greeves.

1831.
D. Henry Flickwir,
James R. Greeves,
Daniel Smith.

1832.
James R. Greeves,
Daniel Smith,
Joseph Hutchinson.

1833.
Daniel Smith,
Joseph Hutchinson,
Daniel R. Knight.

1834.
Joseph Hutchinson,
Daniel R. Knight,
Moses Lancaster.

1835.
Daniel R. Knight,
Moses Lancaster,
John Lindsay.

1836.
Moses Lancaster,
John Lindsay,
William C. Hancock.

1837.
John Lindsay,
William C. Hancock,
Samuel Copeland.

1838.
William C. Hancock,
Samuel Copeland,
Robert A. Govett.

1839.
Samuel Copeland,
Robert A. Govett,
Edward Turner.

1840.
Robert A. Govett,
Edward Turner,
Joseph C. Wills.

1841.
Edward Turner,
Joseph C. Wills,
George R. Lawton.

1842.
Joseph C. Wills,
George R. Lawton,
Jacob Thomas.

1843.
George Myers,
Jacob Thomas,
Theodore Colladay.

1844.
Jacob Thomas,
Theodore Colladay.
Jesse Williamson.

1845.
Theodore Colladay,
Jesse Williamson,
Michael Errickson.

1846.
Jesse Williamson,
Michael Errickson.
William T. Forsyth.

1847.
Michael Errickson,
William T. Forsyth,
Henry Shuster.

1848.
William T. Forsyth,
Henry Shuster,
Joseph Govett.

1849.
Henry Shuster,
Joseph Govett,
Samuel Williamson.

1850.
Joseph Govett,
Samuel Williamson,
James Wood.

1851.
Samuel Williamson,
James Wood,
Henry J. Bockins.

1852.
James Wood,
Henry J. Bockius,
William F. Wilson.

1853.
Henry J. Bockius,
William F. Wilson,
Thomas F. Shuster.

1854.
Richard K. Betts,
Thomas F. Shuster,
John Williams.

1855.
Thomas F. Shuster,
John Williams,
Charles Rubicam.

1856.
John Williams,
Charles Rubicam,
Samuel Rain.

1857.
Charles Rubicam,
Samuel Rain,
Walter Allison.

1858.
Samuel Rain,
Walter Allison,
John Killgore.

1859.
Walter Allison,
John Killgore,
John Ketcham.

1860.
John Killgore,
John Ketcham,
Edward Kelly.

1861.
John Ketcham,
Edward Kelly,
John Rire.

1862.
Edward Kelly,
John Rire,
Jacob Jones.

1863.
John Rire,
Jacob Jones,
Henry Phillippe.

1864.
Jacob Jones,
Henry Phillippe,
Philip Kramer.

1865.
Henry Phillippe,
Philip Kramer,
Edward K. Snow.

1866.
Philip Kramer,
Edward K. Snow,
James G. Steele.

1867.
Edward K. Snow,
James G. Steele,
Wm. Eyre.

1868.
James G. Steele,
Wm. Eyre,
Geo. Day.

1870.
George Day,
Edward T. Miller,
Samuel K. Hopkins.

1872.
Samuel K. Hopkins,
Allen Bard,
James H. Errickson.

1869.
Wm. Eyre,
George Day,
Edward T. Miller.

1871.
Edward T. Miller,
Samuel K. Hopkins,
Allen Bard.

1873.
Allen Bard,
James H. Errickson,
Thomas Marsh.

COMMITTEE ON BOOK OF PRICES.

This Committee was first appointed in 1724, and was regularly continued. The names of its members before 1763 were on the Book of Minutes, missing since about 1847.

1763 to 1767.
Robert Smith,
John Thornhill,
Joseph Thornhill,
Gunning Bedford,
Thomas Nevell,
Benjamin Loxley,
Abraham Carlile,
James Worrell,
Wm. Dilworth,
John Goodwin,
James Pearson,
Joseph Rush.

1767 to 1772.
Robert Smith,
John Thornhill,
Joseph Thornhill,
Gunning Bedford,
Thomas Nevell,
Benjamin Loxley,
Abraham Carlile,
James Worrell,
John Goodwin,
James Pearson,
Joseph Rush,
Joseph Rakestraw.

1772.
Robert Smith,
John Thornhill,
Joseph Thornhill,
Gunning Bedford,
Thomas Nevell,
Benjamin Loxley,
Abraham Carlile,
James Worrell,
John Goodwin,
James Pearson,
Joseph Rush,
Joseph Rakestraw,
Thomas Shoemaker,
James Bringhurst,

George Wood,
Joseph Rhoads,
Wm. Colladay.

1773.
Thomas Nevell,
Robert Smith,
James Worrell,
Thomas Shoemaker,
Benj. Loxley,
Joseph Rhoads,
John Thornhill,
Jas. Bringhurst,
Jos. Rush,
Wm. Lownes,
Jos. Rakestraw,
Gunning Bedford.

1774.
Thomas Nevell,
Robert Smith,
James Worrell,
Thomas Shoemaker,
John Thornhill,
Jas. Bringhurst,
Jos. Rush,
Wm. Lownes,
Jos. Rakestraw,
Gunning Bedford,
James Pearson,
Thomas Proctor.

1775.
Thomas Nevell,
Robert Smith,
James Worrell,
Thomas Shoemaker,
Jas. Bringhurst,
Wm. Lownes,
Jos. Rakestraw,
Gunning Bedford,
Jas. Pearson,
Wm. Colladay,

Robert Allison,
Benj. Loxley.

1776.
Thomas Nevell,
Robert Smith,
James Worrell,
Thomas Shoemaker,
Wm. Lownes,
Jos. Rakestraw,
Gunning Bedford,
Wm. Colladay,
Robert Allison,
Benj. Loxley,
Abraham Carlile,
Jos. Ogilby.
No election of Committee from 1776 to 1780.

1781.
The Committee were authorized to settle accounts and collect rents.
Jos. Rhoads,
Thomas Shoemaker,
Joseph Rakestraw,
Thomas Nevell,
John Thornhill,
Gunning Bedford,
John Keen.

1782.
Jos. Rhoads,
Thomas Shoemaker,
Joseph Rakestraw,
Thomas Nevell,
John Thornhill,
Gunning Bedford,
John Keen.

1783.
Thomas Nevell,
Jos. Rakestraw,

Gunning Bedford,
John Keen,
Robert Allison,
James. Pearson,
Benj. Loxley.

1784 and 1785.
(The Committee were
authorized to transact all
business relating to the
Company.)
Thomas Nevell,
Jos. Rakestraw,
Gunning Bedford.
John Keen,
Robert Allison,
James Pearson.
Benj. Loxley,
Jos. Rush,
Silas Engles,
Geo. Forepaugh.
Geo. Wood.
Wm. Colladay.
Jos. Ogilby.
Making 13.

1786.
Gunning Bedford,
Thomas Nevell,
Jas Pearson,
Silas Engles,
Jos. Ogilby,
Jos. Rakestraw,
Robert Allison,
Sam'l Jones,
Sam'l Pancoast,
Geo. Ingles,
Robert Evans,
Wm. Garrigues,
Thos. Savery,
Geo. Forepaugh.

1787.
Gunning Bedford,
Thomas Nevell,
Jas. Pearson,
Silas Engles,
Jos. Ogilby,
Jos. Rakestraw.

Robert Allison,
William Williams,
Sam'l Jones,
Sam'l Pancoast,
Geo. Ingles,
Robert Evans,
Wm. Garrigues,
Thos. Savery,
Geo. Forepaugh.

1788.
Gunning Bedford,
Jas. Pearson,
Silas Engles,
Jos. Ogilby,
Samuel Pancoast.
Wm. Garrigues,
Samuel Jones,
George Ingles,
Robert Evans,
Thomas Nevell,
George Forepaugh.
Joseph Rakestraw.

1789.
Gunning Bedford.
Jas. Pearson,
Silas Engles,
Jos. Ogilby,
Samuel Pancoast,
Wm. Garrigues,
Samuel Jones,
George Ingles,
Thomas Nevell.

1790.
Gunning Bedford,
Jas. Pearson,
Silas Engles,
Jos. Ogilby,
Samuel Pancoast,
Wm. Garrigues,
Samuel Jones,
Matthew Sadler.
Thomas Nevell.
George Forepaugh.
George Ingles,
Joseph Rakestraw,
Robert Evans,

William Linnard.

1791.
James Pearson,
George Ingles,
Joseph Ogilby,
Wm. Garrigues.
Samuel Jones.
Matthias Saddler.
William Linnard.

1792.
James Pearson,
George Ingles,
Joseph Ogilby,
Wm. Garrigues,
Samuel Jones,
Matthias Saddler.
William Linnard.

1793.
James Pearson.
George Ingles,
Joseph Ogilby,
Samuel Pancoast,
Wm. Garrigues,
Samuel Jones,
William Linnard.

1794.
James Pearson.
George Ingles,
Wm. Garrigues,
Samuel Jones,
William Linnard,
George Forepaugh,
Thomas Savery.

1795.
John Keen,
Robert Allison,
Edward Garrigues,
George Forepaugh,
William Linnard,
William Garrigues,
James Pearson,
Silas Engles,
Joseph Morris.

1796.
William Powell,
John Keen,
William Garrigues,
Edward Garrigues,
George Forepaugh,
William Linnard,
James Pearson.

1797.
John Keen,
Edward Garrigues,
George Forepaugh,
William Linnard,
James Pearson,
William Powell,
Joseph Morris.

1798-1799.
William Powell,
John Keene,
Edward Garrigues,
George Forepaugh,
William Linnard,
Joseph Morris,
Joseph Ogilby.

1800.
John Keen,
Joseph Morris,
Joseph Ogilby,
Daniel Knight,
Joseph Worrell,
William Powell,
James Pearson.

1801.
Daniel Knight,
William Powell,
Joseph Morris,
George Forepaugh,
Alexander Steel,
John Hutchinson,
Thomas Savery.

1802.
Daniel Knight,
William Powell,
Joseph Morris,

George Forepaugh,
William Linnard,
James Pearson,
George Summers.

1803.
Daniel Knight,
William Powell,
Joseph Morris,
George Forepaugh,
William Linnard,
James Pearson,
Jacob Colladay.

1804-1805.
Daniel Knight,
William Powell,
Joseph Morris,
George Forepaugh,
William Linnard,
Jacob Colladay,
Jonathan Roberts.

1806 and 1807.
Daniel Knight,
Joseph Morris,
George Summers,
Jonathan Roberts,
A. C. Ireland,
John D. Smith,
Jacob Lybrand.

1808 and 1809.
Joseph Morris,
George Summers,
Jonathan Roberts,
A. C. Ireland,
Jacob Lybrand,
David Flickwir,
John How.

1810 and 1811.
Joseph Morris,
Jonathan Roberts,
A. C. Ireland,
Jacob Lybrand,
David Flickwir,
John How,
Fred. Forepaugh,

After this, the duties of
the Committee were di-
vided, the "Committee on
Book of Prices" was con-
tinued without re-ap-
pointment until 1817.

1812 to 1817.
Joseph Morris,
George Summers,
A. C. Ireland,
Jacob Lybrand,
Daniel Knight,
George Forepaugh,
Joseph Worrell,
Richard Ware,
John D. Smith.

1817 to 1822.
A. C. Ireland,
Joseph P. Zebley,
John How,
Joseph Eberth,
John O'Neill,
Joseph Morris.

1822 to 1826.
John O'Neill,
James Clark,
Joseph Morris,
Joseph Worrell,
William Wagner,
Joseph Eberth,
John M. Ogden.

1826.
Joseph Worrell,
John Gilder,
A. C. Ireland,
John M. Ogden,
Isaac Shunk,
James Hutchinson,
Michael Baker.

1827.
Joseph Eberth,
William Wagner,
A. C. Ireland,
Jesse Williamson,

Daniel Knight,
Joseph Morris.
John Gilder.

1828.
John Gilder,
A. C. Ireland,
William Wagner,
Joseph Eberth,
Jesse Williamson,
James Hutchinson.
John O'Neill.

1829.
John Gilder,
Geo. Senneff,
James Hutchinson.
Charles Hicks,
Joseph Eberth,
Joseph Strahan,
A. C. Ireland.

1830.
Joseph Eberth,
Joseph Morris,
John O'Neill,
William Wagner,
John Gilder.
Charles Hicks,
James Hutchinson.

1831.
John Gilder,
Charles Hicks,
Joseph Strahan,
James Hutchinson,
John M. Ogden,
John O'Neill,
William Wagner.

1832.
Joseph Morris,
Isaac Shunk,
William Wagner,
John O'Neill,
James Hutchinson.
Charles Hicks,
John Gilder.

1833 to 1835.
Geo. Senneff,
Isaac Shunk,
Joseph Morris,
John O'Neill,
James Hutchinson.
Charles Hicks,
John Gilder.

1836 to 1842.
Joseph Morris,
John Gilder,
Charles Hicks,
Isaac Shunk,
James Hutchinson,
John M. Ogden,
Philip Justus.

1843.
James Hutchinson,
Isaac Shunk,
Charles Hicks,
John M. Ogden,
John Gilder,
Philip Justus,
John Lindsay.

1844.
James Hutchinson,
Isaac Shunk,
John M. Ogden,
John Gilder,
Daniel Smith,
John Lindsay,
D. H. Flickwir.

1845 to 1849.
Samuel Copeland,
James Hutchinson,
Isaac Shunk,
John M. Ogden,
John Gilder,
John Lindsay.
D. H. Flickwir.

1850.
James Hutchinson,
Isaac Shunk,
John M. Ogden,

John Lindsay,
D. H. Flickwir,
James A. Campbell,
Richard K. Betts.

1851 and 1852.
James Hutchinson,
John M. Ogden,
Isaac Shunk,
D. H. Flickwir,
John Lindsay,
Samuel Copeland,
James A. Campbell.

1853.
James Hutchinson,
John M. Ogden,
Isaac Shunk,
D. H. Flickwir,
Samuel Copeland,
James A. Campbell,
Joseph Moore.

1854 and 1855.
James Hutchinson,
John M. Ogden,
Isaac Shunk,
D. H. Flickwir,
Samuel Copeland,
James A. Campbell,
Joseph Moore,
Joseph Hutchinson.

1856 and 1858.
James Hutchinson,
John M. Ogden,
James A. Campbell,
Joseph Moore,
D. H. Flickwir,
Joseph Hutchinson,
Theodore Colladay.

1859.
James A. Campbell,
James Hutchinson,
John M. Ogden,
Joseph Hutchinson,
Richard K. Betts,
Theodore Colladay,

Joseph Moore.

1860.

Increased to nine members, electing three annually, to serve three years.

Richard K. Betts,
John R. Hudden, } 1 year.
Joseph Moore,

Henry Phillippe,
John M. Ogden, } 2 yrs.
Michael Errickson.

James A. Campbell,
Mark Balderston. } 3 yrs.
Samuel Rain.

1861.
Henry Phillippe,
John M. Ogden,
Michael Errickson,
James A. Campbell.
Mark Balderston,
Samuel Rain,
James Hutchinson.
Joseph Moore,
Richard K. Betts.

1862.
James A. Campbell,
Mark Balderston,
Samuel Rain,
James Hutchinson,
Joseph Moore,
Richard K. Betts,
Joseph Hutchinson,
John M. Ogden,
Michael Errickson.

1863.
James Hutchinson,

Joseph Moore,
Richard K. Betts,
John M. Ogden,
Joseph Hutchinson,
Michael Errickson,
James A. Campbell.
Samuel Rain,
Walter Allison.

1864.
Number reduced to five, electing one each year to serve five years.
John M. Ogden,
Joseph Hutchinson,
Michael Errickson,
James A. Campbell,
Samuel Rain,
Walter Allison,
Jas. Hutchinson, 5 years.

1865.
James A. Campbell.
Samuel Rain.
Walter Allison,
James Hutchinson,
John M. Ogden, 5 years.

1866.
James Hutchinson,
John M. Ogden,
Jas. A. Campbell, 3 years
Samuel Rain, 2 years.
Richard K. Betts, 1 year.

1867.
James Hutchinson,
John M. Ogden,
James A. Campbell.
Samuel Rain,
Richard K. Betts, 5 yrs.

1868.
James Hutchinson,
John M. Ogden,
James A. Campbell,
Richard K. Betts,
Samuel Rain, 5 years.

1869.
John M. Ogden,
James A. Campbell,
Richard K. Betts,
Samuel Rain,
James Hutchinson.

1870.
James A. Campbell,
Richard K. Betts.
Samuel Rain,
James Hutchinson,
John M. Ogden.

1871.
Richard K. Betts,
Samuel Rain,
James Hutchinson,
John M. Ogden.
Charles Conard.

1872.
Samuel Rain,
James Hutchinson,
John M. Ogden,
Charles Conard,
William Eyre.

1873.
James Hutchinson,
John M. Ogden,
Charles Conard,
William Eyre,
Richard K. Betts.

MANAGING COMMITTEE.

In 1812, the "business affairs" of the Company were separated from those of the "Book of Prices," and entrusted to a separate Committee, consisting of nine members, three being elected annually, and each serving three years.

1812.
Michael Baker,
Jonathan Roberts.
David Flickwir.
Joseph Morris.
Daniel Knight.
A. C. Ireland,
Jacob Lybrand.
George Summers.
John How.

1813.
Joseph Morris.
Daniel Knight.
A. C. Ireland,
Jacob Lybrand.
George Summers.
John How,
Wm. Garrigues. (resign'd)
William Palmer,
Jesse Williamson.

1814.
Jacob Lybrand,
George Summers.
John How,
Joseph Zebley.
William Palmer,
Jesse Williamson.
Jonathan Roberts.
Michael Baker,
Cornelius Stevenson.

1815.
Joseph Zebley.
William Palmer,
Jesse Williamson.
Jonathan Roberts.
Michael Baker.
Cornelius Stevenson,
A. C. Ireland,
Isaac Forsyth.
Daniel Knight.

1816.
Jonathan Roberts,
Michael Baker,
Cornelius Stevenson,
A. C. Ireland.
Isaac Forsyth.
Daniel Knight.
John D. Smith.
Jacob Colladay.
James Corkrin.

1817.
A. C. Ireland.
Isaac Forsyth.
Daniel Knight.
John D. Smith,
Jacob Colladay.
James Corkrin,
Jesse Williamson.
John O'Neill.
William Wagner.

1818.
John D. Smith,
Jacob Colladay,
James Corkrin,
Jesse Williamson.
John O'Neill.
William Wagner,
Joseph Morris.
George Summers.
William Hause.

1819.
Jesse Williamson,
John O'Neill.
William Wagner.
Joseph Morris.
George Summers.
William Hause,
Joseph Eberth,
Daniel Knight,
James Mitchell.

1820.
Joseph Morris.
George Summers,
William Hause.
Joseph Eberth,
Daniel Knight,
James Mitchell.
John D. Smith. (dec'd,)
Jacob Franks,
John Gilder.

1821.
Joseph Eberth,
Daniel Knight,
James Mitchell.
William Govett,
Jacob Franks.
John Gilder.
Samuel Baker,
Jonathan Roberts,
Jesse Williamson.

1822.
William Govett,
Jacob Franks,
John Gilder.
Samuel Baker.
Jonathan Roberts,
Jesse Williams.
John M. Ogden.
Jacob Ballenger,
Cornelius Stevenson.

1823.
Samuel Baker,
Jonathan Roberts.
Jesse Williamson.
John M. Ogden,
Jacob Ballenger,
Cornelius Stevenson.
James M. Linnard,
Philip Justus,
Michael Baker.

1824.
John M. Ogden,
Jacob Ballenger,
Cornelius Stevenson,
James M. Linnard,
Philip Justus,
Michael Baker,
James Clark,
John Gilder,
John O'Neill.

1825.
James M. Linnard,
Philip Justus,
Michael Baker,
James Clark,
John Gilder,
John O'Neill,
George Linck,
Jesse Williamson,
James Mitchell.

1826.
James Clark,
John Gilder,
John O'Neill,
George Linck,
Jesse Williamson,
James Mitchell,
Joseph Strahan,
Malcom McLeod,
Samuel Baker.

1827.
George Linck,
Jesse Williamson,
James Mitchell,
Joseph Strahan,
Malcom McLeod,
Samuel Baker,
James Weer,
William Govett,
John M. Ogden.

1828.
Jos. Strahan,
Malcolm McLeod,
Samuel Baker,
James Weer,

Wm. Govett,
John M. Ogden,
John O'Neill,
Jacob Kenderdine,
Wm. Randolph.

1829.
James Weer,
Wm. Govett,
John M. Ogden,
John O'Neill,
Jacob Kenderdine,
William Randolph,
James Hutchinson,
Jesse Williamson,
Charles Hicks.

1830.
John O'Neill,
Jacob Kenderdine,
William Randolph,
James Hutchinson,
Jesse Williamson,
Charles Hicks,
Ralph H. Smith,
Cornelius Trimnel,
Cornelius Stevenson.

1831.
James Hutchinson,
Jesse Williamson,
Charles Hicks,
Ralph H. Smith,
Cornelius Trimnel,
Cornelius Stevenson,
Jacob Ballenger,
Jos. Eberth,
Jos. Strahan.

1832.
Ralph H. Smith,
Cornelius Trimnel,
Cornelius Stevenson,
Jacob Ballenger,
Jos. Eberth,
Jos Strahan,
James Mitchell,
D. Henry Flickwir,
James Weer.

1833.
Jacob Ballenger,
Jos. Eberth,
Jos. Strahan,
James Mitchell,
D. Henry Flickwir,
James Weer,
Jesse Williamson,
Wm. Wagner,
Daniel Knight.

1834.
James Mitchell,
D. Henry Flickwir,
James Weer,
Jesse Williamson,
Wm. Wagner,
Daniel Knight,
Daniel Smith,
Charles Hicks,
James Hutchinson.

1835.
Jesse Williamson,
Wm. Wagner,
Daniel Knight,
Daniel Smith,
Charles Hicks,
James Hutchinson,
Jacob Ballenger,
George Linck,
Jos. Hutchinson,

1836.
Daniel Smith,
Charles Hicks,
James Hutchinson,
Jacob Ballenger,
George Linck,
Jos. Hutchinson,
Daniel R. Knight,
Robert O'Neill,
Caleb Maule.

1837.
Jacob Ballenger,
George Linck,
Jos. Hutchinson,
Daniel R. Knight,

6*

Robert O'Neill,
Caleb Maule,
Moses Lancaster,
Philip Justus,
Wm. Bockius.

1838.
Daniel R. Knight,
Robert O'Neill,
Caleb Maule,
Moses Lancaster.
Philip Justus.
William Bockius,
Daniel Smith,
John Lindsay,
Ralph H. Smith.

1839.
Moses Lancaster,
Philip Justus,
William Bockius,
Daniel Smith,
John Lindsay,
Ralph H. Smith,
Wm. C. Hancock,
D. Henry Flickwir,
James Weer.

1840.
Daniel Smith,
John Lindsay,
Ralph H. Smith,
Wm. C. Hancock,
D. Henry Flickwir,
James Weer,
George Linck,
Samuel Copeland,
Jos. Hutchinson.

1841.
Wm. C. Hancock,
D. Henry Flickwir,
James Weer,
George Linck,
Samuel Copeland,
Joseph Hutchinson,
Edward Turner,
Robert A. Govett,
Jesse Williamson,

1842.
George Linck,
Samuel Copeland,
Joseph Hutchinson,
Edward Turner,
Robert A. Govett,
Jesse Williamson,
Daniel R. Knight.
James M. Linnard,
George R. Lawton.

1843.
Edward Turner,
Robert A. Govett,
Jesse Williamson,
Daniel R. Knight,
James M. Linnard,
George R. Lawton,
Peter Weyant,
D. Henry Flickwir,
Robert O'Neill.

1844.
Dnaiel R. Knight,
James M. Linnard,
George R. Lawton,
Peter Weyant.
D. Henry Flickwir,
Robert O'Neill,
George Myers,
Jacob Amos,
Joseph Hutchinson.

1845.
Peter Weyant,
D. Henry Flickwir,
Robert O'Neill,
George Myers,
Jacob Amos,
Joseph Hutchinson.
Jacob Thomas,
Samuel Copeland,
Edward Turner.

1846.
George Myers,
Jacob Amos,
Joseph Hutchinson,
Jacob Thomas,

Samuel Copeland,
Edward Turner,
Theodore Colladay,
John M. Ogden,
James Hutchinson,

1847.
Jacob Thomas,
Samuel Copeland,
Edward Turner,
Theodore Colladay,
John M. Ogden,
James Hutchinson,
Jesse Williamson,
D. Henry Flickwir,
Daniel R. Knight.

1848.
Theodore Colladay,
John M. Ogden,
James Hutchinson,
Jesse Williamson,
D. Henry Flickwir,
Daniel R. Knight,
Michael Errickson,
Henry Little,
Peter Weyant.

1849.
Jesse Williamson,
D. Henry Flickwir,
Daniel R. Knight,
Michael Errickson,
Henry Little,
Peter Weyant.
Jacob Thomas,
George Myers,
Wm. T. Forsyth,

1850.
Michael Errickson,
Henry Little,
Peter Weyant,
Jacob Thomas,
George Myers,
Wm. T. Forsyth,
James Hutchinson,
Theodore Colladay,
Henry Shuster.

1851.
Jacob Thomas,
George Myers,
Wm. T. Forsyth,
James Hutchinson,
Theodore Colladay,
Henry Shuster,
Daniel R. Knight,
John M. Ogden,
Joseph Govett.

1852.
James Hutchinson,
Theodore Colladay,
Henry Shuster,
Daniel R. Knight,
John M. Ogden,
Jos. Govett,
Michael Errickson,
Samuel Williamson,
Michael Shaffer.

1853.
Daniel R. Knight,
John M. Ogden,
Jos. Govett,
Michael Errickson,
Samuel Williamson,
Michael Shaffer,
James Wood,
Joseph Hutchinson,
Jacob Amos.

1854.
Michael Errickson,
Samuel Williamson,
Michael Shaffer,
James Wood,
Joseph Hutchinson,
Jacob Amos,
Henry Shuster,
Theodore Coallday,
Henry J. Bockius.

1855.
James Wood,
Joseph Hutchinson,
Jacob Amos,
Henry Shuster,

Theodore Colladay,
Henry J. Bockius,
James Hutchinson,
George Myers,
Richard K. Betts.

1856.
Henry Shuster,
Theodore Colladay,
Henry J. Bockius,
James Hutchinson,
George Myers,
Richard K. Betts,
Thomas F. Shuster,
Samuel Williamson,
Michael Errickson.

1857.
James Hutchinson,
Michael Shaffer,
Richard K. Betts,
Thomas F. Shuster,
Samuel Williamson,
Michael Erricksou,
John Williams,
Daniel R. Knight,
Charles Conard.

1858.
Thomas F. Shuster,
Samuel Williamson,
Michael Errickson,
John Williams,
Daniel R. Knight,
Charles Conard,
John M. Ogden,
Charles A. Rubicam,
Henry J. Bockius.

1859.
John Williams,
Daniel R. Knight,
Charles Conard,
John M. Ogden,
Charles A. Rubicam,
Henry J. Bockius,
Samuel Rain,
Joseph Hutchinson,
Richard K. Betts.

1860.
John M. Ogden,
Charles A. Rubicam,
Henry J. Bockius,
Samuel Rain,
Joseph Hutchinson,
Richard K. Betts,
Walter Allison,
Michael Errickson,
Thomas F. Shuster.

1861.
Samuel Rain,
Joseph Hutchinson,
Richard K. Betts,
Walter Allison,
Michael Errickson,
Thomas F. Shuster,
D. H. Flickwir,
John Killgore,
Henry Shuster.

1862.
Walter Allison,
Michael Errickson,
Thomas F. Shuster,
D. H. Flickwir,
John Killgore,
Henry Shuster,
John Ketcham,
John Williams,
Henry J. Bockius.

1863.
D. Henry Flickwir,
John Killgore,
Henry Shuster,
John Ketcham,
John Williams,
Henry J. Bockius,
Samuel Rain,
Richard K. Betts,
Edward Kelly.

1864.
John Ketcham,
John Williams,
Henry J. Bockius,
Samuel Rain,

Richard K Betts,
Edward Kelly,
Joseph Hutchinson,
John Rice,
Thomas F. Shuster.

1865.
Samuel Rain,
Richard K. Betts,
Edward Kelly,
Joseph Hutchinson,
John Rice,
Thomas F. Shuster,
D. Henry Flickwir,
Walter Allison,
Jacob Jones.

1866.
Michael Errickson,
William Eyre,
Thomas F. Shuster,
D. Henry Flickwir,
Walter Allison,
Jacob Jones,
Henry Phillippe,
Samuel Williamson,
Henry Shuster.

1867.
D. Henry Flickwir,
Walter Allison,
Jacob Jones,
Henry Phillippe,
Samuel Williamson,
Henry Shuster,

Edward Kelley,
Philip Kramer,
John Ketcham.

1868.
Henry Phillippe,
Samuel Williamson,
Henry Shuster,
Edward Kelley,
Philip Kramer,
Henry Shuster,
Edward K. Snow,
Richard K. Betts,
James A. Campbell.

1869.
Edward Kelley,
Philip Kramer,
Henry Shuster,
Edward K. Snow,
Richard K. Betts,
James A. Campbell,
Jacob Jones,
Walter Allison,
James G Steele.

1870.
Edward K. Snow,
Richard K. Betts,
James A. Campbell,
Jacob Jones,
Walter Allison,
James G. Steele,
Henry Shuster,
William Eyre,

Henry Phillippe.

1871.
Jacob Jones,
Walter Allison,
James G. Steele,
Henry Shuster,
William Eyre,
Henry Phillippe,
George Day,
Philip Kramer,
D. Henry Flickwir.

1872.
Henry Shuster,
William Eyre,
Henry Phillippe,
George Day,
Philip Kramer,
D. Henry Flickwir,
Edward K. Snow,
Richard K. Betts,
Edward T. Miller.

1873.
George Day,
Philip Kramer,
D. Henry Flickwir,
Edward K. Snow,
Richard K. Betts,
Edward T. Miller,
Jacob Jones,
Walter Allison,
Samuel K. Hopkins.

LIBRARY COMMITTEE.

(The Library was placed under the care of a separate Committee in 1853, elected annually.)

1853.
John M. Ogden,
Robert O'Neill,
Daniel R. Knight,
Richard K. Betts,
Charles A. Rubicam.

1854.
John M. Ogden.
James Hutchinson,
John McClure,
William Eyre,
Richard K. Betts.

1855.
John M. Ogden,
James Hutchinson,
John McClure,
William Eyre,
Richard K. Betts.

1856.
John M. Ogden,
James Hutchinson,
John McClure,
William Eyre,
Richard K. Betts.

1857.
John M. Ogden,
James Hutchinson,
John McClure,
Richard K. Betts,
Daniel R. Knight.

1858.
John M. Ogden,
James Hutchinson,
John Lindsay,
Daniel R. Knight,
Richard K. Betts.

1859.
John M. Ogden,
James Hutchinson,
John Lindsay.
Daniel R. Knight,
Richard K. Betts.

1860.
The Committee reduced to 3 members, electing one annually, to serve three years.
John M. Ogden,
Richard K Betts,
James Hutchinson.

1861.
Richard K. Betts,
James Hutchinson,
John M. Ogden.

1862.
James Hutchinson,
John M. Ogden.
Richard K. Betts.

1863.
John M. Ogden.
Richard K. Betts,
James Hutchinson.

1864.
Richard K. Betts,
James Hutchinson,
John M. Ogden.

1865.
James Hutchinson,
John M. Ogden,
Richard K. Betts.

1866.
John M. Ogden,
Richard K. Betts,
James Hutchinson.

1867.
Richard K. Betts,
James Hutchinson,
John M. Ogden.

1868.
James Hutchinson,
John M. Ogden,
Richard K. Betts.

1869.
John M. Ogden,
Richard K. Betts,
James Hutchinson.

1870.
Richard K. Betts,
James Hutchinson.
Edward Kelly.

1871.
James Hutchinson,
Edward Kelly,
Richard K. Betts.

1872.
Edward Kelly,
Richard K. Betts,
James Hutchinson.

1873.
Richard K. Betts,
James Hutchinson,
John M. Ogden.

LIST OF NAMES

OF

THE CARPENTERS' COMPANY OF THE CITY AND COUNTY OF PHILADELPHIA.

ORIGINAL ASSOCIATORS.

DECEASED.		DECEASED.
JOSEPH HENMARSH,†		JOSEPH HARRISON,†
JAMES PORTIUS,	1734.	JOHN NICHOLS,†
SAMUEL POWELL,†		JOHN HARRISON,†
JACOB USHER,†		BENJAMIN CLARK,†
EDMOND WOOLLEY,†		ISAAC ZANE.†

MEMBERS BY ELECTION.

ELECTED.		DECEASED.	ELECTED.		DECEASED.
	*William Clark,†			*Abraham Carlisle.	1778.
	*Edward Warner,†			*James Davis,	1774.
	*Samuel Rhoads.	1784.		*Ellis Price,	1779.
	*Ebenezer Tomlinson,	1767.		*Gunning Bedford,	1802.
	*Reese Loyd,†			*Thomas Nevell,	1797.
	*Joseph Rakestraw.†			*James Armitage,	1807.
	*Tobias Griscom.†			*Samuel Griscom,	1793.
	*John Mifflin,†			*James Pearson,	1813.
	*William Coleman,†			*John Wayne.	1769.
	*John Price,†			*William Roberts	1808.
	*Joseph Hitchcock,†			*Levi Budd,	1790.
	*Jacob Lewis,†			*George Plim,	1775.
	*Joseph Fox,	1780.		*Isaac Lafever,	1779.
	*Joseph Thornhill,	1797.		*Richard Arnitt,	1790.
	*John Thornhill,	1784.		*James Potter,	1809.
1736.	Robert Smith,	1778.		*Benjamin Mifflin,	1786.
	*Benjamin Loxley,	1798.		*George Wood,	1818.
	*James Worrell,	1797.		*Ezekeiel Worrell,	1781.
	*John Goodwin,	1774.		*Josiah Harper,	1767.

* Date of Election not ascertained.   † Date of Decease not ascertained.

ELECTED.		DECEASED.	ELECTED.		DECEASED.
	*Joseph Rakestraw,	1794.	1773.	William Williams,	1794.
	*Silas Engles,	1804.	1773.	Robert Allison.	1811.
	*Joseph Rush,	1787.	1774.	George Forepaugh,	1817.
	*Joseph Rhoads,	1784.	1774.	Samuel McClure,	1796.
	*Isaac Coats,	Rd., 1784.	1775.	Joseph Few,	1798.
	*Nathaniel Irish,	Ex., 1769.	1779.	John Smith,	1804.
	*Patrick Craghead,	1782.	1781.	Matthias Sadler,	1798.
	*William McMullin,	1770.	1782.	James Gibson,	1809.
	*William Dilworth,	1766.	1782.	George Ingles,	1827.
	*Robert Carson,	1775.	1782.	William McDowell,	1790.
1763.	James Bringhurst,	1792.	1782.	Frazer Kinsley,	1790.
1763.	William Rakestraw,	1775.	1782.	Evan Evans,	1786.
1763.	John Hitchcock,	1769.	1782.	William Linnard,	1834.
1763.	Joshua Pancoast,	1770.	1782.	James Corkrin,	1823.
1763.	Lawrence Price,	1768.	1783.	Joseph Thornhill,	1791.
1763.	Evans Peters,	1779.	1784.	Joseph Rakestraw, Jr.,	1791.
	*William Lowncs,	Ex, 1809.	1784.	John King,	1805.
	*Samuel Powell,	1815.	1784.	William Moore,	Ex., 1790.
	*Joseph Gridley,	1782.	1785.	Andrew Boyd,	1797.
	*William Robinson,	1808.	1785.	Conrad Bartling.	1838.
	*James Grainsbury,	1800.	1785.	John Donahue,	Ex., 1790.
	*Jacob Reary,	1782.	1785.	John Rugan,	1836.
1769.	Thomas Shoemaker,	1799.	1785.	Mark Rodes,	1830.
1769.	David Evans,	Ex., 1815.	1785.	John Harrison,	1801.
1769.	William Colladay,	1823.	1785.	John Cooper.	1802.
1770.	Abram Jones,	1781.		*Members of Friendship Car-*	
1770.	Thomas Middleton,	1771.		*penters' Company. Merged*	
1770.	William Boyer,	1775.		*into this Company, 1st mo.,*	
1770.	William Ashton,	Ex., 1798.		*16th, 1786.*	
1770.	John Trip,	1805.		Robert Evans,	1809.
1770.	Andrew Edge.	1786.		Joseph Wetherill,	1820.
1770.	Samuel Jarvis,	1802.		Hugh Roberts,	1790.
1770.	Samuel Wallis,	1798.		William Garrigues,	1832.
1770.	Benjamin Mitchell,	1790.		Isaac Jones,	1807.
1770.	Matthew McGlathery,	1800.		Samuel Pancoast,	1834.
1771.	John Mifflin.	1786.		Matthew Val Keen,	1807.
1771.	Samuel Caruthers,	1780.		William Stevenson,	1817.
1771.	John Allis,	1772.		Robert Morrell,	1806.
1772.	Moses Thomas,	1780.		Richard Mosely,	1800.
1772.	Thomas Procter,	1806.		John Reinhard,	1816.
1772.	Adam Zantzinger.	1798.		Samuel Pastorius,	Ex., 1798.
1772.	John Keen,	1832.		John Barker,	1791.
1772.	Joseph Evans,	1792.		Josiah Matlack,	1802.
1772.	Joseph Govett,	1795.		John Piles,	1790.
1773.	John Lort, Jr.,	1794.		Joseph Clark,	1798.
1773.	Joseph Ogilby,	1809.		William Zane,	Ex., 1805.

* Date of Election not ascertained.

ELECTED.		DECEASED.	ELECTED.		DECEASED.
	Benjamin Mitchell.	1816.	1795.	Jacob Comly,	1826.
	Thomas Savery.	1818.	1795.	George Summers,	1823.
	Nathan Allen Smith,	1824.	1795.	John Hutchinson,	1836.
•	Samuel Talbert,	1790.	1795.	Jacob Evans,	Ex., 1803.
	Samuel Jones,	1796.	1796.	Jacob Nice,	1818.
	John Hall,	1797.	1796.	John Adolph,	1843.
	Jonathan Dilworth, Ex.,	1787.	1796.	John Smith,	Rd., 1820.
	Israel Hallowell,	1790.	1796.	Malcolm McLeod,	1841.
	William Griffiths,	1799.	1796.	Richard Chamberlain,	1824.
	Joseph Howell,	1798.	1796.	Isaac Carlile,	Ex., 1815.
			1796.	Elisha Thomas.	1810.
1786.	Ebenezer Furguson,	1836.	1796.	William Hopkinson, Ex.,	1809.
1786.	Francis McClister, Ex.,	1787.	1796.	David Flickwir.	1813.
1786.	Alexander Hall, Ex.,	1790.	1796.	Jacob Lybrant,	1817.
1787.	Jonathan Evans, Ex.,	1800.	1796.	William Govett,	1852.
1787.	James Craig,	1798.	1797.	John Cox,	1813.
1788.	Joseph Worrell,	1840.	1798.	Isaac Perkins,	1808.
1788.	John Wilson,	1793.	1798.	Jesse Williamson,	1852.
1788.	John Harrison,	1801.	1798.	Jonathan Roberts,	1832.
1788.	James Boyer,	1823.	1799.	Jacob Mansfield,	1803.
1791.	George Snowden, Ex.,	1815.	1799.	Alphonso C. Ireland,	1832.
1791.	Daniel Knight.	1838.	1799.	John Derbyshire,	1811.
1791.	William Krider, Ex.,	1815.	1799.	Peter Gable,	1849.
1791.	Alexander Steel,	1818.	1800.	John How,	1830.
1792.	Jacob Colladay,	1826.	1800.	Frederick Forepaugh,	1811.
1792.	Joseph Morris.	1847.	1800.	Owen Biddle,	1807.
1792.	Abraham Colladay,	1851.	1800.	Joseph Cowgill,	1813.
1792.	Philip Kellinger,	1793.	1800.	William McMullin,	1814.
1792.	Robert Jordan, •	1797.	1800.	William Palmer,	1815.
1792	Benjamin Thornton,	1797.	1801.	Samuel Robinson,	1807.
1792.	Benjamin Paschall,	1801.	1801.	David Gray, Ex.,	1824.
1792.	Matthew Crosier, Ex.,	1805.	1801.	Philip Justus,	1861.
1793.	Samuel Wayne, Ex.,	1809.	1801.	James McGlathery,	1817.
1793.	William Powell,	1824.	1802.	Finnix Stretcher,	1846.
1793.	Edward Garrigues, Rd.,	1845.	1802.	Samuel Baker, Jr.,	1816.
1793.	Samuel Johnson, Ex.,	1805.	1802.	Joseph Corbitt,	1816.
1794.	Samuel Simes,	1795.	1802.	William Reinhard,	1803.
1794.	Edward Mullock,	1801.	1803.	John Rowen,	1820.
1794.	Aaron Clark,	1798.	1803.	James Cooper, Ex.,	1816.
1794.	David Paul,	1852.	1803.	William Coles,	1854.
1794.	Thomas Lancaster,	1858.	1803.	John Sands,	1845.
1794.	Isaac Davis, Ex.,	1799.	1803.	Cornelius Trimnel,	1841.
1794.	Jacob Ziegler,	1822.	1803.	Michael Baker,	1852.
1794.	Daniel Leach,	1798.	1804.	Jacob Reinhard,	1835.
1794.	Charles Rhoads.	1810.	1804.	Thomas Pickands,	1811.
1794.	James Stuart,	1813.	1804.	Thomas Carstairs,	1830.
1794.	John Sproul,	1794.	1805.	Joseph Eberth,	1831.
1794.	Samuel Paul,	1845.	1807.	Isaac Forsythe,	1820.

ELECTED.		DECEASED.	ELECTED.		DECEASED.
1807.	Ralph H. Smith,	1842.	1823.	Theodore Colladay,	1862.
1807.	Henry Hurst,	1831.	1823.	Joseph S. Colladay,	1827.
1808.	John C. Thompson,	1829.	1823.	Charles J. Colladay,	1858.
1809.	Joseph Frank, Jr.,	1828.	1823.	William Bockius,	1848.
1809.	William Wagner,	1865.	1823.	Isaac Shunk,	1855.
1809.	Joseph P. Zebley,	1821.	1823.	Jacob Zeigler,	1848.
1809.	John O'Neil,	1835.	1824.	James R. Greaves,	1870.
1809.	John G. Hoskins, Rd.,	1833.	1824.	D. Henry Flickwir.	
1809.	John Warner,	1843.	1824.	Seth Roberts,	1834.
1809.	Cornelius Stevenson,	1860.	1824.	Joseph Hutchinson.	
1809.	James Mitchell,	1851.	1826.	John Chamberlain,	1868.
1810.	Sampson Davis,	1815.	1827.	Joseph Randall,	1856.
1810.	Joseph Simes,	1846.	1828.	George R. Harmstead,	1863.
1810.	Joseph Strahan,	1834.	1828.	Joseph Smith.	1843.
1810.	Richard Ware, Ex.,	1820.	1828.	Daniel Smith,	1865.
1810.	Samuel Baker,	1827.	1829.	Daniel R. Knight,	1871.
1811.	James Weir,	1856.	1829.	Thomas Hutchinson.	
1811.	John Lancaster,	1834.	1829.	Bethuel A. Moore,	1851.
1811.	Moses Lancaster.		1830.	Jacob Backman,	1862.
1811.	John Gilder,	1854.	1831.	Samuel Copeland,	1860.
1811.	William Hause,	1857.	1831.	William C. Hancock,	1856.
1812.	Charles Blane,	1817.	1831.	John Lindsay,	1863.
1812.	John Parham,	1866.	1831.	Edward Turner,	1852.
1812.	James Lirdel,	1822.	1832.	James A. Campbell.	
1813.	Alexander Wilson, Ex.,	1823.	1833.	George Myers.	
1813.	James Clark,	1811.	1833.	George Haas,	1811.
1813.	Alexander Ramsey.	1822.	1833.	Jonathan Johnson,	1862.
1814.	Joseph Lyndall,	1822.	1833.	Robert A. Govett,	1868.
1814.	James Hall,	1846.	1833.	Joseph Govett.	
1814.	John Howell,	1829.	1833.	James Stewart.	1856.
1814.	William Randolph.	1837.	1833.	William Weer,	1857.
1815.	Charles Hicks,	1855.	1833.	George Day.	
1815.	Jacob Ballinger.	1846.	1833.	S. Smith Leigh,	1871.
1816.	George Linck.	1861.	1833.	Jacob Amos,	1865.
1816.	John M. Ogden.		1833.	William H. Ellis,	1862.
1816.	Isaac H. Griffith,	1820.	1833.	Robert T. Knight,	1873.
1816.	William P. Paxon,	1822.	1834.	Joseph Moore,	1861.
1817.	Samuel Webb, Rd.,	1857.	1834.	Samuel Williamson.	
1817.	Henry Erdman,	1852.	1834.	James Woods.	
1817.	James M. Linnard,	1863.	1834.	Michael Shaffer,	1870.
1817.	Caleb Maule,	1844.	1834.	Jesse Williamson,	1850.
1818.	Jacob Kenderdine,	1844.	1834.	Jacob Thomas,	1855.
1820.	Robert O'Neil.		1835.	Thomas K. Tresse,	1843.
1820.	Henry L. Coryell,	1845.	1835.	James Clark Jr.,	1865.
1822.	James Hutchinson.		1835.	John A. Miskey.	
1822.	John Durrach,	1850.	1835.	John D. Taylor,	1871.
1823.	George Senneff,	1872.	1835.	George R. Lawton.	1859.
1823.	Peter Wyant,	1885.	1835.	Zachariah Howell,	1852.

7

ELECTED.	DECEASED.	ELECTED.	DECEASED.
1836. George Sterr, Sr..	1869.	1854. Henry B. Williamson,	1857.
1836. Joseph C. Wills,	1860.	1854. Henry Phillippe.	
1836. Jacob W. Colladay.		1854. Philip Kramer.	
1836. Presley B. O'Neil.		1854. Edward K. Snow.	
1837. William Durfor.		1855. J. Louis Moore.	
1837. Charles Conard.		1855. Joseph M. Hancock.	
1837. James Leslie,	1860.	1856. Joseph Denegre.	
1837. Henry Little,	1858.	1857. Nathan W. Ellis.	
1837. Henry Shuster.		1859. Thomas C. Lott.	
1838. William T. Forsyth.		1861. Thomas Marsh.	
1838. Ferdinand Conover, Ex.,	1869.	1862. Edward T. Miller.	
1839. John McClure.		1863. George W. Ash.	
1839. John Rice.		1864. Samuel K. Bye.	
1839. Jacob Bartholomew,	1865.	1864. John B. Betts.	
1839. Thomas B. Patterson,	1865.	1864. David Cramer.	
1839. William C. Palmer,	1847.	1864. William H. Cramer.	
1839. John Williams.		1865. James H. Errickson.	
1839. Michael Errickson,	1868.	1865. Allen Bard.	
1841. Richard K. Betts.		1865. James M. Cooper,	1870.
1841. George W. Doane.		1865. William Devitt.	
1841. Henry Bockius,	1873.	1865. Benjamin Ketcham.	
1842. William C. Betts,	1845.	1866. Samuel K. Hopkins.	
1841. Charles Rubicam.		1866. Joseph B. Cooper.	
1844. Jacob S. Price.		1866. Hibberd Yarnall.	
1846. John Ketcham.		1866. Thomas Little.	
1847. Samuel Rain.		1866. John Crump.	
1848. Aaron Doane.		1867. Charles C. Muller.	
1848. Edward Kelly.		1867. S. Ellis Furman.	
1849. Mark Balderston.		1867. W. Henry Furman.	
1849. William F. Wilson,	1853.	1867. Samuel R. Marriner.	
1850. Thomas F. Shuster.		1867. James Buckingham.	
1850. James G. Steel,	1871.	1867. Theodore M. Keeney.	
1851. Levi B. Stokes.		1868. Samuel M. Albertson.	
1851. Charles Shoemaker,	1863.	1868. Thomas Davis.	
1851. William Eyre.		1868. Richard Sharp.	
1851. Robert Hays.		1869. Stephen P. Rush.	
1851. John McArthur.		1869. Oliver Bradin.	
1852. Charles McIntire.		1869. Stacy Reeves.	
1852. Jonathan Rubincam,	1866.	1869. John Duncan.	
1852. George Chandlee,	1865.	1870. Charles S. Close.	
1853. John Kilgore.		1871. Robert M. Strode.	
1853. Jacob Jones.		1872. Edward Mentz.	
1853. John R. Hudders,	1862.	1872. Levi Koder.	
1853. Wesley Ballinger,	1859.	1872. John Eaton.	
1853. George Brown,	1860.	1872. William C. McPherson.	
1853. Walter Allison.		1873. George Watson.	
1853. John D. Jones.			

RULES

FOR THE

Library of the Carpenters' Company

OF THE CITY AND COUNTY OF PHILADELPHIA. *

1st. No person but a member of the Company, and those of his family, residing with him, shall be allowed the use of the Library, except by special permission of the Library Committee.

2d. The Librarian shall loan for six weeks to those entitled thereto one book, and no greater number unless connected so as to be otherwise useless; and may renew it for a similar time, unless application shall have been made by another member for the same book, and the Librarian required to take a memorandum thereof.

3d. Each member shall furnish those of his family, who may use the Library, with a permit directed to the Librarian before their using it; and such member shall be responsible for all books loaned thereon, or fines incurred, until said order is withdrawn.

4th. Books returned are to be delivered into the hands of the Librarian, to be examined whether damaged or not, and any person who shall retain any book or books longer than the time above specified shall forfeit, and pay the Librarian, ten cents per week for each book retained.

5th. It shall be the duty of the Librarian to notify the Secretary of the Library Committee, of all books remaining out beyond the time specified in Rule 2d, and pay all fines received to the Wardens, and furnish them, previous to each stated meeting of the Company, with an account of all fines unpaid, which shall be entered upon the notices of such members, and collected with the other dues of the Company.

6th. In case a book shall have been lost or injured, the damage shall be assessed by the Library Committee, and the amount paid by the borrower before they can be again permitted to use the library.

7th. Any member wanting a book not on the catalogue, must apply to the Library Committee, who may, if they think proper, procure the same.

8th. Any member trangressing the above rules, shall be reported by the Library Committee to the Company at their next stated meeting.

CATALOGUE OF BOOKS

Library of the Carpenters' Company

OF THE CITY AND COUNTY OF PHILADELPHIA.

4226. *Abbott.* Napoleon at St. Helena, or Interesting Anecdotes and Conversations of the Emperor during the five and a half years of his Captivity, collected from the Memorials of Las Casas, O'Meara, Montholon, Antommarchi, and others, by J. S. C. Abbott, with Illustrations. 1855.

634. *Abbott.* Kings and Queens, or Life in the Palace: consisting of sketches of the Empress Josephine and Maria Louisa, Louis Phillippe, Ferdinand, Nicholas, Isabella, Leopold, Victoria, and Louis Napoleon, by J. S. C. Abbott.

4224-25. *Abbott.* The History of Napoleon Bonaparte, by John S. C. Abbott, with maps and illustrations, in 2 vols. 1855.

2226. *Abbott.* Miles Standish, the Puritan Captain, by John S. C. Abbott.

2283. *Abbott.* Daniel Boone, the Pioneer of Kentucky, by John S. C. Abbott.

2225. *Abbott.* Gentle Measures in the Management of the Training of the Young, or the principles on which a firm parental authority may be established, etc., etc., by Jacob Abbott.

1534. *Abbott.* Light, by Jacob Abbott. 1871.

1849. *About.* The Roman Question, by Edward About.

Abyssinia. See Parkyns.

406. *Adams.* Roman Antiquities, or an Account of the Manners and Customs of the Romans, by Alexander Adams.

4627. *Adams.* Life and Public Services of John Quincy Adams, Sixth President of the United States, with the Eulogy delivered before the Legislature of New York, by W. H. Seward. 1849.

2857. *Adams.* The Lives of James Madison and James Monroe, Fourth and Fifth Presidents of the United States, by J. Q. Adams. 1850.

833-42.   *Adams.* The Life and Works of John Adams, Second President of the United States, edited by his Grandson, Charles Francis Adams, 10 vols., portraits.

4721.   *Adams.* Roman Antiquities, or an Account of the Manners and Customs of the Romans, etc., by Alexander Adams, L. L. D.

2297.   *Adams.* The Queen of the Adriatic, or Venice, Past and Present, by W. H. D. Adams.

2823.   *Adams.* Record of Noble Lives, a book of Notable English Biographies, by W. H. D. Adams.

3206.   *Adams.* Light Houses and Light Ships ; a historical and descriptive account of their mode of construction and organization, by W. H. D. Adams.

1927.   *Adams.* Northern Lands, or Young America in Russia and Prussia, a story of travel and adventure, by W. T. Adams.

Adams. See Oliver Optic.

4618-23.   *Addison.* The Works of Joseph Addison, in 6 vols., complete. 1854.

654.   *Adorna.* Life of Madame Catharine Adorna, including some leading facts and traits in her religious character, with explanations, by Thomas C. Upham.

Adventures. See Frost. Goodrich.

2924.   *Æschylus.* The Tragedies of Æschylus, literally translated, with Critical and Illustrative Notes, and an Introduction by T. A. Buckley, to which is added an Appendix, containing the New Readings of Hermann's Posthumous Edition. 1856.

Africa. See Murray, Foote, Taylor, Wilson, and Anderson.

1150.   *Agassiz.* Principles of Zoology, touching the Structure, Development, Distribution, and Natural Arrangement of the Races of Animals, Living and Extinct, by L. Agassiz and A. A. Gould. 1854.

1530.   *Agassiz.* Geological Sketches, by L. Agassiz.

800.   *Agassiz.* A Journey in Brazil, by Professor and Mrs. Louis Agassiz in 1868. See Hart.

1509.   *Agassiz.* Seaside Sketches in Natural History, by E. and A. Agasssiz.

4767.   *Aquilar.* Home Influence, a tale for Mothers and Daughters, by Grace Aquilar.

2227.   *Aquilar.* The Mother's Recompense, a sequel to Home Influence, by G. Aquilar.

3127.   *Aikens.* Memoir of the Court of Elizabeth, Queen of England, by Lucy Aikens. 1870.

2503.   *Akenside.* The Poetical Works of Mark Akenside, with a Life of the Author, by A. Dyce. 1856.

531-532.   *Alcock.* The Capital of the Tycoon, a Narrative of a Three Years' Residence in Japan, by Sir Rutherford Alcock, A. C. B., Her Majesty's Envoy Extraordinary and Minister Plenipotentiary in Japan, with Maps and Engravings. 2 vols.

3263.   *Alcott.* An Old Fashioned Girl, by Louisa M. Alcott.

3261.   *Alcott.* Little Women, or Meg, Jo, Beth, and Amy, by Louisa M. Alcott. Part First.

3262. *Alcott.* Little Women, by Louisa M. Alcott. Part Second.

3264. *Alcott.* Moods, by Louisa M. Alcott.

2334. *Alcott.* Little Men, Life at Plumfield with Jo's boys, by Louisa M. Alcott.

2332. *Alcott.* Aunt Jo's Scrap Bag. My Boys, &c., by Louisa M. Alcott.

2333. *Alcott.* Aunt Jo's Scrap Bag. Shawl Straps, by L. M. Alcott.

1997–1999. *Alexander.* The Daily Chronicle, by Charles Alexander, 1829–30, 3 vols. (Gift of James Hutchinson.

2325. *Alger.* Paul the Pedlar, or the adventures of a Young Street Merchant, by H. Alger, Jr.

2326. *Alger.* Phil, the Fiddler, or the story of a Young Street Musician, by H. Alger, Jr.

2327. *Alger.* Tattered Tom, or the Study of a Street Arab, by H. Alger, Jr.

2328. *Alger.* Slow and Sure, or from the Street to the Shop, by H. Alger, Jr.

323. *Allen.* Philosophy of the Mechanics of Nature, and the Source and Modes of Action of Natural Motive Power, by Z. Allen. 1852.

128–30. *Allibone.* Dictionary of English Literature and English and American Authors, living and deceased, from the earliest accounts to the latter half of the 19th century, by S. Austin Allibone, 3 vols.

4453. *Allison.* Miscellaneous Essays, by Archibald Allison, F. R. S., 1853.

178–81. *Allison.* History of Europe from the Commencement of the French Revolution in 1789 to the Restoration of the Bourbons in 1815, by A. Allison, 4 vols.

3184. *Allison.* Essays on the Nature and Principles of Taste, by A. Allison. 1854.

3614–19. *American.* The American Annual Enclyopædia, and Register of Important Events, embracing Political, Civil, Military, and Social Affairs, Public Documents, Biography, Statistics, Commerce, Finance, Literature, Science, &c., 6 vols.

(See Smith and Watson, Jones and Newman, Chambers, Robertson, Charles, Humboldt, De Tocqueville, Quarterly Review, Hand Book, Magoon.)

858. *America.* The Northern Coast of America, and the Hudson Bay Territories, a narrative of Adventure and Discovery. 1851.

2090–02. *American.* American Artisan, a Journal of Arts, Mechanics, Engineering, and Patent Record, 14 vols.

4011. *American.* American Engineer, A Weekly Scientific Journal of Practical Information, Mechanics, Chemistry, and Art. 1871.

2231. *Ames.* A Memorial of Phebe and Alice Carey, with some of their later poems, by Mary Clemmer Ames.

1531. *Anderson.* The Story of my Life, by Hans Christine Anderson, now first translated into English. 1872.

249. *Anderson.* Lake Ngami, or Explorations and Discoveries during Four Years' Wanderings in the Wilds of Southwestern Africa, by C. J. Anderson, with an Introductory Letter by J. C. Fremont, &c. 1857.

3236. **Andrews.** Sketch of the Official Life of John A. Andrews, as Governor of Massachusetts. 1868.

3862. **Anecdotes.** Anecdotes for the Steamboat and Railroad, selected from the best Anthors, by an Old Traveller. 1854.
See Field, Arvine.

Animated Nature. See "Pictorial Museum."

Angolo. See Grimm.

3875. **Ansted.** Physical Geography, by David Thomas Ansted, M. A. 1869.

Antiquities. See Maunder, Gould.

4587. **Anthon.** A Manual of Greek Literature, from the Earliest Authentic Period to the Close of the Byzantine Era, by C. Anthon. 1853.

•4588. **Anthon.** A Manual of Grecian Antiquities, with Numerous Illustrations, by C. Anthon. 1852.

Annals. See Watson, Fitch, Cyclopædia.

1295-13. **Annual.** The Annual of Scientific Discovery, or Year Book of Facts in Science and Art, exhibiting the most Important Discoveries and Improvements in Mechanics, Useful Arts, &c. &c. 1850-1865, 16 vols.

17-18. **Appleton.** Dictionary of Machines, Mechanics, Engine Work, and Engineering, Illustrated by 4000 Engravings on Wood, 2 vols.

Arabia. See Crichton.

637-8. **Arago.** Biographies of Distinguished Scientific Men, by Francois Arago, 2 vols.

Architecture. See Biddle, Boid, Brown, Barnard, Bullock, Bartholomew, Brandon, Britton, Brooks, Campbell, Cruden, Downing, Dictionary, Designs, Dempsey, Davy, Ferguson, Field, Gibbs, Glossary, Harbershon, Hatfield, Haviland, Hope, Jones, Johnson, Kirby, Leoni, Langly, Lafever, Laing, Lomax, Lugar, Loudon, Minifies, Martin, Mechanics, Middleton, Nicholson, Owen, Perrault, Price, Pope, Pain, Pugin, Papworth, Pitch, Ranlett, Riddell, Ruskin, Rickman, Sloan, Swan, Stuart, Smith, Shaw, Soane, Thompson, Tredgold, Tuthill, Turner, Ware, Woodward, Winkles.

Armenia. See Carson.

3181. **Arnold.** The Great Exhibition, with Continental Sketches, practical and humorous, by Howard Payson Arnold. 1868.

3952-57. **Art.** Art Journal, with Illustrated Catalogue. 1850-1855, 6 vols.

Art. See Pictorial Gallery.

975. **Arthur.** History of Kentucky, from its Earliest Settlement to the Present Time, by T. S. Arthur and W. H. Carpenter.

979. **Arthur.** History of Pennsylvania, from its Earliest Settlement to the Present Time.

977. **Arthur.** History of Georgia, from its Earliest Settlement to the Present Time.

981. **Arthur.** History of Vermont, from its Earliest Settlement to the Present Time.

976. *Arthur.* History of Virginia, from its Earliest Settlement to the Present Time.

971. *Arthur.* History of New York, from its Earliest Settlement to the Present Time.

978. *Arthur.* History of Illinois, from its Earliest Settlement to the Present Time.

973. *Arthur.* History of New Jersey, from its Earliest Settlement to the Present Time.

974. *Arthur.* History of Connecticut, from its Earliest Settlement to the Present Time.

982. *Arthur.* History of Ohio, from its Earliest Settlement to the Present Time.

980. *Arthur.* History of Tennessee, from its Earliest Settlement to the Present Time.

4327. *Arthur.* Orange Blossoms, Fresh and Faded, by T. S. Arthur.

24. *Arvine.* The Cyclopædia of Anecdotes of Literature and the Fine Arts, containing a Copious and Choice Selection of Anecdotes. H. Arvine, 1853.

Asia. See Malcolm, Vamberry.

297. *Assembly.* Acts of General Assembly of the Commonwealth of Pennsylvania, passed 1803.

324. *Assembly.* A Digest of the Acts of Assembly relating to the City of Philadelphia, and the (late) incorporated Districts of the County of Philadelphia, and of the Ordinances of the said City and Districts. 1856.

Athens. See (Stuart) Boecka.

Astronomy. See Herschell, Lardner, Norton, Schœdler, Mitchell.

681. *Atkinson.* Oriental and Western Siberia, a Narrative of Seven Years' Explorations and Adventures in Siberia, Mongolia, the Kirghis Steppes, Chinese Tartary, and part of Central Asia, by Thomas Witlam Atkinson, with a Map and numerous Illustrations.

3071-99. *Atlantic.* The Atlantic Monthly, a Magazine of Literature, Art, and Politeness, 32 vols., 1857 to 1873.

4724. *Atlee.* General and Differential Diagnosis of Ovarium Tumors, &c., by W. Atlee, M. D.

3967-69. *Audubon.* The Quadrupeds of North America, by John James Audubon and the Rev. John Bachman, 3 vols.

3137. *Audubon.* The Life of John James Audubon, the Naturalist; edited by his widow; with an introduction by James Grant Wilson. 1869.

2210. *Autocrat.* The Autocrat at the Breakfast Table, or every man his own Boswell.

B.

1617. *Bache.* Report on Education in Europe to the Trustees of the Girard College for Orphans, by A. D. Bache. 1839. Gift of James Hutchinson.

7*

1648–50. **Bache.** Observations at the Magnetic and Meteorological Observatory of the Girard College, by A. D. Bache. 1840–45. 3 vols. Gift of James Hutchinson.

1438. **Bache.** Plates to accompany the Observations, &c.

1185. **Bacon.** Memoir of Nathaniel Bacon, by William Ware.

766–68. **Bacon.** The Works of Francis Bacon, Lord Chancellor of England, with a Life of the Author by Basil Montague. 3 vols.

Bacon. See Dixon.

2216. **Bagehot.** Physics and Politics, or Thoughts on the Application of the Principles of "Natural Selection" and "Inheritance" to Political Society, by W. Bagehot.

1537. **Baile.** Wonders of Electricity, translated from the French of J. Baile.

3266. **Baily.** Our Own Birds, a Familiar Natural History of the Birds of the United States, by William L. Baily. 1869.

3267. **Baily.** Trees, Plants and Flowers; Where and How they Grow, a Familiar History of the Vegetable Kingdom, by W. L. Baily 1871.

856. **Baily.** Essay on the Formation and Publication of Opinions, the Pursuit of Truth, and on other Subjects, by Samuel Baily.

1134. **Baird.** Modern Greece, a Narrative of a Residence and Travels in that Country, with observations on its Antiquities, Literature, Language, Politics, and Religion, by H. M. Baird, M. A. 1856.

1510. **Baird.** Annual Record of Science and Industry, for 1871, by Spencer F. Baird, with the assistance of eminent men of science.

1876. **Baker.** Eight Years' Wanderings in Ceylon, by Sir S. W. Baker.

2219. **Baker.** The Nile Tributaries of Abyssinia, and the Sword Hunters of the Hamran Arabs, by S. W. Baker.

3229. **Baker.** The Rifle and the Hound in Ceylon, with illustrations, by S. W. Baker. 1869.

3230. **Baker.** Cast up by the Sea, by S. W. Baker. 1871.

3173. **Baldwin.** Pre-historic Nations, or Inquiries concerning some of the Great People and Civilization of Antiquity, and the probable relation to a still older civilization of the Ethiopians or Cushites of Arabia, by John D. Baldwin. 1869.

1544. **Baldwin.** Ancient America, or Notes on American Archæology, by John D. Baldwin. 1872.

1510. **Ballou.** Treasury of Thought, Forming an Encyclopædia of Quotations from Ancient and Modern Authors, by M. M. Ballou.

3798. **Ballou.** History of Cuba, or Notes of a Traveller in the Tropics, being a Political, Historical, and Statistical Account of the Island from its Discovery to the Present Time, by M. M. Ballou. 1854.

3231. **Ballantyne.** Fighting the Flames, a Tale of the Fire Brigade, by R. M. Ballantyne. 1870.

3232. **Ballantyne.** Deep Down, a Tale of the Cornish Mines, by R. M. Ballantyne.

3233. *Ballantyne.* Erling the Bold, a Tale of the Norse Sea-Kings, by R. M. Ballantyne.

2565-72. *Ballads.* English and Scottish, selected and edited, with Notes and Introduction, by F. J. Child, 8 vols.

780-7. *Bancroft.* History of the United States, from the Discovery of the American Continent, by George Bancroft, 8 vols. 1843.

431. *Bardwell.* Healthy Homes, and how to make them, dedicated by permission to the Right Honorable Viscount Palmerston, by William Bardwell, Architect.

2320. *Barker.* Stories About, by Lady Barker.

1877. *Barker.* Station Life in New Zealand, by Lady Barker.

4252. *Barnard.* School Architecture, or Contributions to the Improvement of School Houses in the United States, by H. Barnard. 1854.

288. *Barnard.* National Education in Europe, being an Account of the Organization, Administration, Instruction, and Statistics of Public Schools of Different Grades in the Principal States, by H. Barnard. 1854.

2259. *Barnard.* The New History of Sanford and Merton, being a true Account of Masters Tommy and Harry, with their beloved Tutor, Mr. Barlow, by F. C. Barnard.

199. *Bartholomew.* Specifications for Practical Architecture, preceded by an Essay on the Decline of the Excellence in the Structure and in the Science of Modern English Buildings, with Proposals of Remedies, &c., by the late Alfred Bartholomew. 1846.

2054-5. *Bartlett.* Switzerland, by William Beattie, Illustrated by Views taken on the Spot, by William H. Bartlett, 2 vols.

69. *Bartlett.* Dictionary of Americanisms, a Glossary of Words and Phrases usually Regarded as Peculiar to the United States, by John Russell Bartlett. Third edition, greatly improved and enlarged.

1179. *Barrington.* Personal Sketches of his own Time, by Sir Jonah Barrington, Judge of the High Court of Admiralty in Ireland. 1853.

4625. *Barrington.* A Treatise on Physical Geography, comprising Hydrology, Geognosy, Geology, Meteorology, Botany, Zoology, and Anthropology, by A. Barrington. Edited by C. Burdette. 1850.

2845. *Barton.* Memoirs, Letters, and Poems of Bernard Barton. Edited by his Daughter. 1850.

3918. *Bartram.* Memorials of John Bartram and Humphrey Marshall, with Notes of their Botanical Contemporaries, by W. Darlington.

2849. *Bauer.* Lives of the Brothers Humboldt, William and Alexander. Translated and arranged from the German of Klencke and Schlesier, by Juliette Bauer. 1853.

1131. *Bayard.* Life of the Chevalier Bayard, by W. Gilmore Simms. Engravings.

1539. *Beard.* Stimulants and Narcotics, Medically, Philosophically, and Morally Considered, by George M. Beard. 1871.

1543. **Beard.** Eating and Drinking, a Popular Manual of Food and Diet in Health and Disease, by G. M. Beard.

2502. **Beattie.** The Poetical Works of James Beattie, with a Memoir of the Author, by A. Dyce. 1854.

1109-1110. **Beauchesne.** Louis XVII, his Life, his Sufferings, his Death, the Captivity of the Royal Family in the Temple, by A. De Beauchesne. Translated by W. Hazlitt. 1853. 2 vols.

3178. **Beaumarchais.** Beaumarchais and his Times, Sketch of French Society in the 18th Century, from unpublished Documents, by Louis de Lomenie. Translated by H. S. Edwards. 1857.

243. **Beche.** The Geological Observer, by Sir Henry T. De La Beche. 1851.

3806. **Beck.** The Botany of the United States, North of Virginia, comprising Descriptions of Flowering and Fern-like Plants hitherto found in those States, arranged according to the Natural System, with a Synopsis of the Genera according to the Linnæan System, a Sketch of the Rudiments of Botany, &c., by Lewis C. Beck.

4580. **Becker.** Charicles. Illustrations of the Private Life of the Ancient Greeks, With Notes and Exercises from the German of Professor Becker. 1854.

2927-28. **Beckman.** A History of Inventions, Discoveries, and Origins, by John Beckman, &c. 2 vols. 1846.

Bee. See Langstroth.

1538. **Beecher.** Lecture-room Talk, a Series of Familiar Discourses on Themes of General Christian Experience, by Henry Ward Beecher. 1871.

2229. **Beecher.** Lectures to Young Men on Various Important Subjects, by H. W. Beecher.

1541. **Belcher.** The Mutineers of the "Bounty," the Descendants of Pitcairn and Norfolk Islands, by S. Belcher.

1533. **Bellows.** The Philosophy of Eating, by A. J. Bellows, M. D. 1872.

1547. **Bellows.** How not to be Sick, a Sequel to the Philosophy of Eating, by A. J. Bellows.

3872-3. **Bellows.** The Old World in its New Face, Impressions of Europe, in 1867-68, by H. W. Bellows. 2 vols. 1869.

3265. **Benjamin.** The Choice of Paris, a romance of the Troad, by S. G. W. Benjamin.

2830. **Benjamin.** The Turk and the Greek, or Creeds, Races, Society, and Scenery, in Turkey, Greece, and the Isles of Greece, by S. G. W. Benjamin. 1867.

2215. **Bennett.** Ellenore, from the German of Rothenfels, by F. E. Bennett.

2604. **Bennett.** Winter in the South of Europe, or Mentone, the Riviera, Corsica, Sicily, and Biarritz, as Winter Climates, by J. Henry Bennett.

70-71. **Benton.** Thirty Years' View, or a History of the Working of the American Government for 30 years, from 1820 to 1850, chiefly taken from the Congress Debates, the private papers of General Jackson, and the Speeches of ex-Senator Benton, with his actual View of Men and Affairs, 2 vols.

3801. *Belisle.* History of Independence Hall, by D. W. Belisle.

1950. *Biart.* Adventures of a Young Naturalist, by Lucien Biart.

1386. *Binns.* Digest of the Laws and Judicial Decisions of Pennsylvania, touching the Authority and Duties of Justices of the Peace, by John Binns. 1840.

1145. *Binns.* Recollections of the Life of John Binns; 29 years in Europe and 53 in the United States. 1854.

4093. *Bible.* The Holy Bible, containing the Old and New Testaments, &c., with the Apocrypha. Butler's Edition. 1851.

4041. *Biddle.* The Young Carpenter's Assistant, or a System of Architecture adapted to the Style of Building in the United States, by Owen Biddle. 1805.

4019. *Biddle.* An improved Edition of Biddle's Young Carpenter's Assistant, being a complete System of Architecture for Carpenters, Joiners, and Workmen in General, by John Haviland. 1832.

Biography. See Conrad. Arago.

656. *Biography.* Exemplary Biography of Distinguished Men.

1873. *Bishop.* A Thousand Miles walk across South America, by Nathaniel H. Bishop, with an introduction.

1546. *Black.* The Ten Laws of Health, or how disease is produced and can be prevented, by J. R. Black.

2214. *Blackie.* Four Phases of Morals, Socrates, Aristotle, Christianity, and Utilitarianism, by J. S. Blackie, F. R. S. E.

2296. *Blackmore.* Clara Vaughan, by R. D. Blackmore, 2 vols. in one.

266-67. *Blackstone.* Commentaries on the Laws of England, in four books, with an Analysis of the Work, by Sir William Blackstone, Knt., one of the Justices of the Court of Common Pleas. In two volumes, from the nineteenth London edition. With a Life of the Author, and Notes by Christian, Chitty, Lee, Hovenden, and Ryland; and also references to American Cases, by a member of the New York Bar.

1874. *Bloxam.* Metals and their properties and treatment, by C. L. Bloxam. 1872.

789. *Boeckh.* The Public Economy of the Athenians, by Augustus Boeckh. Translated from the second German edition. With Notes and a Copious Index by Anthony Lamb. Portrait.

1152. *Boid.* A concise History and Analysis of the Principal Styles of Architecture, to which is added a Sketch of the Architecture of England, by Edward Boid. 1835.

412. *Bonaparte.* The Napoleon Dynasty, or the History of the Bonaparte Family, an entirely New Work, by the Berkely Men. 1832.

Bonaparte. See Shoberl. Thiers, D'Abrantes. Forsythe, Watson, Headley, Abbott.

2860-61. *Book.* Book of Prices. Edition of 1786. 2 copies.

2855-56. *Book.* Book of Prices. Edition of 1808. 2 copies.

1418. *Book.* Book of Prices, Edition of 1827.

4044. *Book.* Book of Ornaments, by T. Wallis.

4045. *Book.* Book of Tablets, by T. Pether.

1875. *Books.* Among my Books, Sketches of Persons and Things. 1871.

1535. *Book.* The Book of Travels of a Doctor of Physic, containing his observations made in certain portions of the two continents. 1871.

4616. *Boone.* Daniel Boone and the Hunters of Kentucky, by W. H. Bagot. 1854.

4116. *Boone.* Life of Daniel Boone, the Pioneer of Kentucky, by John M. Peck. See Abbott.

2832. *Borges.* A Trip to the Azores, or Western Islands, by M. Borges and E. Hurquiss. 1867.

1257-66. *Boswell.* The Life of Samuel Johnson, LL.D., including a Journal of his Tour to the Hebrides, by James Boswell, Esq., with numerous Additions and Notes by the Right Hon. J. Wilson Croker; to which is added Two Supplementary Volumes of Johnsoniana, by Hawkins and others, and Notes by various hands, in 10 vols. 1853.

Botany. See Beck.

2212. *Botta.* Hand-Book of Universal Literature, from the best and latest authorities, by A. C. L. Botta.

3203. *Boutel.* Arms and Armour of Antiquity, and the Middle Ages; also a descriptive notice of Modern Weapons, by Charles Boutel. 1871.

5344. *Bourne.* Famous London Merchants, a Book for Boys, by H. R. F. Bourne.

202. *Bowen.* The Pictorial Sketch-Book of Pennsylvania, or the Scenery, Internal Improvements, Resources, Agriculture, &c., popularly described by Eli Bowen. 1852.

4605. *Bowles.* Across the Continent, a Summer Journey to the Rocky Mountains, the Mormons, and the Pacific States, by S. Bowles. 1866.

402. *Bowles.* Our New West, Record of Travel between the Mississippi River and the Pacific Ocean, over the Plains, over the Mountains, through the Great Interior Basin, over the Sierra Nevada, to and up and down the Pacific Coast, with details of the wonderful scenery, by S. Bowles. 1870.

2319. *Boyhood.* The Boyhood of Great Men, intended as an example to Youth.

3176. *Brackenridge.* Recollections of Persons and Places in the West, by H. M. Brackenridge.

72. *Braddock.* The History of an Expedition against Fort Du Quesne in 1755, under Major General Edward Braddock, &c., by W. Sargeant, Member of the Historical Society of Pa. 1855.

866. *Braman.* Information about Texas. Carefully prepared by D. E. E. Braman, of Matagorda, Texas.

1429. *Brandon.* The Open Timber Roofs of the Middle Ages, Illustrated by Perspective and Working Drawings of the best Variety of

Church Roofs, with descriptive Letter Press, by R. and J. A. Brandon. 1849.

4260. *Brande.* A Dictionary of Science, Literature, and Art, comprising the History, Description and Scientific Principles of every Branch of Human Knowledge, with the Derivation and Definition of all the Technical Terms in general use, by W. T. Brande. 1852.

Brazil. See Payne, Ewbank.

2218. *Breck.* New Book of Flowers, by Joseph Breck.

527-8. *Bremer.* The Homes of the New World, or Impressions of America, by Frederica Bremer, 2 vols.

648. *Brewster.* More Worlds than One, the Creed of the Philosopher, and the Hope of the Christian, by Sir David Brewster.

1702. *Bridge.* The New Bridge at Black Friars, London. See Kauptz.

3856-0. *Bridgewater.* The Bridgewater Treatises, or the Power, Wisdom, and Goodness of God, as manifested in the Creation, by Kirby, Kidd, Chalmers, Whewell, in 5 vols.

1548. *Brinton.* The Myths of the New World, a Treatise on the Symbolism and Mythology of the Red Race in America, by Daniel G. Brinton.

4026. *Britton.* Chronological History and Graphic Illustrations of Christian Architecture in England, embracing a Critical Inquiry into the Rise and Perfections of this Style of Architecture, by J. Britton.

2211. *Bristed.* Five Years in an English University, by C. A. Bristed.

430. *Broadhead.* History of the State of New York, first period, 1609 to 1664, by J. R. Broadhead.

2258. *Brock.* Kennath, my King, a Novel, by Sallie A. Brock.

2251. *Brockett.* Walter Powell, of Melbourne and London, Merchant, Philanthropist, and Christian, by L. P. Brockett, M. D.

4027. *Brooks.* Designs for Cottage and Villa Architecture, containing Plans, Elevations, Sections, Perspective Views and Details for the Erection of Cottages and Villas, by S. H. Brooks.

1582. *Brooks.* A Seven Months Run; Up and Down and Around the World, by James Brooks. 1872.

3806-7. *Brougham.* Historical Sketches of Statesmen who flourished in the Time of George III, together with Remarks on the French Revolution, by Henry, Lord Brougham, in 2 vols.

4222-3. *Brown.* The Forum, or Forty Years' full Practice at the Philadelphia Bar, by David Paul Brown. 2 vols. 1856.

21. *Brown.* Encyclopædia of Religious Knowledge; or, Dictionary of the Bible, Theology, Religious Biography, all Religions, Ecclesiastical History, and Missions: Containing definitions of all religious terms, an impartial account of the principal Christian denominations, with their doctrines, rites, and ceremonies, as well as those of the Jews, Mahommedan, and Heathen Nations, by I. Newton Brown.

2061. *Brown.* Sacred Architecture; its Use, Progress, and Present State, embracing the Babylonian, Indian, Egyptian, Greek and Roman

Temples; the Byzantine, Saxon, Lombard, Mormons, and Italian Churches, with an Analytical Inquiry into the Origin, Progress, and Perfection of the Gothic Churches of England, &c., &c., by Richard Brown.

2250. *Brown.* Spare Hours, by John Brown, M. D. First Series.

1536. *Brown.* Spare Hours, a Series of Interesting Sketches, by John Brown, M. D., 2nd Series. 1871.

1220. *Brown.* The Life and Times of Hugh Miller, by Thomas N. Brown. 1858.

2938. *Brown.* The Dervishes, or Oriental Spiritualism, by John P. Brown. 1868.

1545. *Brown.* The Life of Rufus Choate, by S. G. Brown.

997. *Browning.* The Poetical Works of Elizabeth Bennett Browning. 1871.

857. *Browning.* Forty-four Years of a Hunter's Life. Being Reminiscences of Meshack Browning, a Maryland Hunter. Roughly written down by himself. Revised and illustrated by E. Stabler.

625. *Brownlow.* The Recent Debate on Slavery between the Rev. W. G. Brownlow and the Rev. Abram Pryne, with Portraits.

4586. *Bryant.* A Year in China, and a Narrative of Capture and Imprisonment when homeward bound, on board the Rebel Pirate Florida, by Mrs. H. D. Williams. With an introductory note by W. C. Bryant.

4229. *Buck.* A Theological Dictionary, containing Definitions of all Religious Terms, an Impartial Account of the Principal Denominations which have subsisted in the Religious World from the Birth of Christ to the Present Day, together with an Authentic Statement of the most Remarkable Transactions and Events recorded in Ecclesiastical History, by Charles Buck. 1853.

1542. *Buckman.* The Land of Lorne, or a Poet's Adventure in the Scottish Hebrides, &c., by R. Buckman. 1871.

2835-36. *Buffon.* Buffon's Natural History of Man, the Globe, and of Quadrupeds, with additions, &c. 1853. 2 vols.

1434. *Builder.* The City and Country Builder and Workman's Treasury of Designs, or the Art of Drawing and Working the Different Parts of Architecture. Illustrated by upwards of 400 grand designs, and proportioned by aliquot parts. London, 1745.

1435. Same as 1434.

1461. *Bullock.* The American Cottage Builder, a Series of Designs, Plans, and Specifications, from $200 to $20,000, for Homes for the People, by John Bullock, Architect, &c. 1854.

4174-75. *Bulwer.* Historical Characters, Talleyrand, Cobbett, Mackintosh, Canning, by Sir H. L. Bulwer. 2 vols.

1235. *Bulwer.* The Last Days of Pompeii, by Sir H. L. Bulwer.

1236. *Bulwer.* Rienzi, or the Last of the Roman Tribune, by Sir H. L. Bulwer.

1237-38. *Bulwer.* My Novel, or Varieties in English Life, by Sir H. L. Bulwer.

1239. *Bulwer.* Eugene Aram, a Tale, by Sir H. L. Bulwer.

1240. **Bulwer.** Zanoni, by Sir H. L. Bulwer.
1241-42. **Bulwer.** What will he do with it, by Sir H. L. Bulwer. 2 vols.
1243. **Bulwer.** Lelia, or the Siege of Grenada—Calderon, the Courtier—The Pilgrim of the Rhine, by Sir H. L. Bulwer.
1244. **Bulwer.** Devereux, a Tale, by Sir H. L. Bulwer.
1245. **Bulwer.** The Last of the Barons, by Sir H. L. Bulwer.
1246. **Bulwer.** Harrold, the Last of the Saxon Kings, by Sir H. L. Bulwer.
1247. **Bulwer.** The Caxtons, a Family Picture, by Sir H. L. Bulwer.
1248. **Bulwer.** Ernest Maltravers, by Sir H. L. Bulwer.
1249. **Bulwer.** Alice, or the Mysteries, a Sequel to Ernest Maltravers, by Sir H. L. Bulwer.
1250. **Bulwer.** Pelham, or the Adventures of a Nobleman, by Sir H. L. Bulwer.
1251. **Bulwer.** A Strange Story of Haunts and Haunters, by Sir H. L. Bulwer.
1252. **Bulwer.** Lucretia, or the Children of Night, by Sir H. L. Bulwer.
1253. **Bulwer.** The Disowned, by Sir H. L. Bulwer.
1254. **Bulwer.** Godolphin, by Sir H. L. Bulwer.
1255. **Bulwer.** Night and Morning, by Sir H. L. Bulwer.
1256. **Bulwer.** Paul Clifford, by Sir H. L. Bulwer.
3171-72. **Bulwer.** The Life of Henry John Temple, Viscount Palmerston, with selections from his Diaries and Correspondence, by Sir H. L. Bulwer, 2 vols. 1871.
3174-75. **Bunsen.** Memoir of Baron Bunsen, late Minister at the Court of St. James, by his Widow, 2 vols.
1209. **Bunyan.** The Pilgrim's Progress (from this world to that which is to come), by John Bunyan. With a Memoir, by J. M. Hare. 1853.
1215. **Burke.** The Public and Domestic Life of the Right Hon. Edmund Burke, by R. Burke, Esq. 1853.
3864-65. **Burke.** Memoir of the Life and Character of the Right Hon. Edmund Burke. With specimens, &c., &c., by James Prior, 2 vols.
1840. **Burleigh.** The American Manual, or the Thinker, an outline of Government, Nature of Liberty, Laws of Nations, &c.
2584-86. **Burns.** The Poetical Works of Robert Burns, with a Sketch of his Life. 3 vols.
425. **Burns.** The Works of Robert Burns.
1067. **Burr.** The Life and Times of Aaron Burr.
4598. **Burrit.** Thoughts and Things at Home and Abroad, by Elihu Burrit. 1854.
3832. **Burton.** Personal Narrative of a Pilgrimage to El-medinah and Mecca, by Richard F. Burton, Lieutenant, Bombay Army. With Introduction, by Bayard Taylor.
796. **Burton.** The Lake Region of Central Africa, a portion of Exploration, by Richard F. Burton. 1860.
1018. **Burton.** The City of the Saints; and Across the Rocky Mountains to California. By Captain Richard F. Burton, Fellow and Gold Medalist of the Royal Geographical Societies of France and Eng-

land; H. M. Consul in West Africa; Author of "The Lake Regions of Central Africa." With Maps and numerous Illustrations.

2531–2.   **Butler.** The Poetical Works of Samuel Butler. 1853. 2 vols.

1062.   **Butler.** General Butler in New Orleans. History of the Administration of the Gulf in 1863. With an Account of the Capture of New Orleans; and a Sketch of the Previous Career of the General, both Civil and Military, by Thomas Parton. 1864.

143.   **Burton.** The Cyclopædia of Wit and Humor, containing Choice selections &c., &c., of Eminent Humorists of America, Ireland, Scotland and England, by W. E. Burton.

392.   **Byrne.** The Practical Metal Worker's Assistant; containing the Art of Working all Metals and Alloys, forging of Iron and Steel, hardening and tempering, melting and mixing, &c., &c., with their Application to the Art of Electro-metallurgy to Manufacturing Purposes, by Oliver Byrne. 1851.

397.   **Byrne.** The Practical Model Calculator for the Engineer, the Mechanic, Machinist, Manufacturer of Engine Work, Naval Architects, and Millwrights, by Oliver Byrne. 1852.

17–8.   **Byrne.** Dictionary of Machines, Mechanics, Engine Work, and Engineering. Illustrated by 4000 Engravings on Wood, in 2 vols.

1342.   **Byron.** The Works of Lord Byron, including the Suppressed Poems. Also a Sketch of his Life, by J. W. Lake. 1854. See Trelawny.

C.

4290–1.   **Cæsar.** History of Julius Cæsar, by Napoleon III.

2022.   **Cæsar.** Cæsar's Commentaries on the Gallic and Civil Wars, with the supplemental books attributed to Hertius, including the Alexandrian, African, and Spanish Wars, literally translated with notes. 1855.

2335.   **Caldor.** Social Charades and Parlor Operas, by W. T. Caldor.

4595.   **Calhoun.** The Life of John C. Calhoun, by John S. Jenkins.

         California. See Revere, Parkman, Soule, Taylor.

1191.   **Calvert.** Life of Leonard Calvert, first Governor of Maryland, by George W. Burnap.

1553.   **Cameos.** Cameos from English History; from Rollo to Edward the 2d. 1868.

1338.   **Campbell.** The Poetical Works of Rogers, Campbell, J. Montgomery, Lamb, and Kirke White. 1856.

2512.   **Campbell.** The Poetical Works of Thos. Campbell, with Notes and a Biographical Sketch, by W. A. Hill.

841.   **Campbell.** The History of the Colony and Ancient Dominion of Virginia, by Charles Campbell.

3997–9.   **Campbell.** Vitruvius Britannicus, or the British Architect; containing the Plans, Elevations, and Sections of the regular

Building, both public and private, in Great Britain, with a variety of new designs, in 200 large folio plates, by Colon Campbell. 3 vols.

4000. **Campbell.** Same as 3999.

Canada. See Parkman.

4394. **Carleton.** Following the Flag from August, 1861, to November, 1862, with the Army of the Potomac, by Carleton, author of " My Days and Nights on the Battlefield."

4456. **Carlyle.** Critical and Miscellaneous Essays, by Thomas Carlyle. 1853.

Carolina. See Wheeler.

972. **Carpenter.** History of Massachusetts, from the Earliest Settlement to the Present Time, by W. H. Carpenter.

980. **Carpenter.** History of Tennessee, from its Earliest Settlement to the Present Time, by W. H. Carpenter.

1346. **Carpenter.** Reminiscences of Carpenters' Hall in the City of Philadelphia. 1858.

428. **Carpenter.** Articles of the Carpenters' Company of the City and County of Philadelphia, as adopted in 1763; also as amended 1786, and as revised and agreed to 1805-1807 and 1840 ; also the Act of Incorporation, By-Laws, Rules, and Regulations, as passed 1857; together with a Catalogue of Books in their Library.

4164. **Carpenter.** An Act to Incorporate the Carpenters' Company of the City and County of Philadelphia, By-Laws, Rules, and Regulations, together with reminiscences of the Hall, Extracts from Ancient Minutes, Catalogue of Books.

4212. **Carpenters.** An Act to Incorporate the Carpenters' Company of the City and County of Philadelphia; together with the By-Laws, Rules, and Regulations, and Catalogue of Books in their Library. 1857.

1100. **Carpenters.** House Carpenters' Book of Prices, and Rules for Measuring and Valuing all their different kinds of Work: adapted to Federal Currency. 1819. Gift of Robert Warnock.

2833. **Carpenter.** The Inner Life of Abraham Lincoln, Six Months at the White House, by F. B. Carpenter. 1868.

2322. **Carpenter.** Popular Readings in Prose and Verse, by J. E. Carpenter.

Carpentry. See Tredgold, Martin, Mechanics.

Cary. See Ames.

87. **Cassin.** Illustrations of the Birds of California, Texas, Oregon, British and Russian America, intended to contain Descriptions and Figures of all North American Birds not given by former American authors, and a general Synopsis of North American Ornithology, by James Cassin. 1853 to 1855.

Catalogue. See Philadelphia Library.

Cathedrals. See Winkles.

388-89. **Catlin.** Letters and Notes on the Manners, Customs, and

Condition of the North American Indians, by George Catlin. 1844. 2 vols.

3158. *Cavada.* Libby Life, Experience of a Prisoner of War in Richmond, Va., 1863–64, Lieut. Col. F. F. Cavada, U. S. N.

3210. *Casin.* The Phenomena and Laws of Heat, by A. Casin.

1439. *Census.* Statistics of the United States, including Mortality, Property, &c.. 1860, the final exhibit of the Eighth Census.

1556. *Chadbourne.* Instinct, its office in the Animal Kingdom, and its relation to the higher powers of Man, by P. A. Chadbourne.

3153. *Chaillu.* Stories of the Gorilla Country, Narrated for Young People, by Paul du Chaillu.

3154. *Chaillu.* Wild Life under the Equator, by Paul du Chaillu.

3155. *Chaillu.* Lost in the Jungle, Narrated for Young People, by Paul du Chaillu.

1327. *Chaillu.* Explorations and Adventures in Equatorial Africa, with the Manners and Customs of the People, Chase of the Gorilla, Crocodile, Leopard, &c., by Paul du Chaillu.

1549. *Chaillu.* My Apingo Kingdom, with Life in the Great Sahara, and Sketch of the Chase of the Ostrich, Hyena, &c., by Paul du Chaillu. 1871.

1550. *Chaillu.* The Country of the Dwarfs, by Paul du Chaillu.

3859. *Chalmers.* On the Power, Wisdom, and Goodness of God, as Manifested in the Adaptation of External Nature to the Moral and Intellectual Constitution of Man, by Thomas Chalmers.

4346 *Chambers.* Readings in English Literature, a Collection of Specimens from our Best Authors, from the earliest time to 1840, by W. and R. Chambers.

2345. *Chambers.* Historical and Miscellaneous Questions, with Answers, embracing History, Science, Literature, Arts, by W. Chambers.

1069-80. *Chambers.* Chambers' Papers for the People. 1850. 12 vols.

43–44. *Chambers.* The Book of Days. A New, Popular, and Interesting Miscellany. Edited by Robert Chambers. 2 vols. Consists of—

I. Matters Connected with the Church Calendar, including the Popular Festivals, Saints' Days, and other Holidays, with illustrations of Christian Antiquities in general.

II. Phenomena connected with the Seasonal Changes.

III. Folk-lore of the United Kingdom: namely, Popular Notions and Observances connected with Times and Seasons.

IV. Notable Events, Biographies, and Anecdotes connected with the Days of the Year.

V. Articles of Popular Archæology, of an entertaining character, tending to illustrate the progress of civilization, manners, literature, and ideas in these kingdoms.

VI. Curious, Fugitive, and Inedited Pieces. 2 vols.

1278-83. *Chambers.* Repository of Instructive and Amusing Tracts, by William and Robert Chambers. 6 vols.

28-34. *Chambers.* Encyclopædia. A Dictionary of Universal Knowledge for the People. Illustrated. 7 vols.

4441-46. **Chambers.** A Biographical Dictionary of Eminent Scotchmen. Edited by Robert Chambers. 6 vols.

1284-87. **Chambers.** Select Writings of Robert Chambers, Essays, Familiar, Humorous, Moral, Economical, Philosophical, Sentimental, and Historical. 4 vols. 1854.

1139. **Chambers.** Things as they are in America, by Wm. Chambers. 1854.

40-41. **Chambers.** Information for the People. Edited by Wm. and Robert Chambers. 2 vols.

1268-77. **Chambers.** Chambers' Miscellany of Useful and Entertaining Tracts. William and Robert Chambers. 10 vols.

2033-36. **Chambers.** Cyclopædia of Literature; a History, Critical and Biographical, of British Authors, from the Earliest to the Present Times. Edited by Robert Chambers. 2 vols.

1883. **Chambers.** Memoir of Robert Chambers, with Autobiographical Reminiscence of Wm. Chambers.

2282. **Chamberlain.** The Servant Girl of the Period, the Greatest Plague of Life, &c., by Charles Chamberlain, Jr.

1081. **Channing.** A Physician's Vacation, or a Summer in Europe, by Walter Channing. Revised to the Present Time. 1854.

4395. **Chaplin.** The Life of Henry Dunster, First President of Harvard College, by J. Chaplin.

4725-26. **Chapman.** Travels in the South of Africa, comprising Fifteen Years Hunting and Trading, by J. Chapman. 2 vols.

1517. **Chapman.** Evolution of Life, by H. C. Chapman, M. D.

1148. **Chasles.** Anglo-American Literature and Manners, by P. Chasles, Professor in the College of France.

2549-50. **Chatterton.** The Poetical Works of Thomas Chatterton, with Notices of his Life. A History of the Rowley Controversy, and a Glossary. A Selection of his Letters, Notes, Critical and Explanatory. 2 vols.

1882. **Chavasse.** Advice to a Wife on the Management of her own Health, &c., by P. H. Chavasse.

1881. **Chavasse.** Advice to a Mother on the Management of her Children, and in the Treatment on the moment in some of the most Pressing Illnesses and Accidents, by P. H. Chavasse.

1880. **Chavasse.** Counsel to a Mother, being a continuation of "Advice to a Mother," by P. H. Chavasse.

Chemistry. See Liebig, Johnston, Crooks.

3886. **Chester.** Pictorial Plan, with Hand-Book of Chester, City, Walls, Racecourse, Antiquities, &c.

3797. **Chesterfield.** Letters from the Earl of Chesterfield to his Son.

Chicago. See Goodspeed.

Chief Justices. See Santvoord.

2565-72. **Child.** Ballads, English and Scottish. Selected and Edited, with Notes and Introduction, by Francis J. Child. 8 vols.

2222. **Child.** Looking towards Sunset, from Scenes Old and New, Original and Selected, by M. T. Child.

Choate. See Browne.

4490. *Chimneys.* An Essay on the Construction and Building of Chim-
neys, including an Inquiry into the Common Cause of their
Smoking, and the most Effectual Remedy for so intolerable a
Nuisance, by Robert Clavering. 1793.

China. Chinese. See Williams, Bryant.

5840. *Choules.* The Cruise of the Steam Yacht North Star; a Narrative
of Mr. Vanderbilt's Party to England, Russia, Denmark, France,
Spain, Italy, Malta, Turkey, Madeira, &c., by J. O. Choules.
1854.

Choate. See Brown.

Christ Church. See Dorr.

Chronology. See Shallus, Haydn.

2541-3. *Churchill.* The Poetical Works of Charles Churchill, with
copious Notes, and a Life of the Author, by W. Tooke. 3 vols.
1854.

3841-4. *Cicero.* The Orations of Marcus Tullius Cicero, translated by E.
D. Young, B. A., in 4 vols. 1853.

3839. *Cicero.* The Academic Questions, Treatise de finibus and Tusculan
Disputations of M. T. Cicero, with a Sketch of the Greek Phil-
osophers mentioned by Cicero, by C. D. George. 1853.

3840. *Cicero.* The Treatise of M. T. Cicero on the Nature of the Gods; on
Divination; on Fate; on the Republick; on Laws ; and on standing for the Consulship; by C. D. Young. 1853.

3838. *Cicero.* The Three Books of Offices, on Moral Duties; also his Cato
Major, Essay on old Age, on Friendship, Paradoxes, Scipio's
Dream; and Letters to Quintus on the Duties of a Magistrate,
translated by C. D. Edmonds. 1853.

1879. *Cities.* Lost Cities brought to Light, by the Author of "Steps up the
Ladder."

3802-3. *Claiborne.* Life and Correspondence of John A. Quitman, by
J. F. H. Clairborne, 2 vols.

615. *Clay.* Annals of the Swedes on the Delaware, 1624 to 1858, by Rev.
J. C. Clay.

227. *Clay.* The Private Correspondence of Henry Clay, edited by Calvin
Colton, LL. D. 1856.

423. *Clay.* Report of the Committee of Management of the Common
Council of New York, of the Obsequies of Henry. 1852.

2252. *Clay.* Life of Henry Clay: the Statesman and Patriot, containing
Numerous Anecdotes.

1288. *Clinton.* The Life and Writings of De Witt Clinton, by W. W.
Campbell. 1849.

1651-68. *Coast.* Report of the Superintendent of the Coast Survey, 1856
to 1863. *Gift of A. D. Bache.*

Coal. See Taylor. Historical.

2824. *Codman.* · Ten Months in Brazil, with Incidents of Voyages and
Travels, Descriptions of Scenery and Character ; Commerce and
Productions, by John Codman. 1867.

3226. *Coffin.* The Seat of Empire, by C. Carleton Coffin. 1870.

2340. *Coffin.* Winning his Way, by C. C. Coffin.

2501. **Collins.** The Poetical Works of William Collins. 1853.

1552. **Collins.** The Autobiography of Stephen Collins, M. D. 1872.

2551-52. **Coleridge.** The Poetical and Didactic Works of J. T. Coleridge, with a Life of the Author, by C. E. Norton, 2 vols.

2255. **Collier.** A History of English Literature, in a Series of Biographical Sketches, by W. F. Collier, LL. D.

2321. **Collier.** The Great Events of History from the beginning of the Christian Era till the Present Time, by W. F. Collier.

4579. **Colton.** Lacon, or Many Things in Few Words, addressed to those who Think, by C. C. Colton, A. M. 1855.

3978. **Colton.** A General Atlas, containing 170 Steel Plates, Maps, and Plans, by G. W. Colton, with Geographical, Statistical, and Historical Descriptions.

Colonial Records. See Pennsylvania.

Columbus. See Irving.

192. **Combe.** A System of Phrenology, by George Combe, Revised and Enlarged. 1851.

3716. **Commerce.** Report of the Secretary of the Treasury on the Commerce and Navigation of the United States.

873-4. **Congress.** Journal of Congress, containing the Proceedings from Sept., 1774, to Dec. 31st, 1776, 2 vols. *The second volume the gift of Thomas F. Mitchell.*

Connecticut. See Arthur.

4423. **Conrad.** Sanderson's Biography of the Signers of the Declaration of Independence, revised and edited by Robert T. Conrad. 1847.

Constantinople. See Fisher.

76. **Constitution.** The Constitution of the Several States of the Union and United States, including the Declaration of Independence and Articles of Confederation. 1853. See Curtis.

426. **Contributionship.** Address before the Centennial Meeting of the Philadelphia Contributionship for the Insurance of Houses from Loss by Fire. 1852.

633. **Cook.** Voyages of Captain Cook around the World. With an Account of his Life during the Previous and Intervening Periods, by Dr. Kippis, F. R. S.

1153. **Cooke.** A Commentary of Medical and Moral Life; or Mind and the Emotions, considered in relation to Health, Disease, and Religion, by W. Cooke, M. D., 1853.

414. **Cooke.** The Constitutional History of the United States, from the Adoption of the Articles of Confederation to the Close of Jackson's Administration, by William Archer Cooke.

795. **Cooper.** A Dictionary of Practical Surgery, comprehending all the most interesting Improvements, an Account of the Instruments and Remedies employed in Surgery, the Etymology and Signification of the Principal Terms, &c. With numerous Notes and Additions, derived from the Practice of American Surgeons, together with a Supplementary Index, in which the Science of Surgery is brought down to the present Period, by David M. Reese, M. D., LL. D.

261. *Councils.* Ordinances and Joint Resolutions of the Select and Common Councils of the Consolidated City of Philadelphia, as passed by them, and approved by the Mayor. 1864.

1014–5. *Cousin.* Course of the History of Modern Philosophy, by M. F. Cousin, translated by O. W. Wright, 1852.

1046. *Cousin.* Lectures on the True, the Beautiful, and the Good, by M. V. Cousin.

Coughs. See Hall.

322–23. *Covode.* Report of the Investigation into Naval Contracts, 2 vols.

1518. *Cowan.* The Science of a New Life, by John Cowan. 1871.

2533–35. *Cowper.* The Poetical Works of William Cowper, 3 vols. 1853.

1140. *Coxe.* Impressions of England, and Sketches of English Scenery and Society.

1324. *Craig.* History of the Protestant Church in Hungary, from the beginning of the Reformation to 1850, by the Rev. J. Craig, D.D. 1854.

533. *Creasy.* The Fifteen Decisive Battles of the World; from Marathon to Waterloo, by E. S. Creasy, A. M.

647. *Crichton.* History of Arabia and its People, containing an account of the Country and its Inhabitants, the Life and Religion of Mahomed, the Conquest, Arts, and Literature of the Saracens, the Caliphs of Damascus, Bagdad, Africa, and Spain, the modern Arabs, the Wahabees, the Bedouins, &c., by Andrew Crichton. 1852.

4722–23. *Crittenden.* The Life of John J. Crittenden, with his Correspondence and Speeches, by his Daughter, Mrs C. Coleman, 2 vols.

Cromwell. See Guizot.

3828. *Crosland.* Memorable Women, the Story of their Lives, by Mrs. N. Crosland. 1854.

1511. *Crooks.* The Hand-Book of Chemical Technology of R. Wagner, with extensive additions, by Wm. Crooks.

2045. *Cruden.* Convenient and Ornamental Architecture, consisting of Original Designs for Plans, Elevations, and Sections, beginning with the Farm House, and regularly ascending to the most grand and magnificent Villa, by John Cruden. 1791.

2035. *Cruden.* A Concordance of the Holy Scriptures of the Old and New Testaments, or a Dictionary and Alphabetical Index of the Bible, by Alexander Cruden, M.A., with a Life of the Author.

2347. *Crusoe.* The Life and Adventures of Robinson Crusoe, of York, Mariner.

Cuba. See Ballou.

1551. *Cummings.* Wild Men and Wild Beasts, or scenes in Camp and Jungle, by Lt. Col. Gordon Cummings. 1872.

1554–55. *Cummings.* Five Years of a Hunter's Life in the Far Interior of South Africa, by B. G. Cummings, 2 vols.

3934. *Cummings.* Designs for Street Fronts, Suburban Houses and Cottages, including Details, Exterior and Interior, by Cumming and Miller. 1866.

114   THE CARPENTERS' COMPANY.

1878.   *Curtess.*   The Profile House, White Mountain Series, by Perry Curtess.

Curiosities.   See Watson, Smith, Spooner.

91.   *Curtis.*   History of the Origin, Formation, and Adoption of the Constitution of the United States, with Notices of its principal Framers, by G. T. Curtis.

2914.   *Curran.*   The Life of the Right Honorable John Philpot Curran, late Master of the Rolls in Ireland, by his Son, W. H. Curran. Additions and Notes by R. S. Mackenzie. 1855.

4584.   *Curzon.*   Armenia.   A Year at Erzeroom and on the Frontiers of Russia, Turkey, and Persia, by the Hon. Robert Curzon. 1854.

1803.   *Cushing.*   Rules of Proceedings and Debate, in Deliberative Assemblies, by Luther Cushing.

4581.   *Custine.*   Russia, translated from the French of the Marquis de Custine. 1854.

4727.   *Cutts.*   Scenes and Characters of the Middle Ages, by E. L. Cutts.

3966.   *Cuvier.*   The Animal Kingdom, arranged after its organizations, forming a Natural History of Animals, and an Introduction to Comparative Anatomy, by the late Baron George Cuvier. 1851.

3614-9.   *Cyclopædia.*   The American Annual Cyclopædia and Register of Important Events of the year 1861; embracing Political, Civil, Military, and Social Affairs, Public Documents, Biography, Statistics, Commerce, Finance, Literature, Science, Agriculture, and Mechanical Industry.   1862, 1863, and 1864.

Cyclopædia.   See Rees, Arvine, American, Homans.

D.

1016-7.   *D'Abrantes.*   Memoir of Napoleon, his Court and Family, by the Duchess D'Abrantes, 2 vols.   1855.

1565.   *Dahlgren.*   Memoir of Ulric Dahlgren, by his father, Rear Admiral Dahlgren.

1512.   *Dana.*   Corals and Coral Islands, by J. D. Dana.   1872.

3285.   *Dana.*   To Cuba and Back; a Vacation Voyage, by R. H. Dana. 1868.

2291.   *Dana.*   Two Years Before the Mast; a Personal Narrative, by R. H. Dana.

247.   *Dana.*   A System of Mineralogy, comprising the most Recent Discoveries, &c., &c., &c., by James D. Dana, 2 vols. in one.   1854.

3836-7.   *Dale.*   The History of the Peloponnesian War, by Thucydides, a new and literal version, from the text of Arnold, collated with Bakker, Galler, and Poppo, by H. Dale, M. A., 2 vols.

2885.   *Darby.*   Odd Hours of a Physician, by John Darby.   1872.

659.   *Dante.*   The Vision of Hell, Purgatory, and Paradise, of Dante Alighieri, translated by the Rev. H. F. Cary, A. M., with the Life of Dante, &c., &c.   1856.

3918. *Darlington.* Memorials of John Bartram and Humphrey Marshall, with Notices of their Botanical Contemporaries, by W. Darlington.

3134. *Darwin.* On the Origin of Species, by Means of Natural Selection, &c., by Charles Darwin.

1562-3. *Darwin.* The Descent of Man, and Selections in Relation to Sex, by Charles Darwin, 2 vols.

4316. *Darwin.* The Expression of Emotions in Man and Animals, by Charles Darwin, M. A.

Dates. See Haydn, Shallus.

545-7 *D'Aubigne.* History of the Reformation in Europe in the Times of Calvin, by J. H. M. D'Aubigne, 3 vols.

2240. *Davidson.* The True History of Joshua Davidson, Communist.

3835. *Davidson.* The Works of Virgil, literally translated into English Prose, with Notes, by Davidson, &c. 1853.

1197. *Davie.* The Life of William Richardson Davie, by F. M. Hubbard.

19. *Davies.* A Treatise on Shades and Shadows and Linear Perspective, by Charles Davies. 1835.

4275. *Davy.* The Architect, Engineer, and Operative Builder's Constructive Manual, being a Practical and Scientific Treatise on the Construction of Artificial Foundations for Buildings, Railways, &c., &c., by Christopher Davy. 1841.

4427. *Day.* Historical Collections of the State of Pennsylvania, containing a copious selection of the most interesting Facts, Traditions, Biographical Sketches, Anecdotes, &c., relating to its history and antiquity, both general and local, by Sherman Day. 1843.

2865. *Deans.* History of the Ottoman Empire from the Earliest Period to the Present Time, by William Deans. 1854.

1193. *Decatur.* Life of Stephen Decatur, a Commodore in the Navy of the United States, by A. Slidell MacKenzie.

138. *Delafield.* Art of War in Europe, in 1854-5-6.

139. *Delafield.* Report of Col. R. Delafield, U. S. Army, and Major of the Corps of Engineers, on the Art of War in Europe. 1854-6.

2821-2. *Dempsey.* Rudimentary Treatise on the Drainage of Districts and Lands, and Drainage and Seweraging of Towns and Buildings, by G. D. Dempsey. 2 vols. 1854.

427. *Dempsey.* The Builder's Guide, a Practical Manual for the use of Builders, clerks of works and professional students, and others engaged in designing or superintending the construction of buildings, comprising a description of materials, details of parts, calculating strengths, scantlings, dimensions, &c., by G. D. Dempsey. 1851.

Democracy. See Jones.

68. *Denny.* The Record of the Court at Upland, in Pennsylvania, 1676 to 1681, and a Military Journal kept by Major E. Denny, 1781 to 1795.

Denominations. See Religious Denominations.

3205. *Depping.* Wonders of Bodily Strength and Skill in all Ages and all Countries. Translated from the French of G. Depping. 1871.

2891–05. *De Quincey.* De Quincey's Writings, embracing his Opium Eater, Biographical Essays, Miscellaneous Essays, Cæsars, Literary Reminiscences, Narrative Papers, Essays on the Poets, and on Philosophical Writers, Autographs, Sketches, Historical Essays, Letters to a Young Man; in 15 vols. 1854.

1436. *Designs.* Designs for Ornamental Gates, Lodges, Palisading, and iron work of the Royal Parks, with other designs equal in utility and taste; intended for those designing and making parks, terraces, pleasure walks, recreative grounds, &c., principally taken from the executed works of Burton, Nash, Smirke, Soane, Stephenson, Vanbrugh, and Wren.

4043. *Designs.* Designs for Urns.

4044. *Designs.* Designs for Ceilings, Panels in Painting, Patterns, &c.

4045. *Designs.* Tablets.

870–1. *De Stael.* Germany, by Madame the Baroness De Stael Holstein, with notes and appendixes by O. W. Wright. 2 vols.

3712. *De Tocqueville.* Democracy in America, by A. De Tocqueville.

95. *De Tocqueville.* The Republic of the United States of America and its Political Institutions reviewed and examined, by Alexis De Tocqueville, translated by H. Reeves, with notes by J. C. Spencer. 1851.

1557. *De Vere.* Wonders of the Deep: a companion to "Stray Leaves from the Book of Nature," by M. S. De Vere.

1564. *De Vere.* The Great Empress; a Portrait, by M. S. De Vere.

4364. *De Vere.* The Romance of American History: Early Annals, by M. S. De Vere.

4304. *De Vere.* Americanisms; the English of the New World, by M. S. De Vere.

1566. *Dewey.* Life and Letters of Catharine M. Sedgwick, edited by Mary E. Dewey.

De Witt. See "Witt."

144. *Dick.* Encyclopedia of Practical Receipts and Processes, containing over 6,400 receipts; embracing thorough information in plain language applicable to almost every possible industrial and domestic requirement, by William B. Dick.

184–91. *Dickens.* Household Words, a weekly Journal, edited by Charles Dickens, 8 vols.

2811. *Dickens.* The Pickwick Papers.

2806. *Dickens.* Sketches.

2807. *Dickens.* New Stories.

2820. *Dickens.* Barnaby Rudge.

2815. *Dickens.* Martin Chuzzlewit.

2814. *Dickens.* The Old Curiosity Shop.

2805. *Dickens.* A Message from the Sea, and the Uncommercial Traveller, by Charles Dickens.

2812. *Dickens.* Great Expectations.

2817. *Dickens.* Dombey and Son.
2803. *Dickens.* Little Dorrit.
2809. *Dickens.* The Lamplighter's Story ; Hunted Down ; The Detective Police, and other Stories.
2804. *Dickens.* Oliver Twist.
2813. *Dickens.* A Tale of Two Cities.
2808. *Dickens.* David Copperfield.
2816. *Dickens.* Christmas Stories.
2810. *Dickens.* Bleak House.
2818. *Dickens.* Nicholas Nickleby.
2801. *Dickens.* American Notes, Commercial Traveller, by Charles Dickens.
2802. *Dickens.* Our Mutual Friend, by Charles Dickens.
2819. *Dickens.* Works of Charles Dickens, Mysteries of Edwin Drood.
1558-59. *Dictionary.* The Dictionary of Useful Knowledge. 2 vols.
4494. *Dictionary.* A Dictionary of Architecture, being a definition of terms and description of towns, buildings, antiquities, &c.
Dictionary. See Chambers—Jameson—Stuart—Appleton—Fleming and Tibbins—Ure—Smith—McCulloch—Ogilvie—Brande—Maunder—Smith—Putnam—Haydn—Glossary—Bee—Johnson —Hall—Bartlett—Gardiner—Lanman—Quotations.
1560. *Dictionary.* The Dictionary of Daily Wants, by the Author of "Useful Knowledge."
1561. *Dictionary.* Dictionary of Medical and Surgical knowledge.
3596. *Digest.* A Digest of Laws and Ordinances, relating to the City of Philadelphia. 1869.
660, 442-77. *Directory.* Philadelphia Directory for the years 1813, 1849, 1851,1852,1856, and 1858-73.
4428. *D'Israeli.* Curiosities of Literature, and the Literary Character Illustrated, by J. C. D'Israeli, with Curiosities of American Literature, by R. Griswold. 1853.
4591-94. *D'Israeli.* Curiosities of Literature, by Isaac D'Israeli, with a view of the Life and Writings of the Author, by his Son. In four volumes.
529-30. *D'Israeli.* The Amenities of Literature, consisting of Sketches and Characters of English Literature, by Isaac D'Israeli. A new Edition. Edited by his Son, the Right Hon. B. D'Israeli, Chancellor of Her Majesty's Exchequer. In two volumes.
2851. *Dixon.* The Personal History of Lord Bacon, from unpublished documents.
1094. *Dixon.* Life of William Penn, by William H. Dixon.
3142. *Dixon.* Free Russia, by W. H. Dixon. 1870.
1084. *Dixon.* Spiritual Wives, by W. H. Dixon. 1868.
Doctor. See Book.
2239. *Dollinger.* Fables respecting the Popes in the Middle Ages, by Dr. J. J. J. V. Dollinger.
2546. *Donne.* The Poetical Works of John Donne, with a Memoir, by Isaac Walton.

account of the Works of Albert Durer, &c., &c , with Examples of Ancient Painted and Stained Glass, &c., &c. 2 vols. 1846.

2884. *Dutch.* Pennsylvania Dutch, and other Essays. 1872.

3826. *Dwight.* The Lives of the Signers of the Declaration of Independence, by X. Dwight. 1851.

1186. *Dwight.* Life of Timothy Dwight, President of Yale College, by W. H. Sprague.

4488. *Dyer.* The History of the Kings of Rome, with a dissertation on its Sources and Evidences, by T. H. Dyer, LL. D. 1868.

E.

Earthwork. See Warner.

1567. *Eassie.* Healthy Homes, a Hand-Book to the History, Defects and Remedies of Drainage, Ventilation,Warming, &c., by Wm. Eassie.

1516. *Eastlack.* Hints on Household Taste in Furniture, Upholstery, and other details, by C. L. Eastlack.

Ecclesiastical. See Socrates—Burke—Religious—Eusebius—Neander—Miller—Mosheim—Muston.

1888 *Edgar.* Sea Kings and Naval Heroes, a Book for Boys, John G. Edgar.

2339. *Edgar.* Footprints of Famous Men, designed as Incitements to Intellectual Industry, by John F. Edgar.

1568. *Edwards.* Pearls, or the World's Laconics, being choice thoughts of the best Authors, in Prose and Poetry, by T. Edwards.

4060-82. *Egypte.* Description del'Egypte, ou Recueil des Observations et des Recherches qui ont ete faites en Egypte pendant l'Expedition de l'Armee Francaise. 23 vols. 1809.

Egypt and Egyptians. See Russell—Wilkinson—Stephens—Rollin—Lansing—Harman.

4338. *Eggleston.* How to Educate Yourself, with or without Masters, by G. C. Eggleston.

1099. *Election.* Election Laws of the Commonwealth of Pennsylvania, 1858.

2223-4. *Eliot.* Middlemarsh, a Story of Provincial Life, a Novel, by George Eliot. 2 vols.

2234. *Ellet.* Domestic History of the American Revolution, by M. Ellet.

2238. *Ellet.* Pioneer Women of the West, by M. Ellet.

1085. *Ellet.* The Queens of American Society, by M. Ellet.

678. *Ellet.* The Mississippi and Ohio Rivers, containing plans for the protection of the Delta from inundations; an investigation of the practicability and cost of improving the navigation of the Ohio and other rivers, by means of reservoirs, by Charles Eilet, Jr.

407-11. *Elliot.* The Debates in the several State Conventions on the Adoption of the Federal Constitution, as recommended by the General Convention at Philadelphia, in 1787. Together with the

Journal of the Federal Convention, Luther Martin's letter, Yates'
minutes, Congressional opinions, Virginia and Kentucky Resolutions of 1798-99, and other illustrations of the Constitution.
Including the Madison Papers, containing the Debates on the
adoption of the Federal Constitution in the Convention held at
Philadelphia in 1787, with a diary of the Debates of the Congress
of the Confederation, as reported by James Madison. Published
under the sanction of Congress. By Jonathan Elliot. Complete
in five vols.

1194. *Ellis.* The Life of William Penn, by George E. Ellis.

90. *Elton.* With the French in Mexico, by J. F. Elton. 1867.

622. *Elwyn.* A Glossary of supposed Americanisms. Collected by Alfred
L. Elwyn, M. D.

2235. *Emanuel.* Diamonds and Precious Stones; their History, Value,
and Distinguishing Characteristics, by H. Emanuel.

862. *Emerson.* The Principles of Mechanics, explaining and demon-
strating the General Laws of Motion, Laws of Gravity, &c., by
William Emerson. 1825. See Johnson.

609. *Emerson.* Miscellanies, embracing Nature, Addresses and Lectures, by R. W. Emerson.

610. *Emerson.* Representative Men, Seven Lectures, by R. W. Emerson.

611. *Emerson.* English Traits, by Ralph Waldo Emerson.

612. *Emerson.* Poems. With Portrait, by Ralph Waldo Emerson.

613. *Emerson.* Conduct of Life, by R. W. Emerson.

3128-9. *Emerson.* The Prose Works of R. W. Emerson. 2 vols. 1870.

1889. *Emerson.* Society and Solitude; Twelve Chapters, by R. W.
Emerson.

Encyclopædia of Religious Knowledge. See Brown.

1735-48. *Encyclopædia.* Encyclopædia Americana, a Popular Dictionary of Arts, Sciences, Literature, History, Politics and Biography,
including a copious collection of Original Articles in American
Biography, by Lieber and Wigglesworth. 1844. 14 vols.

1711-32. *Encyclopædia.* The London Encyclopædia, or Universal Dictionary of Science, Art, Literature and Practical Mechanics.
1829. 22 vols.

Encyclopædia. See Loudon—Herbert—Johnson—Brown—Lomax—Chambers.

England. See Hume—Strickland—Miller—Lingard—Laud—May
—Coxe—Ray—Guizot—Doran.

1111-2. *Erman.* Travels in Siberia, including Excursion northward down
the Obi, to the Polar Circle, and southward to the Chinese Frontier, by Adolph Erman; from the German, by W. D. Cooley.
2 vols. 1850.

3945. *Espy.* Second Report on Meteorology to the Secretary of the Treasury, by James P. Espy.

Essayists. See Bailey—Macauly—Allison—Smith—Wilson—Carlyle—Jeffreys—Alfourd—Stephens—Mackintosh—Rumford—
Lardner—Tuckerman—Legh—Tatler—Guardian.

2338. *Etiquette.* The Habits of Good Society; a Handbook of Etiquette for Ladies and Gentlemen.

Eulogy. See Marshall.

Europe. See Allison—Taylor—Silliman—Kaepen—Hallam—Howard—Channing—Fuller—Thomas.

4214. *Eusebius.* The Ecclesiastical History of Eusebius Pamphylus, Bishop of Cæsarea, in Palestine, translated, &c., by C. F. Cruse; and an Historical View of the Council of Nice, by J. Boyle. 1850.

3157. *Evans.* Glimpses at Sea and Land, during a six months trip to Europe, by Mary L. Evans.

4271-2 *Everett.* Orations and Speeches on various Occasions, by Edward Everett. 2 vols.

4377. *Everett.* Address on the Cause of the Struggle, and the great Issues before the Country, by Edward Everett. See Moore.

2342. *Everts.* Christian Womanhood, Life of M. K. Everts, with an Introduction.

256. *Ewbank.* A Descriptive and Historical Account of Hydraulic and other Machines for raising water, ancient and modern, with observations on various subjects connected with the Mechanic Arts, including the progressive development of the Steam Engine, by Thomas Ewbank. 1842.

232. *Ewbank.* Life in Brazil, or a Journal of a Visit to the Land of the Cocoa and the Palm; with an Appendix, containing Illustrations of Ancient South American Arts, in recently discovered implements and products of domestic industry, and works in Stone, Pottery, Gold, Silver, Bronze, &c., by Thomas Ewbank. 1856.

F.

203. *Fairbairn.* On the Application of Cast and Wrought Iron to Building Purposes, by Wm. Fairbairn, C. E., &c. 1854.

1572. *Fairbanks.* History of Florida, from its discovery by Ponce De Leon, in 1511 to the close of the Florida War, by G. R. Fairbanks.

45, 46, 47. *Fairmount.* Annual Report of the Commissioners of Fairmount Park, 1869 to 1873.

2514. *Falconer.* The Poetical Works of William Falconer, with a Life, by J. Mitford. 1854.

2330. *Faraday.* Michael Faraday, the Story, Study, &c., of his Life, by J. H. Gladstone.

3222. *Farrar.* Recollections of Seventy Years, by Mrs. John Farrar.

4501. *Farrar.* A Critical History of Free Thought in Reference to the Christian Religion. Eight Lectures, by A. S. Farrar.

4745. *Fay.* Norman Leslie, a New York Story, by Theodore S. Fay.

682-83. *Felton.* Greece, Ancient and Modern; Lectures before the Lowell Institute, by C. C. Felton, LL.D. 1867.

9

4498. **Female Poets.** The American Female Poets, with Biographical and Critical Notices, by Caroline May. 1854.

3604-06. **Ferdinand.** History of the Reign of Ferdinand and Isabella, the Catholic, by William Prescott. In 3 vols. 1853.

194. **Fergusson.** The History of the Progress and Termination of the Roman Republic, by Adam Fergusson. With a notice of the Author, by Lord Jeffery. 1856.

2304. **Fergusson.** Picturesque Illustrations of Ancient Architecture in Hindostan, by James Fergusson, Esq. 1848.

1130. **Ferris.** Utah and the Mormons. The History, Government, Doctrines, Customs, and Prospects of the Latter-day Saints, from Personal Observation, &c., by B. G. Ferris. 1854.

1573. **Fichte.** The Science of Rights, by J. G. Fichte.

1571. **Field.** Yesterday with Authors, by James T. Field.

260. **Fields.** The Scrap Book; consisting of Tales and Anecdotes, Biographical, Historical, Patriotic, Moral, Religious, and Sentimental Pieces, in prose and poetry: compiled by Wm. Fields. 1856.

2030. **Field.** City Architecture; or Designs for Dwellings, Stores, Hotels, &c., in 20 plates, with description, and an Essay on the Principles of Design, by M. A. Field. 1853.

3704. **Figuier.** The Ocean World, being a Description of the Sea and its Living Inhabitants, by L. Figuier.

3706. **Figuier.** The Insect World, being a popular Account of the Order of Insects, the Habits and Economy of some of the most Interesting Species, by L. Figuier.

3705. **Figuier.** The Vegetable World, being a History of Plants, with their Botanical Description and Peculiar Properties, by L. Figuier.

3707. **Figuier.** Reptiles and Birds; a Popular Account of the Various Orders; their Habits, Economy &c., by L. Figuier.

3709. **Figuier.** Mammalia, their Various Order and Habits Popularly Illustrated by Typical Species, by L. Figuier. 1870.

3710. **Figuier.** The World before the Deluge, by L. Figuier. 1869.

1515. **Figuier.** The Human Race, by L. Figuier.

300. **Finance.** Report of the Secretary on the State of the Finances.

246. **Finlay.** Greece under the Romans. An Historical View of the Condition of the Greek Nation, from the time of its Conquest by the Romans, until the Extinction of the Roman Empire in the East, B. C. 146 to A. D. 717, by George Finlay. 1854.

250. **Finlay.** History of the Byzantine Empire, from 716 to 1057, by George Finlay. 1853.

251. **Finlay.** History of the Byzantine and Greek Empires, from 1057 to 1453, by George Finlay. 1854.

252. **Finlay.** History of Greece, from its Conquest by the Crusaders to its Conquest by the Turks, and of the Empire of Trebizond, 1204 to 1461, by George Finlay. 1851.

2351. **Fisher.** Views in Ireland. Illustrated from Original Drawings by Petre, Bartlett, and Bayne, with Descriptions, by G. N. Wright.

2352. **Fisher.** Illustrations of Constantinople and its Environs.

78. *Fisher.* The National Magazine and Industrial Record, by Redwood Fisher. (*Gift of Thomas Gilpin.*)

65. *Fisher.* The Reformation, by George P. Fisher.

1188. *Fitch.* Life of John Fitch, by Charles Whittlesey.

1181. *Fitch.* Life of John Fitch, the Inventor of the Steamboat, by Thompson Westcott. With numerous Illustrations.

3713. *Fitch.* Annals of the Army of the Cumberland; comprising Biographies, Descriptions of Departments, Accounts of Expeditions, Skirmishes, and Battles; also its police Record of Spies, Smugglers, and Prominent Rebel Emissaries, &c., by John Fitch. 1864.

1569. *Flagg.* The Woods and By-ways of New England, by Wilson Flagg.

1177-8. *Flagg.* Venice, the City of the Sea, from the Invasion by Napoleon in 1797 to the Capitulation to Radetsky in 1849, with a Contemporaneous View of the Peninsula, by Edward Flagg. 1853. 2 vols.

1890. *Flammarion.* The Wonders of the Heavens, with Forty-eight Engravings, by Camille Flammarion.

182. *Flanders.* The Lives and Times of the Chief Justices of the Supreme Court of the United States, by Henry Flanders. First series, Jay to Rutledge. 1855.

14. *Fleming.* A New and Complete French and English and English and French Dictionary, compiled by Fleming and Tibbins on the basis of the Royal Dictionary.

2285. *Fleming.* Guy Earlscourt's Wife; a Novel, by M. Agnes Fleming.

2825. *Flint.* The Rail Roads of the U. S.; their History and Statistics, Progress, Resources, Expenses, &c., by Henry N. Flint. 1868.

Florida. See Irving—Fairbanks.

2217. *Flowers.* Wax Flowers; and how to make them, with New Methods of Sheeting Wax—Modelling Fruit.

1570. *Fontaine.* How the World was Peopled; Ethnological Lectures, by E. Fontaine.

3200. *Fonvielle.* Thunder and Lightning; translated from the French.

2260. *Foussagrives.* The Mother's Work with Sick Children, by Prof. J. B. Foussagrives.

3164. *Forward.* An Historical and Descriptive Narrative of the Cave of Kentucky; its Atmospheric Condition, Chemistry, Geology, Zoology, by W. S. Forward.

1123. *Foote.* Africa and the American Flag, by Commodore A. H. Foote. 1854.

1121-2. *Forsythe.* History of the Captivity of Napoleon at St. Helena, from the letters and journals of the late Sir Hudson Lowe, and official documents not before made public, by William Forsythe. 1853. 2 vols.

Foundations. See Davy.

1357-9. *Fox.* Book of Martyrs; the Acts and Monuments of the Church, by John Fox, in 3 vols. Reprinted from the edition of 1563. 1851.

405. *Fox.* The Life of George Fox, with a Dissertation on his Views concerning the Doctrines, Testimonies and Discipline of the Christian Church, by Samuel M. Janney. 1853.

3699. *Fox.* First Annual Message of Daniel M. Fox, Mayor of the City of Philadelphia. 1870.

4700. *Fox.* Dorothy Fox; by the Author of "How It All Happened." Parr.

France. See Dumas—Redhead—Thiers—Napoleon.

4311. *Franklin.* Autobiography of Benjamin Franklin, &c., &c., by J. Bigelow.

4617. *Franklin.* A Narrative of the Discovery of the Fate of Sir John Franklin, by Captain McClintock.

4429-0. *Franklin.* Memoirs of Benjamin Franklin, written by himself, and continued by his grandson and others, with Correspondence, Letters, Essays, and Diplomatic Transactions at London and Versailles. 1840. 2 vols.

4431-0. *Franklin.* The Works of Benjamin Franklin; containing several Political and Historical Tracts, not included in any former edition, and many Letters, official and private, not hitherto published, with Notes and a Life of the Author. 10 vols.

2951,3024. *Franklin.* Journal of the Franklin Institute and American Mechanics' Magazine, devoted to the Useful Arts, Internal Improvements, and General Science. 1826 to 1866. 74 vols.

Franklin. See Kane, Leslie, Sparks.

1127. *Freedley.* A Practical Treatise on Business; or how to get, save, spend, give, and bequeath money, with an inquiry into the chances of success and causes of failure in business, by E. T. Freedley; also prize essays, statistics, and numerous private letters from successful and distinguished business men. 1853.

4326. *Freedley.* Opportunities for Industry, and the Safe Investment of Capital; or a Thousand Chances to Make Money, by E. T. Freedley.

3225. *Frere.* Old Decan Days, or Hindoo Fairy Legends current in Southern India, by M. Frere. 1869.

French. See Pulszky, Lamartine, Hoddie.

605. *French.* Farm Drainage; the Principles, Processes, and Effects of Draining Land with stones, wood, open ditches, and especially with tiles; including tables of rain-fall, evaporation, filtration, excavation, capacity of pipes, &c., &c., by Henry B. French.

843. *Frick.* Physical Technics; or, Practical Instructions for Making Experiments in Physics, and the Construction of Physical Apparatus with the most Limited Means, by Dr. J. Frick, Director of the High School in Freiburg, and Professor of Physics in the Lyceum. Translated by John D. Easter, Ph. D., Professor of Natural Philosophy and Chemistry in the University of Georgia. Illustrated with over 800 engravings of the various apparatus used in experimentation.

4471. *Frost.* Pictorial Life of Andrew Jackson, embellished by numerous Engravings, by John Frost. 1847.

4460-1. **Frost.** Pictorial History of the United States of America, from the Discovery by the Northmen in the 10th Century to the Present Time, by John Frost. 1854. 2 vols.

429. **Frost.** Great Men and Great Events, from the Earliest Period to the Present Time, by John Frost. 1854.

537. **Frost.** Perilous Adventures and Thrilling Incidents, and Narratives of Travelers in Europe, Asia, Africa, and America, in Various Periods of History, by John Frost, LL. D. 1853.

Frothingham. The Rise of the Republic of the United States, by Richard Frothingham.

4319-20. **Froude.** Short Studies on Great Subjects, by J. A. Froude, first and second series. 2 vols.

2287. **Fuller.** Mistaken; or the Seeming and the Real, by Lydia Fuller.

1066. **Fuller.** At Home and Abroad; or Things and Thoughts in America and Europe, by Margaret Fuller Ossoli. Edited by her brother, A. B. Fuller. 1856.

1065. **Fuller.** Woman in the 19th Century, and Kindred Papers relating to the Spheres, Condition, and Duties of Woman, by M. F. Ossoli. Edited by her brother, A. B. Fuller. 1855.

2913 **Furness.** Julius, and others Tales from the German, by W. H. Furness. 1856.

G.

3920. **Gallatin.** The Speech of Albert Gallatin, a Representative from the County of Fayette, in the House of Representatives of the Comomnwealth of Pennsylvania, on the important question touching the Validity of the Elections held in the four western counties of the State, in 1794, with relation to the Western Insurrection.

424. **Gardner.** New Medical Dictionary. Containing an Explanation of the Terms in Anatomy, human and comparative, Physiology, Practice of Medicine, Obstetrics, Surgery, Therapeutics, Materia Medica, Chemistry, Botany, Natural Philosophy, with the Formulas of the principal Pharmacopœias, and valuable practical articles on the Treatment of Disease. On the Basis of Hooper and Grant. Adapted to the present State of Science, and for the Use of Medical Students and the Profession.

2228. **Garland.** The Speaker's Garland and Literary Bouquet, combining Choice Selections, 4 vols. in one, for use of Lyceums, &c.

1574. **Garrett.** Premiums Paid to Experience, incidents in my Business Life, by Edward Garrett.

772. **Gartland.** The Life of John Randolph of Roanoke, by Hugh A. Gartland. 1854.

1129. **Gasparin.** America before Europe; Principles and Interests, by Count Agenor de Gasparin. 1862.

3884. **Gasparin.** The Uprising of a Great People; the United States in

1861; to which is added a Word of Peace on the differences between England and the United States, by Count A. de Gasparin. 1862.

Gates. See Designs.

1214. *Gautier.* Wanderings in Spain, by Theophile Gautier. 1853.

2517–18. *Gay.* The Poetical Works of John Gay, with a Life of the Author, by Dr. Johnson. 1854. 2 vols.

413. *Gayarre.* Louisiana, its History as a French Colony, by Charles Gayarre. 1852.

390. *Gayarre.* History of Louisiana, the Spanish Domination, by Charles Gayarre. 1854.

23. *Gazetteer.* A new and complete Pronouncing Gazetteer, or Geographical Dictionary of the World, containing a notice and the pronunciation of the names of nearly 100,000 places, with the most recent and authentic information respecting the Countries, Islands, Rivers, Mountains, Cities, Towns, &c., &c., edited by J. Thomas and T. Martin. 1855.

3692. *Gazetteer.* A New and Complete Gazetteer of the United States, giving a full and comprehensive review of the present Condition, Industry and Resources of the American Confederacy, &c. &c., by Baldwin and Thomas. 1854.

1360–63 *Gazetteer.* A Gazetteer of the World, or Dictionary of Geographical Knowledge, compiled from the most recent authorities, and forming a complete body of modern Geography, Physical, Statistical, Historical, and Ethnographical, edited by a member of the Royal Geographical Society. 1853. 14 vols.

126–27. *Gell.* Pompeiana, the Topography, Edifices, and Ornaments of Pompeii; the result of excavations since 1819, by Sir William Gell. 2 vols.

1946. *General.* The General, or Twelve Nights in a Hunter's Camp: a Narrative of Real Life, Illustrated, by G. G. White.

Geology. See Lyell, Beche, Miller, Hooker.

Geography. See Barrington.

Georgia. See Arthur.

Germany. See Wight.

3878–3. *Gibbon.* The History of the Decline and Fall of the Roman Empire, by Edward Gibbon, Esq., with notes, by H. H. Milman, in 6 vols. 1854.

241. *Gibbon.* The Miscellaneous Works of Edward Gibbon, with a Memoir of his Life and Writings, composed by himself. 1837. Ornamented notes by John, Lord Sheffield.

4009. *Gibbs.* A Book of Architecture, containing Designs of Buildings and Ornaments, by James Gibbs. 1739.

4008. *Gibbs.* Rules for Drawing the several parts of Architecture in a more exact and easy manner than has been heretofore practised, by which all fraction in dividing the principal members and their parts is avoided, by James Gibbs. 1753.

2974. *Gibbs.* Same as 4009.

2329. **Giberne.** Not Forsaken; or the Old House in the City, by Agnes Giberne.

1068. **Gibson.** The Prison of Weltevreden; and a Glance at the East India Archipelago, by Walter Gibson. 1855.

3183. **Gilfillan.** Modern Literature and Literary Men, being a second Gallery of Literary Portraits, by George Gilfillan. 1856.

1038. **Gillespie.** A Manual of the Principles and Practice of Roadmaking; comprising the Location, Construction and Improvement of Roads and Railroads, by W. M. Gillespie. 1853.

195. **Gillies.** The History of Ancient Greece, its Colonies and Conquests, to the Division of the Macedonian Empire; including the History of Literature, Philosophy, and the Fine Arts, by John Gillies. 1856.

4098-9. **Gillis.** The United States Astronomical Expedition to the Southern Hemisphere, during the Years 1849, '50, '51, '52. Lieut. J. M. Gillis, Superintendent. Chili: its Geography, Climate, Earthquakes, Government, Social Condition, Mineral and Agricultural Resources, Commerce, &c., by Lieut. J. M. Gillis. 2 vols. 1856.

Girondists. See Lamartine.

2846. **Gironiere.** Twenty Years in the Phillippines, translated from the French of P. de La Gironiere, &c. 1854.

2292. **Gladden.** Plain Thoughts on the Art of Living, designed for Young Men and Women, by W. Gladden.

140. **Glaisher.** Travels in the Air, by James Glaisher and others. 1871.

2330. **Gladstone.** See Faraday.

2331. **Gladwyn.** On Papa's Lap; or Talks with my Children, by G. Gladwyn.

Glass. See Durer.

1576. **Gleason.** Talks to my Patients; hints on Getting Well and Keeping Well, by R. B. Gleason.

1440. **Globe.** Congressional Globe for 2d Session of 39th Congress, part 1st.

1441. **Globe.** " " " " part 2d.

1442. **Globe.** " " " " part 3d.

1443. **Globe.** " " 1st Session 40th Congress, complete in one volume.

1444. **Globe.** Congressional Globe for 2d Session of 40th Congress, part 1st.

1445. **Globe.** " " " " part 2d.

1446. **Globe.** " " " " part 3d.

1447. **Globe.** " " " " part 4th.

1448. **Globe.** " " " " part 5th.

1449. **Globe.** " " Supplement Trial of Impeachment.

1450. **Globe.** " " for 3d Session 40th Congress, part 1st.

1451. **Globe.** " " " " part 2d.

1452. **Globe.** " " " " part 3d.

1453. **Globe.** " " 1st Session 41st Congress, complete.

4219-21. **Glossary.** Glossary of Terms used in Roman, Grecian, Italian, and Gothic Architecture, 5th edition, enlarged, exemplified by 1700 wood-cuts. 3 vols. 1850.

1891. *Goodeve.* The Elements of Mechanics, by T. M. Goodeve. 1872.

Goodrich. Man upon the Sea; Remarkable Voyages.

4297. *Goodspeed.* History of the Great Fire in Chicago, and the West, by E. J. Goodspeed. 1871.

Gothic. See Pugin, Kirkman.

66. *Gould.* The Naturalist's Library, containing scientific and popular descriptions of Man, Quadrupeds, Birds, Fishes, Reptiles, Insects, &c., &c., by A. A. Gould. 1854.

2295. *Gould.* Marjorie's Quest, by J. T. Gould.

3167. *Gould.* Curious Myths of the Middle Ages, by J. Baring Gould. 1868.

401. *Gough.* Autobiography and Personal Recollections of John B. Gough, with 26 years experience as a Public Speaker. 1870.

3866-69. *Goldsmith.* The Miscellaneous Works of Oliver Goldsmith, including a variety of new pieces first collected by James Prior. 4 vols.

2505. *Goldsmith.* The Poetical Works of Oliver Goldsmith, with a Life, by J. Mitford. 1853.

15. *Goodrich.* Select British Eloquence, embracing the best speeches, entire, of the most eminent Orators of Great Britain, for the last two centuries; with Sketches of their Lives, &c., by Chauncey A. Goodrich. 1855.

778. *Goodrich.* Man upon the Sea; or a History of Maritime Adventure, Exploration, and Discovery, from the earliest ages to the present time, comprising a detailed account of remarkable voyages, ancient as well as modern, by Frank B. Goodrich.

35-36. *Goodrich.* Illustrated History of the Animal Kingdom, being a systematic and popular treatise on the Habits, Structure, and Classification of Animals, by S. G. Goodrich.

1187. *Gorton.* Life of George Gorton, one of the first Settlers of Warwick, R. I., by John M. Mackie.

2506. *Gray.* The Poetical Works of Thomas Gray, with a Life of the Author, by J. Mitford. 1853.

Greece. See Baird, Findlay, Middleton, Anthon, Barker.

Greeley. See Parton.

4292-93. *Greeley.* The American Conflict, a History of the Great Rebellion in the U. S. in 1861-65, its Causes, Incidents, Results, &c. &c., by Horace Greeley, 2 vols. 1867.

1192. *Greene.* Life of Nathaniel Greene, Major-General in the Army of the Revolution, by his grandson, George W. Greene.

3876. *Greene.* Historical View of the American Revolution, by G. W. Greene. 1869.

Greenland. See Hayes.

4339. *Greenwood.* The Seven Curses of London, by James Greenwood.

4307. *Greenwood.* Wild Sports of the World; a Book of Nature, History and Adventure, by James Greenwood.

1063. *Greenwood.* Haps and Mishaps of a Tour in Europe, by Grace Greenwood. 1854.

1035-6. *Gregory.* Mathematics for Practical Men, being a common-place book of principles, theories, rules and tables, in various departments of pure and mixed Mathematics, by O. Gregory. 1825.

2837. *Grey.* The Early Years of His Royal Highness, the Prince Consort; compiled under the direction of Her Majesty, the Queen, by C. Grey. 1868.

2941-2. *Grier.* The Mechanic's Calculator, comprehending rules and tables in the various departments of Mathematics and Mechanics, by William Grier. 1836.

4308-9. *Grimm.* Life of Michael Angelo, by H. Grimm; translated by F. E. Bunnett. 2 vols.

2230. *Grindon.* Life; its Nature, Varieties and Phenomena, by L. H. Grindon.

75. *Grinnell.* Expedition in Search of Sir John Franklin, a Personal Narrative, by E. K. Kane, M. D., U. S. N.

4097. *Griswold.* The Republican Court, or American Society in the Days of Washington, by Rufus Griswold. See D'Israeli.

4428. *Griswold.* Curiosities of Literature, and the literary character illustrated, by J. C. D'Israeli; with Curiosities of American Literature, by R. W. Griswold.

3926-8. *Guardian.* The Guardian, with a Preface by Chalmers. 3 vols.

2046. *Guest.* A Compendious History of Cotton Manufacturing, with a disproval of the claim of Sir Richard Arkwright to the invention of his Ingenious Machinery, by Richard Guest. 1823.

3218. *Guillemin.* The Sun, by A. Guillemin; from the French, by A. L. Phipson. 1871.

4336. *Guizot.* A French Country Family, by M. De Wm. Guizott.

2847-8. *Guizot.* History of Oliver Cromwell and the English Commonwealth, from the Execution of Charles the First, to the Death of Cromwell, by M. Guizot. 2 vols.

4628-1. *Guizot.* The History of Civilization from the Fall of the Roman Empire to the French Revolution, by F. Guizot. 4 vols.

777. *Gurney.* Memoirs of Joseph John Gurney, with selections from his Journal and Correspondence. Edited by Joseph Bevan Braithwaite.

1089. *Gurowski.* Russia as it is, by Count A. D. Gurowski. 1854.

148. *Guthrie.* The Sunday Magazine, by Mrs. Guthrie.

1575. *Guthrie.* Studies of Character from the Old Testament, by Thomas Guthrie. 1872.

4462. *Gwilt.* Sciography, or Examples of Shadows, with Rules for their Projection, by Joseph Gwilt. 1833. See Nicholson.

H.

248. *Habersham.* The North Pacific Surveying and Exploring Expedition; or, My Last Cruise; where we went and what we saw: being an Account of Visits to the Malay and Loo-Choo Islands, the Coasts of China, Formosa, Japan, Kamtschatka, Siberia, and the Amoor River, by A. W. Habersham.

1710.   *Habershon.* The Ancient Half-timbered Houses of England, by
        M. Habershon, Architect. 1836.

4333.   *Hack.* Stories from English History during the Middle Ages, by
        Maria Hack.

1147.   *Hale.* The Library of Standard Letters, comprising Selections from
        the Correspondence of Eminent Men and Women, with Biograph-
        ical Sketches, Notes, and an Index. Edited by Sarah Josepha
        Hale. Letters of M. DeSevigne. 1856.

1132.   *Hale.* Kansas and Nebraska; the History, &c., &c.; an Account of
        the Emigrant Aid Companies, &c., &c., by Edward E. Hale. 1854.

4466.   *Hale.* A Complete Dictionary of Poetical Quotations, comprising
        the most excellent and appropriate passages in the old British
        Poets ; with choice and copious selections from the best modern
        British and American Poets. Edited by Sarah Josepha Hale.
        1856.

4255-6. *Half Hours.* Half Hours with the Best Authors. Complete in
        2 vols. See Knight.

2038-0. *Hall.* Ireland, its Scenery, Character, &c., by Mr. and Mrs. S.
        C. Hall. 3 vols.

1049.   *Hall.* Lives of the Queens of England, before the Norman Conquest,
        by Mrs. M. Hall. 1854.

2859.   *Hall.* Life of Maximilian, the late Emperor of Mexico, with a Sketch
        of the Empress Carlotta, by F. Hall. 1868.

1947.   *Hall.* Coughs and Colds; or the Prevention, Cause and Cure of
        various Affections of the Throat, with Cures illustrating the
        Efficacy of Out-door Activity, and Horse Back Exercises, &c., &c.

1895.   *Hall.* Fun Better Than Physic ; or Everybody's Life Preserver, by
        W. W. Hall.

1578.   *Hall.* Sleep : or the Hygiene of the Night, by W. W. Hall. 1871.

4472-3. *Hallam.* Introduction to the Literature of Europe in the 15th,
        16th, and 17th Centuries, by Henry Hallam. 2 vols.

242.   *Hallam.* View of the State of Europe during the Middle Ages, by
        H. Hallam. Complete in one vol. 1854.

193.   *Hallam.* The Constitutional History of England, from the Acces-
        sion of Henry VII to the Death of George III, by H. Hallam.
        1851.

4298.   *Hallowell.* Geometrical Analysis, or the Solution of various Geo-
        metrical Problems, &c., &c., by Benjamin Hallowell.

2245.   *Hammond.* Sleep and its Derangements, by W. A. Hammond.

4382.   *Hamerton.* Thoughts About Art, by P. G. Hamerton.

1008.   *Hamilton.* The Federalist. A Commentary on the Constitution
        of the United States. A Collection of Essays, by Alexander
        Hamilton, Jay, and Madison. Also the Continentalist and other
        Papers, by Hamilton. Edited by John C. Hamilton.

826-2. *Hamilton.* History of the Republic of the United States of
        America, as traced in the Writings of Alexander Hamilton and
        his Contemporaries, by John C. Hamilton. 7 vols.

998.   *Hamilton.* The Life of John Jay and Alexander Hamilton.

1579. *Hamilton.* The Battle of the Books; recorded by an Unknown Writer, for the Use of Authors and Publishers, by Gail Hamilton.

2298. *Hamilton.* Skirmishes and Sketches, by Gail Hamilton.

2301. *Hamilton.* Wool Gathering, by Gail Hamilton.

2300. *Hamilton.* Gala Days, by Gail Hamilton.

2302. *Hamilton.* Country Living and Country Thinking, by Gail Hamilton.

2290. *Hamilton.* Stumbling Blocks, by Gail Hamilton.

4386. *Hamley.* Our Poor Relations; a Phelozoic Essay, by Col. E. B. Hamley.

2867. *Hand Book.* Hand Book of American Literature, Historical, Biographical and Critical.

1004-7. *Hardee.* Rifle and Light Infantry Tactics, for the Exercise and Manœuvre of Troops when acting as Light Infantry or Riflemen, by W. J. Hardee. 1861.

4347. *Hare.* Wanderings in Spain, by A. J. C. Hare.

4321. *Hare.* Guesses at Truth, by Two Brothers.

4340. *Hare.* Walks in Rome, by A. J. C. Hare.

2295. *Harland.* The Empty Heart, or Husks; For Better or For Worse, by Maria Harland.

2280. *Harland.* Husbands and Homes, by Maria Harland.

2281. *Harland.* Helen Gardner's Wedding Day, or Col. Floyd's Words: a Battle Summer, by M. Harland.

2278. *Harland.* True as Steel; a Novel, by M. Harland.

2276. *Harland.* The Hidden Path, by Maria Harland.

2279. *Harland.* Alone, by Maria Harland.

2277. *Harland.* Sunny-Bank; a Novel, by Maria Harland.

2274. *Harland.* Moss-Side; a Novel, by Maria Harland.

4305. *Harman.* A Journey to Egypt, the Holy Land, in 1869-70, by H. M. Harman.

149. *Harper.* Harper's New Monthly Magazine, vol. 43.

525. *Harris.* An Introductory Outline of the Progress of Improvement in Ventilation, by Elisha Harris, M. D. See Reid.

3708. *Hartt.* Scientific Results of a Journey to Brazil, by Louis Agassiz; Geology and Physical Geography of Brazil, by C. F. Hartt. 1870.

1335. *Hatfield.* The American House Carpenter; a Treatise upon Architecture, Cornices and Mouldings; Framing, Door Windows, Stairs, &c.; together with the most Important Principles of Practical Geometry, by R. C. Hatfield. 1844.

1344. *Haupt.* General Theory of Bridge Construction, containing Demonstration of the Principles of the Art, and their Applications to Practice; furnishing the means of Calculating the Strain upon the Chords, Ties, Beams, Camber Braces, and other parts of a Bridge or Frame of any description, with Practical Illustrations, by Herman Haupt. 1853.

1750-2. *Haviland.* The Builder's Assistant, containing the five orders of Architecture; selected from the best specimens of the Greek and

Roman, with the figure, dimension of heights, projection and profile, by John Haviland. 3 vols. 1825. See Biddle.

4341. *Haweis.* Music and Morals, by H. R. Howeis, M. A.

790. *Hawks.* Peruvian Antiquities, by M. E. Revero and J. J. Von Tschudi. Translated by F. L. Hawks. 1853.

2293. *Hawthorne.* Septimus Felton, or the Elixir of Life, by N. Hawthorne.

4360. *Hawthorne.* The Scarlet Letter and the Blithedale Romance, by N. Hawthorne.

4356. *Hawthorne.* The House of the Seven Gables, and the Snows Image, by N. Hawthorne.

4355. *Hawthorne.* Passages from the English Note-Books of N. Hawthorne.

1892-93. *Hawthorne.* Passages from the French and Italian Note-Books of N. Hawthorne, 2 vols.

4354. *Hawthorne.* Passages from the American Note-Books of N. Hawthorne. 1873.

4357. *Hawthorne.* Mosses from an old Manse, by N. Hawthorne.

4358. *Hawthorne.* Twice told Tales, by N. Hawthorne.

4359. *Hawthorne.* The Marble Fawn, or the romance of Montebeni, by N. Hawthorne.

290. *Haydn.* Dictionary of Dates and Universal Reference, relating to all Ages and Nations, comprehending every remarkable occurrence, ancient and modern, &c. &c. ; the whole comprehending a body of information, classical, political, and domestic, from the earliest accounts to the present time, by Joseph Haydn. 1851.

1894. *Hay.* Castilian Days, by John Hay. 1871.

4470. *Hayes.* The Open Polar Sea, a narrative of a voyage of discovery towards the North Pole, in the Schooner United States, by Dr. I. I. Hayes. 1867.

3874. *Hayes.* The Artic Boat Journey in the Autumn of 1854, by Isaac I. Hayes. 1869.

4344. *Hayes.* The Land of Desolation, being a personal observation and adventure in Greenland, by Isaac I. Hayes.

4322. *Hayes.* Cast-Away in the Cold, or an old man's story of a young man's adventures, as related by Captain John Hardy, Mariner, by Dr. Isaac Hayes.

4759. *Haslett.* Glennair, or Life in Scotland, by Helen Haslett.

3703. *Hazard.* Cuba with Pen and Pencil, by Samuel Hazard.

4310. *Hazard.* Santo Domingo, Past and Present, with a Glimpse at Hayti, by Samuel Hazard.

176. *Hazzard.* Annals of Pennsylvania, from the Discovery of the Delaware, by Samuel Hazzard, from 1609 to 1682.

1388, 1403. *Hazzard.* The Register of Pennsylvania, devoted to the Preservation of Facts and Documents, and every other kind of useful Information respecting the State of Pennsylvania. 16 vols.

727-3. *Hazzard.* Pennsylvania Archives; selected and arranged from Original Documents, conformably to an Act of the General Assembly, by Samuel Hazzard. 1644 to 1779. 7 vols. *Gift of Charles O'Neill.*

3195. *Headley.* The Life of the Empress Josephine, first wife of Napoleon, by P. C. Headley. 1854.

3194. *Headley.* The Life of General Lafayette, Marquis of France, General in the U. S. Army, by P. C. Headley. 1853.

3197. *Headley.* The Adirondack, or Life in the Woods, by J. T. Headley. 1853.

3191. *Headley.* Letters from Italy, by J. T. Headley.

3190. *Headley.* Miscellanies, by J. T. Headley. Authorized edition. 1850.

3188-9. *Headley.* Washington and his Generals, by J. T. Headley. 2 vols. 1854.

3192-3. *Headley.* Napoleon and his Marshals, by J. T. Headley. 2 vols. 1815.

3196. *Headley.* The Imperial Guard of Napoleon from Marengo to Waterloo, by J. T. Headley. 1855.

3198. *Headley.* The Life of Mary Qeeen of Scots, by P. C. Headley. 1854.

1117. *Heard.* History of the Sioux War and Massacres of 1862 and 1863, by Isaac V. D. Heard, with Portraits and Illustrations.

4385. *Heard.* Curiosities of the Law Reporters, by F. F. Heard. 1871.

1141. *Helper.* The Impending Crisis in the South, and how to meet it, by H. B. Helper.

4577-8. *Helps.* The Spanish Conquest in America, and its Relation to the History of Slavery and to the Government of Colonies, by Arthur Helps. In 2 vols. 1856.

2838. *Helps.* Leaves from the Journal of our Lives in the Highlands from 1848 to 1861, and Extracts from the same Journal of Earlier Visits, &c., &c., by Arthur Helps. 1868. (Victoria and Albert.)

1341. *Hemans.* The Poetical Works of Mrs. Felicia Hemans, complete in one volume, with a Critical Preface, and Biographical Memoir. 1854.

1331. *Henry.* The Life of Patrick Henry, by William Wirt, 4th edition. 1831.

1183. *Henry.* Life of Patrick Henry, by Alexander H. Everett.

4250-1. *Herbert.* The Engineer and Mechanics' Encyclopædia, comprehending Practical Illustrations of the Machinery and Process employed in every description of Manufacture of the British Empire, by Luke Herbert. 1837.

2548. *Herbert.* The Poetical Works of George Herbert, with Memoir by the Rev. Robert Aris Willmott.

3223. *Heroes.* Pictures of Heroes and Lessons from their Lives.
Hero. See Mulock.

2925. *Herodotus.* An Analysis and Summary of Herodotus, with a Synchronistical Table of Principal Events, by J. T. Wheeler.

134 THE CARPENTERS' COMPANY.

2933. *Herodotus.* Herodotus, a new and literal version, from the text
of Bache, with a Geographical and General Index, by H. Carey.
1854.

2587-8. *Herrick.* The Poetical Works of Robert Herrick. Hesperides,
or the Works both Human and Divine. With a Biographical
Notice, by S. W. Singer. 2 vols.

1032. *Herschell.* Outlines of Astronomy, by Sir John F. W. Herschell.
1852.

541. *Hervey.* Meditations and Contemplations, by James Hervey, A.M.,
to which is prefixed a Life of the Author.

2246. *Heywood.* How will it End, a Romance, by J. C. Heywood.

4362. *Higginson.* Atlantic Essays, by Thomas Wentworth Higginson.

639-40. *Hillard.* Six Months in Italy, by George Stillman Hillard,
2 vols. 1854.

2256. *Hillern.* A Two-Fold Life, by W. V. Hillern.

1577. *Hinton.* Life in Nature, the Living Form and World, by James
Hinton. 1872.

74. *Historical.* Memoirs of the Historical Society, containing an
Account of the Society of the Cincinnati, and a Journal of their
Meetings in 1784—History of Western Insurrection in Pennsyl-
vania in 1794—Presentation of the Belt of Wampum—The
French Neutrals or Acadian Exiles—The Case of Major Andre,
with a Review of Mahon's England.

2070. *Historical.* Constitution of the Society—Memoir on the Locality
of Penn's Treaty—Notes on the Provincial Literature of Penn-
sylvania—Memoir of the Controversy between Penn and Lord
Baltimore—Relating to Washington's Farewell Address—Hecke-
welder's History of the Indian Nation—First Settlement of
Buckingham and Solebury—Account of the Discovery of
Anthracite Coal—Conynham's Historical Notes—Bettle's Negro
Slavery—Life and Character of Robert Proud—Letter of William
Penn—Biographical Sketch of Sir W. Keith.

2071. *Historical.* Minutes of the Committee of Defence of Philadelphia.
1814-15.

2072-73. *Historical.* Correspondence between Penn and Logan, Secretary of the Province, 1700 to 1750, from original Letters, &c.,
with Notes, by the late Deborah Logan, 2 vols. 1870.

1133. *Hitchcock.* Religious Truths, illustrated from Science, in Addresses
and Sermons on special occasions, by Edward Hitchcock. 1854.

4718. *Hobbs.* Architecture, containing Designs and Ground Plans for
Villas, Cottages, and other Edifices, &c., by J. H. Hobbs and
Son, Arch.

277. *Hodde.* History of Secret societies, and of the Republican Party
of France, from 1830 to 1848, containing Sketches of Louis
Phillippe, and the Revolution of February, together with
Portraits, Conspiracies, and unpublished facts, by L. De La
Hodde. 1856.

2262. *Hodge.* Little Hodge, by the author of "Ginx's Baby."

1580. *Holland.* Recollections of Past Life, by Sir Henry Holland. 1872.

2242. **Holland.** The Bay-Path, a Tale of New England Colonial Life, by J. G. Holland.
2343. **Holland.** Lessons in Life, a Series of Familiar Essays, by Timothy Titcomb (Dr. Holland).
2244. **Holland.** Miss Gilbert's Career, an American Story, by J. G. Holland.
2243. **Holland.** Plain talk on Familiar Subjects, a Series of Popular Lectures, by J. G. Holland.
4393. **Holland.** Gold-Foil Hammered from Popular Proverbs, by Timothy Titcomb (Dr. Holland).
39. **Holly.** Country Seats, containing Lithographic Designs for Cottages, Villas, Mansions, &c.; also Country Churches, City Buildings, Railway Stations, &c., by Henry Hudson Holly.
641. **Holmes.** Poems by Oliver Wendell Holmes, new and enlarged edition. 1856.
2273. **Holmes.** Tempest and Sunshine; or Life in Kentucky, by M. J. Holmes.
2268. **Holmes.** Rose Mather; a Tale, by M. J. Holmes.
2272. **Holmes.** Darkness and Daylight, by M. J. Holmes.
2209. **Holmes.** The Poet at the Breakfast Table; his Talk with his Fellow Boarders and his Readers, by M. J. Holmes.
2271. **Holmes.** Dora Deane; or the East India Uncle—Maggie Miller, or Old Hagar's Secret, by M. J. Holmes.
2270. **Holmes.** Edna Browning; or the Leighton Homestead. A Novel, by M. J. Holmes.
2265. **Holmes.** Lena Rivers, by M. J. Holmes.
2267. **Holmes.** The English Orphans; or A Home in the New World, by M. J. Holmes.
2269. **Holmes.** Meadow-Brook, by M. J. Holmes.
2266. **Holmes.** The Homestead on the Hill-Side; and other Tales, by M. J. Holmes.
25. **Homans.** A Cyclopædia of Commerce and Commercial Navigation, edited by J. Smith Homans, Corresponding Secretary of the Chamber of Commerce of the State of New York, and editor of "The Bankers' Magazine and Statistical Register," and by J. Smith Homans, Jr., B. S.
4583. **Homans.** The Personal Adventures of "Our Own Correspondent in Italy," showing how an article campaigner can find good quarters when other men lie in the fields, &c., by M. B. Homans. 1853.
2346. **Home.** Our Forest Home; its Inmates and what became of them, by the author of "Robert Jay's Victory."
Homes. See Barnwell—Bremer.
3180. **Homer.** The Iliad of Homer, translated by Alexander Pope, with an Introduction and Notes, by T. A. Buckley. 1853.
4596. **Homer.** The Iliad of Homer, translated into English blank verse, by William Cowper.
3179. **Homer.** The Odyssey of Homer, translated by A. Pope, with Notes by T. A. Buckley. 1854.

2544-5. **Hood.** Poems by Thomas Hood, with some Account of the Author. 2 vols. 1854.

4299. **Hood.** The World of Moral and Religious Anecdote, gathered from Words, Thoughts and Deeds of Men, Women and Books. E. P. Hood.

4300. **Hood.** The World of Anecdote, Fact, Incident and Illustrations; Historical and Biographical; Recent and Remote, by E. P. Hood.

628. **Hooker.** Science for the School and Family, Mineralogy and Geology, by Worthington Hooker, M. D.

12. **Hope.** An Historical Essay on Architecture, by the late Thomas Hope. Illustrated from Drawings made by him in Italy and Germany. 1835.

13. **Hope.** Illustrations to Hope's Essay on Architecture, from Drawings made by the Author in Germany, France, Italy, &c. 1835.

4337. **Hope.** Hope till the Doctor comes, and how to help him, by Geo. H. Hope, M. D.

1581. **Hopkins.** Lectures on Moral Science; delivered before the Lowell Institute, By M. Hopkins.

2831. **Hoppin.** Old England; its Scenery, Art, and People, by James M. Hoppin. 1868.

2924. **Horace.** The Works of Horace; translated literally into English Prose, by C. Smart, A. M. Revised, with a copious selection of Notes. 1855.

4585. **Hotz.** The Moral and Intellectual Diversity of Races, with particular reference to their respective Influence on the Civil and Political History of Mankind, from the French of Count A. de Gobineau, with Introduction and Notes, by H. Hotz, and Appendix, &c., by J. C. Nott. 1856.

4384. **Hours.** Leisure Hours in Towns; by the Author of Recreations of a Country Parson.

2516. **Howard.** The Poetical Works of Henry, Earl of Surrey, with a Memoir.

1267. **Howard.** John Howard, and the Prison World of Europe, from Original and Authentic Documents, by H. Dixon. 1854.

1221. **Howitt.** An Art Student in Munich, by Anna Mary Howitt. 1854.

4348. **Howitt.** Vignettes of American History, by Mary Howitt.

3138. **Howell.** Suburban Sketches, by W. D. Howell. 1871.

2828. **Howell.** Italian Journeying, by W. D. Howell. 1867.

2906. **Howell.** Venetian Life, by W. D. Howell. 1867.

684-5. **Hosier.** The Seven Weeks War; its Antecedents and its Incidents, by H. M. Hosier. 2 vols. 1867.

4361. **Hubback.** May and December; a Tale of Wedded Life, by Mrs. Hubback.

2911. **Hufeland.** Art of Prolonging Life, by Hufeland. Edited by E. Wilson.

1582. **Hugo.** The Destroyer of the Second Republic, being Napoleon the Little, by Victor Hugo. 1870. Translated from the French.

855. **Humboldt.** The Life, Travels, and Books of Alexander Von Humboldt.

852. *Humboldt.* The Travels and Researches of Alexander Von Humboldt, by William Macgillivray, with a Narrative of Humboldt's most recent Researches, including his celebrated Journey to the Ural Mountains and the Caspian Sea. 1853.

3852-4. *Humboldt.* Personal Narrative of Travels to the Equatorial Regions of America, during the years 1799, 1823, by Alexander Von Humboldt and Aime Bonpland. 3 vols. 1852.

3855. *Humboldt.* Views of Nature, or Contemplation on the Sublime Phenomena of Creation, with Illustrations, by Alexander Von Humboldt. 1850.

3818-1. *Humboldt.* Cosmos; a Sketch of a Physical Description of the Universe, by Alexander Von Humboldt. 1849.

2850. *Humboldt.* Aspects of Nature in Different Lands and Different Climates, with Scientific Elucidations, by Alexander Von Humboldt.

2849. *Humboldt.* The Lives of the Brothers Humboldt, Alphonso and William. Translated by Bauer.

4234-7. *Hume.* The History of England, from the Invasion of Julius Cæsar to the Revolution of 1688, by David Hume, and from 1688 to the Death of George II, by T. Smollett. 4 vols. 1835.

Hungary. See Paget, Craig.

600. *Hunt.* Worth and Wealth; a collection of Maxims, Morals, and Miscellanies, for Merchants and Men of Business, by Freeman Hunt. 1856.

Hunter. Hunter's Camp. See General.

Husbandry. See Liebig.

1188. *Hutchinson.* Life of Anne Hutchinson, with a Sketch of the Antinomian Controversy in Massachusetts, by George E. Ellis.

2926. *Hutchinson.* Memoirs of the Life of Colonel Hutchinson, written by his Widow; to which is prefixed the Life of Mrs. Hutchinson, written by herself. Also added an Account of the Siege of Latham House. 1848.

3135. *Huxley.* On the Origin of Species, or the Causes of the Phenomena of Organic Nature, a Course of Six Lectures to workingmen, by T. H. Huxley. 1870.

Hydraulics. See Ewbank.

I.

Ireland. See Miles, Keyser.

Illinois. See Arthur.

2056-7. *Illustrations.* Illustrations of Paris, by A. Pugin, 2 vols. 1831.

2060. *Illustrations.* Illustrations of London, by T. H. Shepherd.

2054-5. *Illustrations.* Illustrations of Switzerland, by Beattie, 2 vols.

2353. *Illustrations.* Illustrations of England.

2358. *Illustrations.* Illustrations of Aberdeen, Perth, Bedford, and Berkshire.

2359. *Illustrations.* Illustrations of Bath, Bristol, and Edinburgh.

2350.   *Illustrations.*   Illustrations of Kent, Bath, and Bristol, by Virtue.

2351.   *Illustrations.*   Illustrations of Ireland, from Original Drawings by Petric, Bartlett, and Baynes, with descriptions by G. N. Wright, by Fisher.

2352.   *Illustrations.*   Illustrations of Constantinople and its Environs, by Fisher.

2458.   *Illustrations.*   Illustrations of Lancashire.

    Independence.   See Conrad, Dwight.

    India.   See Murray.

    Indians.   See Schoolcraft, Drake, Catlin.

861.   *Infantry.*   Abstract of Infantry Tactics, including Exercises and Manœuvres of Light Infantry and Riflemen, for the use of the Militia of the United States.

4318.   *Ingham.*   The Ingham Lectures, a Course of Lectures on the Evidence of Natural and Revealed Religion, before the Wesleyan University, Ohio.

379-1.   *Ingersoll.*   Historical Sketch of the Second War between the United States of America and Great Britain, declared by Act of Congress, the 18th of June, 1812, and concluded by Peace, the 15th of February, 1815. 3 vols.

1029.   *Insect.*   Episodes of Insect Life, by Acheta Domestica, M. E. S., 1st, 2d, and 3d Series. 3 vols. 1852.

4493.   *Internal Navigation.*   A Connected View of the whole Internal Navigation of the United States, Natural and Artificial, Present and Prospective. 1826.

    Inventions.   See Beckman.

    Ireland.   See Hall, Fisher.

1146.   *Irish.*   The Irish Abroad and at Home, at the Court and in the Camp, with Souvenirs of "the Brigade," Reminiscences of an Emigrant Milesian. 1856. .

3937.   *Iron.*   Designs of Ornamental Gates,' Lodges, Palisading and Iron Work of the Royal Parks, with other designs equal in utility and taste, intended for those designing and making Parks, Terraces, Pleasure Walks, Recreative Grounds, &c., &c.

    Iron.   See Fairbairn.

3820.   *Irving.*   The Conquest of Florida by H. De Soto, by Theodore Irving, M. A. 1851.

3808-24.   *Irving.*   The Works of Washington Irving, in 15 vols., embracing his Mahomet, New York, Bracebridge Hall, Crayon Miscellany, Granada, Alhambra, Columbus, Goldsmith, Sketch-Book, Tales of a Traveller, Astoria, Bonneville Adventures.

    Italy.   See Hillard, Homan.

J.

3861.   *Jackman.*   The Australian Captive; or, an Authentic Narrative of Fifteen Years in the Life of William Jackman, &c. 1853.

4471. *Jackson.* Pictorial Life of Andrew Jackson, embellished with numerous Engravings, by John Frost. 1847.

2872. *Jackson.* The Mountain. In three books.

Book I. Atlas. Natural Science of the Mountain, or what the Mountain is in a critical inventory of the Planet. Skeleton, skin appendages, and circulating fluids.

Book II. Æsculapius. Doctoreal uses of the Mountain. Hygeia.

Book III. Antæus the Giant. The Mountain telling its whole story of fate to man—creeping in his bones, boiling in his blood, flashing in his brain. Pan a symbol of the Universe. By R. M. S. Jackson, M. D., Member of the Academy of Natural Sciences, &c., &c.

4094. *Jamison.* A Dictionary of Mechanical Science, Arts, Manufactures, and Miscellaneous Knowledge, by Alexander Jamison. 1828.

405. *Janney.* The Life of George Fox, with a Dissertation on his Views concerning the Doctrines, Testimonies, and Discipline of the Christian Church, by Samuel M. Janney. 1853.

416. *Janney.* The Life of William Penn, with Selections from his Correspondence and Autobiography, by Samuel M. Janney. 1852.

1896. *Janus.* The Pope and the Council, by Janus.

Japan. See Macfarlane, Perry, Alcock.

1095. *Jarves.* Reminiscences of Glass-making, by Deming Jarves.

998. *Jay.* Life of John Jay and Alexander Hamilton.

81-9 *Jefferson.* The Writings of Thomas Jefferson ; being his Autobiography, Correspondence, Reports, Messages, Addresses, and other Writings, official and private, from the Original Manuscripts. Edited by H. A. Washington. 9 vols. 1853.

Jefferson. See Randolph.

4457. *Jeffrey.* Contributions to the Edinburgh Review, by Francis Jeffrey. 1853.

1086. *Jeffrey.* The Life of Lord Jeffrey, with a Selection from his Correspondence, by Lord Cockburn. 1856.

4595. *Jenkins.* The Life of John C. Calhoun, by Ida S. Jenkins. 1856.

2910. *John.* Purple Tints of Paris; Character and Manners of the New Empire, by Bayle St. John.

2261. *John.* The Arctic Crusoe; a Tale of the Polar Sea, or Arctic Adventures on the Sea of Ice, by Perry B. St. John.

1583. *Johnson.* Lucretius on the Nature of Things, &c., by C. F. Johnson, with Introduction and Notes. 1872.

4012. *Johnson.* The Practical Draughtman's Book of Industrial Designs, and Machinist's and Engineer's Drawing Companion, forming a complete course of Mechanical Engineering and Architectural Drawing, translated from the French of M. Armagund, the elder, &c., by William Johnson.

4095-6. *Johnson.* A Dictionary of the English Language, in which the words are deduced from their originals, by Samuel Johnson. 2 vols.

1257-6. **Johnson.** The Life of Samuel Johnson, LL. D., including the Journal of his Tour to the Hebrides, by James Boswell, with additions and notes, by J. Wilson Croker, M. P., to which is added two supplementary volumes of Johnsoniana, by Hawkins and others. In 10 vols. 1853.

16. **Johnston.** The Farmer's and Planter's Encyclopædia of Rural Affairs, embracing all the most recent Discoveries in Agricultural Chemistry, adapted to the Comprehension of unscientific readers, by Cuthbert W. Johnston. Adapted to the United States, by Gouverneur Emerson. 1852.

2918-9. **Johnston.** The Chemistry of Common Life, by James F. Johnston M. A., 2 vols. 1856.

4624. **Johnston.** Lectures on the Application of Chemistry and Geology to Agriculture, by J. F. W. Johnston.

627. **Johnston.** The English Classics; or Historical Sketches of the Literature of England, from the earliest times to the reign of George the Third.

542-3. **Johnston.** Lives of the English Poets, with Critical Observations on their works. With Notes by Peter Cunningham, and a Life of the Author, by Macaulay. 2 vols.

1422-3. **Jones.** The American Architect, comprising original Designs of Cheap Country and Village Residences, with details; the Designs by John W. Ritch, Architect. 1st and 2d series.

2051. **Jones.** Jones's Views of the Seats, Mansions, and Castles of Noblemen and Gentlemen in England, Wales, Scotland, and Ireland, and other Picturesque Scenery, accompanied with an Historical Description of the Mansions, list of Pictures, Statues, &c.

2058-9. **Jones.** Views in England, Kent, Bath, Bristol.

3871. **Jones.** Wild Western Scenes: A Narrative of Adventures in the Western Wilderness, wherein the exploits of Daniel Boone, the great American pioneer, are particularly described. Also, accounts of bear, dear, buffalo, and wolf hunts, desperate conflicts with the savages, fishing and fowling adventures, &c., &c., by J. B. Jones.

4600. **Jones.** Mirror of Modern Democracy; a History of the Democratic Party, from its organization in 1825 to its last great achievement, the Rebellion of 1861; to which is prefixed a sketch of the old Federal and Republican Parties, by William D. Jones.

608. **Jones.** Life of John Paul Jones, Chevalier of the Military Order of Merit and the Russian Order of St. Anne, &c., &c. Compiled from his original journals and correspondence; including an account of his services in the American Revolution, and in the war between the Russians and the Turks in the Black Sea. Illustrated with 88 Engravings from original drawings, by James Hamilton.

4764. **Jones.** Una and her Paupers: Memorials of Agnes Elizabeth Jones, by her sister, with an Introduction by Florence Nightingale, and Preface by H. W. Beecher.

1584. **Jones.** The War-Path, a Narrative of Adventures in the Wilderness, with minute details of the captivity of sundry persons—Amusing Incidents—Fearful Battles with the Indians—Encounters with Beasts and Snakes, by J. B. Jones. -

4350. **Jonquil.** Was She Engaged, by Jonquil.

4216-7. **Josephus.** The Works of Flavius Josephus, containing 20 books of the Jewish Antiquities, seven books of the Jewish War, and the Life of Josephus, &c., &c., with notes, by William Whiston. 2 vols. 1854.

655. **Junius.** The Letters of Junius. 2 vols. in one. 1854.

Justices. See Binns, Read, Santvoord, Story.

K.

1325-6. **Kaepen.** The World in the Middle Ages, an Historical Geography, with accounts of the Origin and Development, the Institutions and Literature, the Manners and Customs of the Nations of Europe, Western Asia, and Northern Africa, from the close of the Fourth to the middle of the Fifteenth Century, by A. S. Kaepen. 2 vols. 1854.

75. **Kane.** The United States Grinnell Expedition in Search of Sir John Franklin, a Personal Narative, by Elisha Kent Kane, M. D., U. S. N. 1854.

275-6. **Kane.** Arctic Explorations; the Second Grinnell Expedition in Search of Sir John Franklin, 1853, '54, '55, by Elisha Kent Kane, M. D., U. S. N., 2 vols. 1856.

Kansas. See Hale.

538. **Kay.** The Social Condition and Education of the People of England, by Joseph Kay. 1863.

2583. **Keats.** The Poetical Works of John Keats, with a Life by J. Russell Lowell.

4378. **Kellogg.** The Hardscrabble of Elm Island, by E. Kellogg.

2318. **Kellogg.** The Ark of Elm Island, by E. Kellogg.

3834. **Kelly.** The Elegies of Propertius, Satyricon, and of Petronius Arbiter, Kisses of Johannes Secundus, and Love Epistles of Aristaenetus, edited by W. W. Kelly. 1854.

1118. **Kemble.** Journal of a Residence on a Georgia Plantation in 1838, 1839, by Frances Anne Kemble.

4303. **Kenly.** Memoir of a Maryland Volunteer, War with Mexico in 1846 -48, by J. R. Kenly.

3168. **Kennan.** Tent Life in Siberia, and Adventures among Koraks and other Tribes in Kamtschatka and Northern Asia, by George Kennan.

1585. **Kennedy.** Political and Official Papers, by John P. Kennedy.

Kentucky. See Arthur.

1143. **Keyser.** The Religion of the Northmen, by Rudolph Keyser, translated by B. Pennock. 1854.

3858.   *Kidd.* On the Adaptation of External Nature to the Physical Condition of Man, with reference to the supply of his wants and the exercise of his intellectual faculties, by John Kidd.

4332.   *Kimball.* Life in Santo Domingo; by a Settler, with an Introduction, by R. B. Kimball.

1586.   *King.* Mountaineering in the Sierra Nevada, by Clarence King. 1872.

799.   *King.* The Microscopist's Companion, a popular manual of Practical Microscopy, to which is added a Glossary of Terms, &c., &c., by John King, M. D.

634.   *Kings.* Kings and Queens, or Life in the Palace. Sketches of Josephine, Maria Louisa, Louis Phillippe, Ferdinand, Nicholas, Isabella, Leopold, Victoria, and Louis Napoleon.

2003.   *Kirby.* The Description and Use of a New Instrument called an Architectonic Sector, by which any part of Architecture may be drawn with facility and exactness, by Joshua Kirby. 1761.

2002.   *Kirby.* The Perspective of Architecture, a work entirely new, deduced from the principles of De Brook Taylor, by John Kirby. 1761.

3856–7.   *Kirby.* On the History, Habits, and Instinct of Animals, by William Kirby, M. A. 2 vols.

1019–0.   *Kirk.* History of Charles the Bold, Duke of Burgundy, by John Foster Kirk, 2 vols.

1197.   *Kirkland.* The Life of Samuel Kirkland, Missionary to the Indians, by S. K. Lathrop.

4254.   *Knight.* Half Hours in English History, selected and arranged by Charles Knight.

4255–6.   *Knight.* Half Hours with the best Authors, by Chas. Knight, 2 vols.

1124.   *Knight.* Knowledge is Power; a View of the Productive Forces of Modern Society, and the Results of Labor, Capital, and Skill, by Charles Knight; revised by D. A. Wells, &c. 1856.

4489–2.   *Knight.* Mechanics' Magazine, a Weekly Periodical, by Knight & Long. 1825 to 18—. 4 vols.

3827.   *Knox.* An Historical Account of St. Thomas, W. I., with its Rise and Progress in Commerce, Missions and Churches, Climate and its Adaption to Invalids, &c., &c., and incidental Notes of St. Croix and St. John's, by J. P. Knox. 1852.

77.   *Koran.* The Koran, commonly called the Alcoran of Mahommed, with Notes, &c., by George Sale. 1855.

L.

3194.   *Lafayette.* The Life of General Lafayette, Marquis of France, General in the United States Army, &c., by P. C. Headley. 1852.

4040.   *Lafever.* The Beauties of Architecture, illustrated in 48 original plates, by M. Lafever. 1835.

4013. **Laferer.** The Modern Builder's Guide, illustrated by 87 copperplate engravings, by M. Lafever. 1841.

2873. **Lagny.** The Knout and the Russians, or the Muscovite Empire, the Czar, and his People, by G. De Lagny.

4048. **Laing.** Hints for Dwellings, consisting of Original Designs for Cottages, Farm Houses, Villas, &c., by D. Laing. 1823.

3829-1. **Lamartine.** History of the Girondists, or Personal Memoirs of the Patriots of the French Revolution, from unpublished sources, by A. D. Lamartine. 3 vols. 1854.

1205-6. **Lamartine.** Memoirs of Celebrated Characters, by Alphonse de Lamartine. 2 vols. 1854.

4270. **Lamb.** The Works of Charles Lamb, complete in one volume, with a Sketch of his Life by Sir T. N. Talfoerd. 1857.

1338. **Lamb.** The Poetical Works of Rogers, Campbell, J. Montgomery, Lamb, and Kirke White. 1856.

2050. **Lancashire.** Lancashire, illustrated in a series of Views of Towns, Public Buildings, Antiquities, Castles, Seats of Noblemen, &c.

4088-9. **Land.** The Land We Live In; a Pictorial and Literary Sketch Book of the British Empire. In 2 vols.

1434-5. **Langley.** A System of Architecture, with New Designs, by B. Langley. 1741.

4047. **Langley.** The City and Country Builder, and Workman's Treasury of Designs, or the Art of Drawing and Working the Ornamental Parts of Architecture, illustrated by 400 grand designs, by B. Langley. 1745.

604. **Langstroth.** A Practical Treatise on the Hive and Honey Bee, by L. L. Langstroth, with an Introduction by Robert Baird.

236-7. **Lanman.** Adventures in the Wilds of the United States and British American Provinces, by Charles Lanman. 2 vols. 1856.

776. **Lanman.** Dictionary of the United States Congress, containing Biographical Sketches of its Members from the Foundation of the Government, with an Appendix, compiled as a Manual of Reference for the Legislator and Statesman, by Charles Lanman.

3211. **Lanoye.** Rameses the Great, or Egypt 3300 years ago, from the French of F. De Lanoye.

3217. **Lanoye.** The Sublime of Nature, compiled from the descriptions of Travellers and celebrated Writers, by F. De Lanoye.

619. **Lansing.** Egypt's Princes, a Narrative of Missionary Labor in the Valley of the Nile, by Gulian Lansing.

1920. **Laporte.** Sailing on the Nile, by Laurient Laporte. 1872.

853. **Lardner.** Hand-Book of Natural Philosophy and Astronomy, by D. Lardner. 1851.

2858. **Lardner.** Popular Essays on Scientific Subjects, comprising Steam, Artificial Light, Photography, Electro-metallurgy, Electric Telegraph, Pottery, Glass Manufactures, Railways, Steam Marine, Rotation of the Earth, &c., by Dionysius Lardner, with additions. 1852.

1898. **Lanman.** The Japanese in America, by Charles Lanman, American Secretary of Japanese Legation, &c. 1872.

4449–0.   *Layard.*   Nineveh and its Remains, with an account of a Visit to the Chaldean Christians of Kurdistan, and the Yezidis, or Devil Worshippers, and an Inquiry into the Manners and Customs of the Ancient Assyrians, by A. H. Layard. 2 vols. 1850.

4264.   *Layard.*   Discoveries in the Ruins of Nineveh and Babylon, with Travels in Armenia, Hindostan, and the Desert, being the result of a Second Expedition undertaken for the Trustees of the British Museum, by A. H. Layard. 1853.

3863.   *Ledderhose.*   The Life of Philip Melancthon, by C. F. Ledderhose. 1855.

1196.   *Ledyard.*   The Life of John Ledyard, the American Traveller, by Jared Sparks.

644.   *Lee.*   The Australian Wanderers, or the Adventures of Captain Spencer, his Horse and Dog, by Mrs. R. Lee. 1854.

1190.   *Lee.*   Life of Charles Lee, by Jared Sparks.

3215.   *Lefebre.*   Wonders of Architecture from the French of M. Lefebre, to which is added a Chapter on English Arcitecture, by R. Donald. 1811.

4100–17.   *Legal Intelligencer.*   The Legal Intelligencer, conducted by Henry E. Wallace, Esq. 1857–73.

679–0.   *Legh.*   The Music of the Eye, or Essays on the Principles of the Beauty and Perfection of Architecture, as founded on and deduced from Reason and Analogy, by Peter Legh. 1831.

1185.   *Leisler.*   The Adventures of Jacob Leisler, a Chapter of American History, by C. P. Hoffman.

1897.   *Leifchild.*   The Higher Ministry of Nature viewed in the Light of Modern Science, and as an aid to advanced Christian Philosphy, by John R. Leifchild. 1872.

1826–27.   *Lenormant.*   A Manual of the Ancient History of the East to the Commencement of the Medean Wars, by F. Lenormant. 1871. 2 vols.

4006–7.   *Leoni.*   The Architecture of Andrea Palladio, in 4 books, containing a short Treatise of the Five Orders, and the most necessary observations concerning all sorts of Buildings, as also the different construction of Private and Public Houses, Highways, Bridges, Market Places, &c. &c., by Giacomo Leoni. 2 vols. 1742.

1825.   *Leonowens.*   The English Governess at the Siamese Court; being Recollections of Six Years in the Royal Palace at Bangkok. 1871.

4301.   *Leonowens.*   The Romance of the Harem, by Mrs. Anna H. Leonowens.

2937.   *Leslie.*   Discovery and Adventures in the Polar Seas and Regions, with illustrations of their Climates, Geology and Natural History, by Sir John Leslie and others, with a Narrative of the recent Expedition in Search of Sir John Franklin. 1853.

539–0.   *Lewis.*   The Physiology of Common Life, by George H. Lewis. 2 vols.

4125.   *Library.*   Catalogue of the Pennsylvania State Library.

2841–2. *Lieber.* On Civil Liberty and Self-Government, by Francis Lieber, LL. D. 2 vols. 1853.

4503. *Liebig.* The Natural Laws of Husbandry, &c., &c., by Justus Von Liebig.

198. *Liebig.* Liebig's Complete Works on Chemistry, comprising his Agricultural, Animal, Familiar Letters, Origin of the Potato Disease, and its relation to Physiology and Pathology, by Justus Liebig.

Life. See Wilson.

605. *Lincoln.* Our Martyr President, Abraham Lincoln. Voices from the Pulpit in New York and Brooklyn. Orations by George Bancroft, and Oration at the Burial by Bishop Simpson.

1195. *Lincoln.* The Life of Benjamin Lincoln, Major-General in the Army of the Revolution, by F. Bowen.

2833. *Lincoln.* The Inner Life of Abraham Lincoln, six months at the White House, by F. B. Carpenter. 1868.

1430. *Lincoln.* The Assassination of A. Lincoln, late President of the United States of America, and the attempted Assassination of W. H. Seward, &c., &c., Expressions of Sympathy and Condolence, &c. 1867.

1198–04. *Lingard.* A History of England, from the First Invasion by the Romans to the Accession of William and Mary, in 1656, by John Lingard, in 7 vols.

1828. *Linn.* Living Thoughts of Leading Thinkers; a thesaurus, by S. P. Linn. 1872.

3720. *Lippincott.* A Complete Pronouncing Gazetteer of the World.

676. *Lives.* Lives of Great and Celebrated Characters of all Ages and Countries, comprising Heroes, Conquerors, Statesmen, Authors, Artists, Extraordinary Humorists, Misers, &c., &c., and other curiosities of Human Nature; compiled by Leary and Getz.

4268. *Livingstone.* Travels and Researches in South Africa, including a Sketch of Sixteen Years' Residence in the Interior of Africa, and a Journey from the Cape of Good Hope to Loanda, on the West Coast, thence across the Continent down the Zambesi to the Eastern Ocean, by David Livingstone.

4353. *Livingstone.* Livingstone and his African Explorations, together with a full account of the Young, Stanley, and Dawson Search Expeditions, &c.

Livingstone. See Stanley.

2929–2. *Livy.* The History of Rome, by Titus Livius, translated by D. Spellan, A. M. 4 vols.

4090–1. *Lomax.* Encyclopædia of Architecture; a new and improved edition of Nicholson's Dictionary of the Science and Practice of Architecture, Building, &c. Edited by E. Lomax and T. Gunvon. 2 vols.

London. See Schlesinger, Miller, Shepherd, Reynolds.

662–3. *Longfellow.* Poems by Henry Wadsworth Longfellow. 2 vols.

4734. *Lord.* The Old Roman World; the Grandeur and Failure of its Civilization, by John Lord, LL. D.

146 THE CARPENTERS' COMPANY.

4735. **Lord.** Ancient States and Empires, by John Lord.
4737–8. **Lossing.** The Life and Times of Philip Schuyler, by Benson J· Lossing. 2 vols.
2036–7. **Lossing.** The Pictorial Field Book of the Revolution; or Illustrations by Pen and Pencil of the History, Biography, Scenery, Relics and Tradition of the War for Independence, by B. J. Lossing. 1851.
3690. **Loudon.** The Encyclopædia of Cottage, Farm and Villa Architecture and Furniture, containing numerous designs for dwellings,· from the Cottage to the Villa, by J. C. Loudon. 1836.
4218. **Loudon.** The Landscape Gardening and Landscape Architecture of the late Humphrey Repton; being his entire works on these subjects, &c., by J. C. Loudon. 1840.
Louis. See Beauchesne.
Louisiana. See Gayarre.
3165. **Lowell.** Among My Books, by J. Russell Lowell. 1870.
3166. **Lowell.** My Study Windows, by J. Russell Lowell. 1871.
4374. **Lowell.** Fireside Travels, by J. Russell Lowell.
4701. **Lubbock.** Pre-Historic Times; as illustrated by Ancient Remains, and the Manners and Customs of Modern Savages, by Sir John Lubbock.
3144. **Lubbock.** The Origin of Civilization and the Primitive Condition of Man; Mental and Social Condition of Savages, by Sir John Lubbock. 1871.
146–7. **Lubke.** History of Sculpture from the Earliest Ages to the Present Time, by Dr. W. Lubke. 2 vols.
4739. **Ludlow.** The Heart of the Continent, a Record of Travel across the Plains and in Oregon, with an examination of the Mormon Principle, by F. H. Ludlow.
4016. **Lugar.** The Country Gentleman's Architect; containing a variety of Designs for Farm Houses and Farm Yards, of different magnitudes; arranged on the most approved principles for Arable, Grazing, Feeding, and Dairy Farms, by B. Lugar. 1823.
4016. **Lugar.** Architectural Sketches for Cottages, Rural Dwellings, and Villas, in the Grecian, Gothic, and fancy styles, with plans suitable to persons of genteel life and moderate fortunes, by B. Lugar. 1823.
1329. **Luther.** The Life of Martin Luther, and the Reformation in Germany, &c., &c., by Thomas Stork. 1854.
255. **Lyell.** A Manual of Elementary Geology; or, the Ancient Changes of the Earth and its Inhabitants, as Illustrated by Geological Monuments, by C. Lyell. 1852.
3697–8. **Lyell.** Principles of Geology; or, the Modern Changes of the Earth and its Inhabitants, considered as Illustrated by Geology, by Charles Lyell. 1853. 2 vols.
3726. **Lyell.** The Geological Evidence of the Antiquity of Man, with remarks on Theories of the Origin of Species by Variation, by Sir Charles Lyell. 1871.

2834. **Lyle.** Lights and Shadows of Army Life; or, Pen Pictures from the Battle-field, the Camp, and the Hospital, by W. W. Lyle, &c., &c.

4273. **Lynch.** Expedition to the Dead Sea and Jordan, by W. S. Lynch, U. S. N., Commander of the Expedition, with Maps, &c. 1850.

M.

4152. **Macaulay.** Essays, Critical and Miscellaneous, by T. Babington Macaulay.

1908. **MacDonald.** Wilfred Cumbermede, by George MacDonald.

3234. **MacDonald.** Ranald Bannerman's Boyhood, by Geo. MacDonald.

1830. **MacDonald.** Annals of a quiet Neighborhood, by Geo MacDonald.

1831. **MacDonald.** David Elgarbrod, by George MacDonald.

4606. **Mace.** The History of a Mouthful of Bread, and its effects on the organization of Man and Animals, by J. Mace. 1866.

1101. **Macfarlane.** Japan; an Account, Geographical and Historical, from the Earliest Period at which the Islands comprising this Empire were known to Europeans, down to the Present Time; also the Expedition fitted out in the United States, by C. Macfarlane. 1852.

4733. **Macgregor.** The Rob Roy on the Jordan, Nile, Red Sea, and Gennesareth, by J. Macgregor.

1090-1. **Mackay.** Memoirs of Extraordinary Popular Delusions, by Charles Mackay. 2 vols. 1850.

616-8. **Mackenzie.** A Year in Spain, by A. Slidell Mackenzie. 3 vols.

1182. **Mackie.** From Cape Cod to Dixie and the Tropics, by J. Milton Mackie.

4459. **Mackintosh.** The Miscellaneous Works of the Right Honorable Sir James Mackintosh. Complete in 1 vol. 1853.

2236. **Mackellar.** Rhymes atween Times, by Thomas Mackellar.

3133. **Macleod.** Days in North India, by Norman Macleod. 1870.

4732. **Macleod.** The New Cyclopædia of Illustrative Anecdote, Religious and Moral; Original and Selected, by D. Macleod.

145. **Macleod.** Good Words for 1870, by Norman Macleod.

Madagascar. See Sibree.

4590. **Madeira.** Sketches and Adventures in Madeira, Portugal, and the Andalusias of Spain, by the Author of Daniel Webster and his Contemporaries. 1856.

386. **Madison.** History of the Life and Times of James Madison, by William C. Rives. 1 vol.

2857. **Madison. Monroe.** The Lives of James Madison and James Monroe, Fourth and Fifth Presidents of the United States, by J. Quincy Adams, with Historical Notices of their Administrations. 1850.

Magazine. See Knight.

2909. **Magoon.** Living Orators in America, by E. L. Magoon. 1854.

544. **Magoon.** Westward Empire; or, the Great Drama of Human Progress, by E. L. Magoon. 1856.

4276. **Mahan.** An Elementary Course of Civil Engineering, for the use of the Cadets of the United States Military Academy. D. H. Mahan. 1853.

4599. **Malcolm.** India and the Indian Mutiny, comprising a complete history of Hindostan, by H. F. Malcolm.

1222. **Malcom.** Travels in Southeastern Asia, embracing Hindostan, Malaya, Siam, and China, with a full Account of the Burman Empire, by Howard Malcom.

Mankind. See Gliddon, Hotz, Draper, Cooke, Buffon.

1899. **Mann.** A Few Thoughts for Young Men; a Lecture before the Boston Mercantile Library, by Horace Mann. 1871.

4329. **Manning.** Half Truths and the Truth; Lectures on the Origin and Development of prevailing Forms of Unbelief, &c., &c., by J. M. Manning.

1126. **Mansfield.** The Life of General Winfield Scott, by E. D. Mansfield. 1846.

1033. **Mansfield.** The Mexican War; a History of its Origin, and a Detailed Account of the Victories which Terminated in a Surrender of the Capital; with the Official Despatches. the Treaty of Peace, &c., by E. D. Mansfield. 1851.

4373. **March.** The Old Stone House, by Ann March.

4377. **Marcy.** The Prairie Traveller; a Hand-Book for Overland Expeditions, &c., by R. B. Marcy.

4751. **Marcy.** Border Reminiscence, by R. B. Marcy.

4306. **Marcy.** Thirty Years of Army Life on the Border, comprising Descriptions of the Indian Nomads, Travels, Habits of Animals, &c., &c., by Col. R. B. Marcy.

3213. **Margalle.** Meteors, Areolites, Storms, and Atmospheric Phenomena; from the French of Margalle, &c., &c.

1839. **Marion.** The Wonders of Vegetation, from the French of F. Marion, &c. 1872.

3207. **Marion.** Wonderful Balloon Ascents, or the Conquest of the Skies, a History of Balloons and Balloon Voyages, by F. Marion. 1870.

3209. **Marion.** The Wonders of Optics, by F. Marion. 1871.

Marlitt. See Wister.

1041-5. **Marshall.** The Life of George Washington, Commander-in-chief of the American Forces during the War which established the Independence of his Country, and First President of the United States, by John Marshall. 6 vols. 1804.

4479. **Marshall.** Eulogy on the Life and Character of John Marshall, Chief Justice of the Supreme Court of the United States.

Marshall. See Duane, Darlington.

1755. **Martin.** The Carpenter and Joiner's Instructor, Geometrical Lines, Strength of Materials, and Mechanical Principles of Framed Work, by Thomas Martin. 1826.

2547. **Marvell.** The Poetical Works of Andrew Marvell, with Memoir, by Henry Rogers.

1900. *Marvel.* Dream Life; a Fable of the Seasons, by T. Marvel. 1871.

4392. *Marvel.* Reveries of a Bachelor, or a Book of the Heart, by J. Marvel.

1836. *Mason.* The Story of a Workingman's Life, with Sketches of Travels in Europe, Asia, Africa, and America, by F. Mason.

1185. *Mason.* Life of John Mason, of Connecticut, by George E. Ellis.

Massachusetts. See Carpenter, Young.

4755. *Mateer.* The Land of Charity, an Account of Travancore and its Devil Worship, by S. Mateer.

4762. *Matthew.* Getting on in the World, or Hints on Success in Life, by W. Matthew, LL.D.

Mathematics. See Gregory, Dupin.

804. *Matthias.* Rules of Order, a Manual for conducting business in Meetings and Deliberative Bodies.

2324. *Mattocks.* Minnesota, a Home for Invalids, by B. Mattocks, M.D.

657. *Maunder.* The Treasury of Natural History; or, a Popular Dictionary of Animated Nature, &c.; to which is added a Syllabus of Practical Taxidermy and Glossarial Appendix, by Samuel Maunder. 1852.

4352. *Maurice.* Sacred Morality, Twenty-one Lectures delivered in the University of Cambridge, by E. D. Maurice.

1834. *Maury.* Memoirs of a Huguenot Family, translated and compiled from the Original Autobiography of James Fontaine, by Ann Maury.

391. *Maury.* Physical Geography of the Sea and its Meteorology, by M. F. Maury, LL.D. The eighth edition, revised and enlarged.

1903. *Maxwell.* Theory of Heat, by J. Clark Maxwell, M. A. 1872.

1060-1. *May.* The Constitutional History of England, since the Accession of George III, 1760 to 1860, by Thomas Erskine May. 2 vols.

4498. *May.* The American Female Poets, with Biographical and Critical Notices, by Caroline May. 1854.

3170. *Mayfield.* A Wreath of Rhymes, by Millie Mayfield. 1849.

801. *Mayhew.* The Illustrated Horse Doctor; being an Accurate and Detailed Account, accompanied by more than Four Hundred Pictorial Representations, of the Various Diseases to which the Equine Race is subjected; together with the Latest Mode of Treatment, and all the Requisite Prescriptions written in plain English. By Edward Mayhew, M.R.C.V.S.

802. *Mayhew.* The Illustrated Horse Management; contains Descriptive Remarks upon Anatomy, Medicine, Shoeing, Teeth, Food, Vices, Stables; likewise a Plain Account of the Situation, Nature, and Value of the Various Points; together with Remarks on Grooms, Dealers, Breeders, Breakers, and Trainers; also on Carriages and Harness, by Edward Mayhew.

4754. *Maynard.* The Naturalist's Guide in collecting objects of Natural History, a Catalogue of Birds, &c., by C. J. Maynard.

1829. *Mayo.* Kaloolah; Adventures of Jonathan Romer, of Nantucket, by W. S. Mayo. 1872.

150 THE CARPENTERS' COMPANY.

1902. *McCabe.* Planting the Wilderness; or, the Pioneer Boys; a Story of Frontier Life, by J. D. McCabe.

137. *McClellan.* The Art of War in Europe.

4617. *McClintock.* The Voyage of the "Fox" in the Arctic Seas. A Narrative of the Discovery of the Fate of Sir John Franklin and his Companions. Preface by Sir Roderick Murchison, F.R.S , with Maps and Illustrations, by Captain Francis L. McClintock.

4747. *McClure.* Three Thousand Miles Through the Rocky Mountains, by A. K. McClure.

4262-3. *McCulloch.* A Dictionary, Geographical, Statistical, and Historical, of the various countries, places, and principal natural objects in the world, by J. R. McCulloch. 2 vols.

4257-8. *Meade.* Old Churches, Ministers, and Families of Virginia, by Bishop Meade, of Virginia. 2 vols.

1037. *Mechanics.* The Mechanic's Companion; or, the Elements and Practice of Carpentry, Joining, Bricklaying, Masonry, Slating, Plastering, Painting, Smithing, and Turning. 1829.

Mechanics. See Knight, Emerson.

4741. *Mechanic.* The Young Mechanic, Instruction for use of Tools, Construction, Models, &c.. &c.

2826. *Meline.* Two Thousand Miles on Horseback; Santa Fe and Back: a Summer Tour Through Kansas, Nebraska, Colorado, and New Mexico in 1866, by J. F. Meline.

3863. *Melancthon.* The Life of Philip Melancthon, by C. D. Ledderhose. 1855.

1835. *Melek-Hanuus.* Thirty Years in the Harem; or the Autobiography of Melek-Hanuus, wife of H. H. K. Mehemet Pasha. 1872.

4743. *Men.* Men of the Times; a Dictionary of Contemporaries, &c., &c., of both Sexes.

3208. *Menault.* The Intelligence of Animals, with Illustrative Anecdotes, by E. Menault. 1871.

Mensuration. See Nicholson.

1907. *Meredith.* Every Day Errors of Speech, by L. P. Meredith, M. D. 1872.

1830. *Messages.* The Addresses and Messages of the Presidents of the United States, from Washington to Tyler, embracing the Executive Proclamations, Recommendations, Protests and Vetoes; Declaration of Independence, Constitution of the United States, &c. 1842.

4463. *Messages.* Messages of the President on Enlistments by Great Britain and Construction of Treaty of 1850.

291, 4049. *Messages.* Maps and Views to accompany the Messages and Documents.

2626. *Messages.* President to Congress, 39th Congress, 1st Session.

2627-30. *Messages.* " Foreign Affairs. 4 vols.

2631-3. *Messages.* " 39th Congress, 2d Session. 3 vs.

2634-43. *Messages.* " 41st Congress. 10 vols.

2644-50. *Messages.* " " 3d Session. 7 vs.

2651–3. *Messages.* President to Congress, 41st Congress, Revenue Commissioner. 3 vols.
2654–7. *Messages.* President to Congress, Secretary of Treasury. 4 vs.
2658. *Messages.* " Revenue.
2659. *Messages.* " Treasurer.
2660. *Messages.* " Internal Revenue. 1867.
2661–3. *Messages.* " Land Office. 3 vols. 1866–8.
2664–70. *Messages.* " Patents. 7 vols.
2671–4. *Messages.* " Secretary of State. 4 vols. 1865–8.
2675–80. *Messages.* President to Congress, Agriculture. 6 vols. 1863–8.
2681. *Messages.* " Retrenchment. 1868.
2682. *Messages.* " Levee. 1867.
2683. *Messages.* " Mineral Resources. 1869.
2684. *Messages.* " New Orleans Riots. 1866.
3716. *Messages.* " Commerce and Navigation.
Metal Worker. See Byrne.
Meteorology. See Espy.
3204. *Meunier.* Adventures on the Great Hunting Grounds of the World, by Victor Meunier. 1870.
Mexico. See Mansfield, Prescott, Ripley, Wilson.
Microscope. See King.
3975. *Middleton.* Grecian Remains in Italy : a Description of Cyclopean Walls and Roman Antiquities, with Topographical and Picturesque Views of Ancient Latium, by J. J. Middleton. 1812.
631. *Middleton.* The Architect and Builder's Miscellany, or Pocket Library ; containing Original Picturesque Designs in Architecture, for Cottages, Farm, Country and Town Houses, by Charles Middleton.
603. *Miles.* Norðurfari, or Rambles in Iceland, by Pliny Miles. 1854.
4365–6. *Milford.* Our Village ; Sketches of Rural Character and Scenery, by M. R. Milford. 2 vols.
3934. *Miller.* Designs for Street Fronts, Suburban Houses, and Cottages, including Details, &c., by C. Miller.
1904. *Mille.* The Seven Hills, by Prof. J. De Mille.
1905. *Mille.* Picked Up Adrift, by J. De Mille.
4389. *Mille.* The Treasure of the Seas, by J. De Mille.
3919. *Miller.* Geology of Bass Rock, with its Civil and Ecclesiastical History, by Hugh Miller. 1854.
708. *Miller.* First Impressions of England and its People, by Hugh Miller. 1853.
709. *Miller.* The Old Red Sandstone ; or, New Walks in an Old Field, by H. Miller. 1854.
710. *Miller.* The Footprints of the Creator; or, the Asterolepis of Stromness, by Hugh Miller. 1854.
711. *Miller.* My Schools and Schoolmasters; or, the Story of my Education, by Hugh Miller.
1216. *Miller.* Picturesque Sketches of London, Past and Present, with numerous Engravings, Churches, and Public Buildings, by Thomas Miller.

1021-2. *Miller.* Bench and Bar of Georgia. Memoirs and Sketches, with an Appendix ; containing a Court Roll from 1790 to 1857, &c., by Stephen F. Miller. 2 vols.

706. *Miller.* The Testimony of the Rocks, by Hugh Miller.

707. *Miller.* Popular Geology ; a Series of Lectures, by Hugh Miller.

1220. *Miller.* The Life and Times of Hugh Miller, by Thomas M. Brown.

20. *Milner.* The Gallery of Nature, a Pictorial and Descriptive Tour through Creation, illustrative of the wonders of Astronomy, Physical Geography, and Geology, by Rev. Thomas Milner. 1852.

2526-8. *Milton.* The Poetical Works of John Milton, with a Life, by J. Mitford. 3 vols. 1853.

Minnesota. See Mattock.

Mineralogy. See Dana, Schœdler, Hooker.

2032. *Minifics.* The Text-Book of Mechanical Drawing for the use of Mechanics and Schools, with illustrations for drawing plans, sections and elevations of Buildings, Machinery, &c., by William Minifics. 1848.

Mississippi. See Squier, Schoolcraft, Shea, Ellet.

2916. *Mitchell.* Mitchell's World, an accompaniment to Mitchell's Map of the World on Mercator's Projection, containing an index to the various countries, &c.

3711. *Mitchell.* The Planetary and Stellar Worlds, a popular exposition of the great discoveries and theories of modern Astronomy, in a series of 10 lectures, by O. M. Mitchell.

4612. *Mitchell.* Popular Astronomy ; a concise elementary treatise on the Sun, Planets, Satellites, and Comets, by O. M. Mitchell.

1833. *Mitchell.* The Astronomy of the Bible, by O. M. Mitchell. 1871.

1514. *Mitchell.* Injuries of Nerves and their Consequences, by S. Weir Mitchell, M. D. 1872.

1901. *Mitchell.* Wear and Tear; or, Hints for the Over-worked, by S. Weir Mitchell, M. D. 1872.

1832. *Mitchell.* Wonders of the Moon, translated from the French of A. Guillemin, &c., with additions, by Maria Mitchell.

1837. *Mivart.* On the Genesis of Species, by St. George Mivart, F. R. S. 1871.

3212. *Monnier.* The Wonders of Pompeii, by M. Monnier. 1871.

4761. *Monroe.* Public and Parlor Readings, Prose and Poetry, for use of Reading Clubs, &c., by L. B. Monroe. Humorous.

2232. *Monroe.* Public and Parlor Readings, Prose and Poetry, for use of Reading Clubs, &c., by L. B. Monroe. Miscellaneous.

Mont Blanc. See Smith.

766-8. *Montagu.* The Works of Francis Bacon, Lord Chancellor of England, with a Life of the Author, by Basil Montague. 3 vols.

1056-9. *Montaigne.* The Works of Michael de Montaigne ; comprising his essays, letters, and journey through Germany and Italy ; with notes from all the commentators, biographical and biblio-graphical notices, &c., &c., by W. Haslitt, edited by O. W. Wright. 4 vols.

4607. *Monteage.* Debtor and Creditor Made Easy, or a short instruction for the attaining the right use of accounts, after the best methods used by Merchants, fitted to the trades or ways of dealing, &c., by Stephen Monteage. 1690.

1338. *Montgomery.* The Poetical Works of Rogers, Campbell, J. Montgomery, Lamb, and Kirke White. 1856.

1838. *Montgomery.* Thrown Together, a Story, by F. Montgomery.

1906. *Montgomery.* Misunderstood, by Florence Montgomery.

92. *Morgan.* The American Beaver and his Works, by Lewis H. Morgan. 1868.

80. *Monument.* Report of the Committee for the Erection of a Monument to the Signers of the Declaration of Independence, in Independence Square, Philadelphia.

136. *Mordecai.* Art of War in Europe in 1855 and 1856. Report of Major Alford Mordecai, of Ordnance Department.

1337. *Moore.* The Poetical Works of Thomas Moore, including his melodies, ballads, &c., complete in one volume.

4277–4. *Moore.* The Rebellion Record; a Diary of American events, with documents, narrative, illustrative incidents, and poetry, edited by F. Moore, with an Address on the cause by Edward Everett. 8 vols.

200–1. *Moore.* The Complete Works of Hannah Moore. 2 vols. 1854.

42. *Morton.* An Illustrated System of Human Anatomy, Special, General, and Microscopic, by Samuel George Morton, M. D., author of Crania Americana, Crania Egyptiaca, &c. With three hundred and ninety-one engravings on wood.

2067. *Mosheim.* An Ecclesiastical History, ancient and modern; from the Birth of Christ to the beginning of the 18th century, in which the rise, progress and variations of Church power are considered in their connection with the state of learning and philosophy, and the political history of Europe, during that period, by J. L. Mosheim; continued to the year 1826, by Charles Coote, &c. 1854.

1010–1. *Motley.* History of the United Netherlands, from the death of William the Silent to the Synod of Dort; with a full View of the English-Dutch Struggle against Spain, and of the Origin and Destruction of the Spanish Armada, by John Lothrop Motley, LL.D., D. C. L., Author of "The Rise of the Dutch Republic." 2 vols.

1338–0. *Motley.* A History of the Rise of the Dutch Republic, by J. L. Motley. 3 vols.

2241. *Moustache.* Two Lives in One, by Vieux Moustache.

4705. *Muhlbach.* Mahommed Ali and his House, by L. Muhlbach.

4704. *Muhlbach.* Frederick the Great and his Family, by L. Muhlbach.

4703. *Muhlbach.* Louisa of Prussia and her Times, by L. Muhlbach.

4706. *Muhlbach.* Old Fritz and the New Era, by L. Muhlbach.

4707. *Muhlbach.* Queen Hortense; a Life Picture of the Napoleon Era, by L. Muhlbach.

4708. *Muhlbach.* Napoleon and the Queen of Prussia, by L. Muhlbach.

11

N.

1211. *Neale.* Narrative of a Residence at the Capital of the Kingdom of Siam, with a description of the Manners, Customs, and Laws of the Modern Siamese, by F. A. Neale. 1852.

4288-2. *Neander.* General History of the Christian Religion and Church, from the German of Dr. Augustus Neander; translated by J. Torrey. 5 vols. 1851.

4763. *Neele.* The Romance of History, England, by H. Neele.

794. *Neill.* History of Minnesota, from its Earliest Explorations under the French and British Governments to the present time, by Rev. Edward Duffield Neill, Secretary of the Minnesota Historical Society.

New Jersey. See Arthur.

New York. See Clay, Watson, Broadhead, Valentine, Arthur.

2684. *New Orleans.* Report of Select Committee on the New Orleans Riot. 1867.

1841. *Nevin.* Black Robes, or Sketches of Missions and Ministers in the Wilderness and on the Border, by Robert P. Nevin.

4467-8. *Nicaragua.* Nicaragua; its People, Scenery, Monuments, and the proposed Interoceanic Canal, with numerous original Maps and Illustrations, by E. F. Squier. 2 vols. 1852.

4090-1. *Nicholson.* Dictionary of the Science and Practice of Architecture, Building, &c. Improved and edited by E. Lomax and T. Gunyon.

4028. *Nicholson.* The Builder and Workingman's New Director, comprising Explanations of the General Principles of Architecture, of the Practice of Building, and of the several Mechanical Arts connected therewith; also the Elements and Practice of Geometry in its application to the Building Art. A new edition, revised and much enlarged from the original work, by Peter Nicholson, Architect. 1853.

3612. *Nicholson.* Principles of Architecture, comprising fundamental Rules of the Art, with their application to practice; also Rules for Shadows and for the five Orders, by Peter Nicholson, Architect, revised and corrected by Joseph Gwilt. 1848.

2063-4. *Nicholson.* The New Practical Builder and Workingman's Companion, containing a full Display and Elucidation of the most recent and skilful Methods pursued by Architects and Artificers, &c., by Peter Nicholson. 2 vols. 1828.

1753-4. *Nicholson.* The Operative Mechanic and British Machinist; being a practical Display of the Manufactures and Mechanical Arts in the United Kingdom, by John Nicholson. 2 vols. 1826.

1758-0. *Nicholson.* The Principles of Architecture; containing the fundamental Rules of the Art in Geometry, Arithmetic, and Mensuration, the true Method of drawing the Ichnography and Orthography of Objects, &c., by Peter Nicholson. 3 vols. 1827.

4023 *Nicholson.* Same as 4025.

4028. *Nicholson.* The Builder and Workman's New Director, comprehending Definitions and Descriptions of the component parts of

Buildings, the Principles of Construction, &c., by P. Nicholson. 1825.

132. *Nicholson.* A Practical Treatise on Mensuration, for the use of Carpenters, Builders, Surveyors, and Artificers in general, Measurement of curved Surfaces clearly explained, by Peter Nicholson.

4022. *Nicholson.* The Carpenter and Joiner's Assistant, containing practical rules for making all kinds of joints, and various methods of hinging them together, for hanging of doors on straight, and circular plans for fitting up windows and shutters to answer various purposes, with rules for hanging them, with examples of various roofs constructed, and on the strength of timber, with practical illustrations, by Peter Nicholson. *Gift of James Hutchinson.*

4025. *Nicholson.* The Carpenter's New Guide: being a complete Book of Lines for Carpentry and Joinery, treating fully on practical Geometry, Soffits, Brick and Plaster Groins, by Peter Nicholson. 1793.

1842. *Nicholson.* A Manual of Zoology for the use of Students, with a General Introduction on the principles of Zoology, by H. A. Nicholson. 1872.

1218. *Nineveh.* The Ruined City of the East, Nineveh, with numerous Illustrations. See Layard.

867. *Nolte.* Fifty Years in both Hemispheres, or Reminiscences of the Life of a former Merchant, by Vincent Nolte, late of New Orleans : translated from the German. 1854.

3717. *Nordhoff.* California; or Health, Pleasure, and Residence; a Book for Travellers and Settlers, by Chas. Nordhoff.

636. *Norton.* The Undying One, Sorrows of Rosalie, and other Poems, by the Hon. Mrs. Norton. 1814.

623. *Norton.* The Dream and other Poems, by the Hon. Mrs. Norton. 1851.

4243. *Norton.* An Elementary Treatise on Astronomy, in 4 parts, containing a systematic and comprehensive exposition of the Theory and the more important problems, with Solar, Lunar, and other Astronomical Tables, by William Norton. 1854.

4455. *North.* The Recreations of Christopher North, complete in one volume.

North, C. See Wilson.

North Carolina. See Wheeler.

Northmen. See Keyser.

690. *Nott & Gliddon.* Types of Mankind, or Ethnological Researches, based upon the Ancient Monuments, Paintings, Sculptures, and Crania of Races, and upon their natural, geographical, philological, and Biblical History, illustrated by Selections from the unedited papers of S. G. Morton, M. D., &c., by J. C. Nott, and George B. Gliddon. 1854.

885. *Nott & Gliddon.* Indigenous Races of the Earth, or New Chapters of Ethnological Inquiry. Contributed by Alfred Maury,

Francis Pulzky, J. Aitken Meigs, M. D., presenting fresh investigations, documents, and materials, by the editors, J. C. Nott, M. D., and George R. Gliddon, authors of "Types of Mankind."

4368. **Nuttall.** Dictionary of Scientific Terms, by P. A. Nuttall.

O.

3964–5. **Ogilvie.** The Imperial Dictionary, English, Technological and Scientific, adapted to the Present State of Literature, Science, and Art, on the Basis of Webster's English Dictionary, and Supplement, by John Ogilvie. 1853. 2 vols.

3962. **Ogilvie.** A Supplement to the Imperial Dictionary, &c.

1184. **Oglethorpe.** Life of James Oglethorpe, by William O. B. Peabody.

Ohio. See Taylor, Arthur, Ellett.

1137. **Oliphant.** The Russian Shore of the Black Sea, in the Autumn of 1852, with a Voyage down the Volga, and a Tour through the Country of the Don Cossacks, by L. Oliphant. 1854.

797. **Oliphant.** Narrative of the Earl of Elgin's Mission to China and Japan, in the Years 1857, '58, '59, by Laurence Oliphant, Private Secretary to Lord Elgin. Illustrations.

1923. **Oliphant.** Agnes Hopton's Schools and School-days, the experience of a little girl, by Mrs. Oliphant.

1924. **Oliphant.** The Laird of Norlaw, by L. Oliphant.

1909. **Optic.** Desk and Debit; or the Catastrophes of a Clerk, by Oliver Optic.

1910. **Optic.** The Soldier Boy: or Tom Somers in the Army, a Story of the Great Rebellion, by Oliver Optic.

1911. **Optic.** Fighting Joe; or the Fortunes of a Staff Officer, a Story of the Great Rebellion, by Oliver Optic.

1912. **Optic.** The Young Lieutenant; or the Adventures of an Army Officer, a Story of the Great Rebellion, by Oliver Optic.

1913. **Optic.** The Sailor Boy; or Jack Somers in the Navy, a Story of the Great Rebellion, by Oliver Optic.

1914. **Optic.** The Yankee Middy; or the Adventures of a Naval Officer, a Story of the Great Rebellion, by Oliver Optic.

1915. **Optic.** Brave Old Salt: or Life on the Quarter Deck, a Story of the Great Rebellion, by Oliver Optic.

1916. **Optic.** Plane and Plank; or the Mishaps of a Mechanic, by Oliver Optic.

1917. **Optic.** Sea and Shore; or the Tramps of a Traveller, by Oliver Optic.

1918. **Optic.** Field and Forest; or the Fortunes of a Farmer Boy, by Oliver Optic.

1919. **Optic.** Bivouac and Battle: or the Struggles of a Soldier, by Oliver Optic.

1920. **Optic.** Cringle and Crosstree; or the Sea Swashes of a Sailor, by Oliver Optic.

1949. *Optic.* Up the Baltic; or Young America in Norway, Sweden, and Denmark, a Story of Travel and Adventure, by Oliver Optic.

3237. *Optic.* Rich and Humble; or the Mission of Bertha Grant. A Story for Young People, by Oliver Optic.

3238. *Optic.* In School and Out; or the Conquest of Richard Grant. A Story for Young People, by Oliver Optic.

3239. *Optic.* Watch and Wait; or the Young Fugitive. A Story for Young People, by Oliver Optic. 1870.

3240. *Optic.* Work and Win; or Neddy Newman on a Cruise. A Story for Young People, by Oliver Optic.

3241. *Optic.* Hope and Have; or Fanny Grant among the Indians   A Story for Young People, by Oliver Optic.

3242. *Optic.* Haste and Waste; or the Young Pilot of Lake Champlain, by Oliver Optic.

3243. *Optic.* The Boat Club; or the Bunkers of Rippleton. A Tale for Boys, by Oliver Optic.

3244. *Optic.* All Aboard; or Life on the Lake. A Sequel to the Boat Club, by Oliver Optic.

3245. *Optic.* Now or Never; or the Adventures of Bobby Bright. A Story for Young Folks, by Oliver Optic.

3246. *Optic.* Try Again; or the Trials and Triumphs of Harry West, by Oliver Optic.

3247. *Optic.* Little by Little; or the Cruise of the Fly-Away, by Oliver Optic.

3248. *Optic.* Poor and Proud; or the Fortunes of Katy Redburn, by Oliver Optic.

3268. *Optic.* Lightning Express, by Oliver Optic.

3269. *Optic.* Switch Off; or the War of the Students, by Oliver Optic.

3270. *Optic.* On Time; or the Young Captain of the Ucayga Steamer, by Oliver Optic.

3271. *Optic.* Bear and Forbear; or the Young Skipper of Lake Ucayga, by Oliver Optic.

3272. *Optic.* Through by Daylight; or the Young Engineer on the Lake Shore Railroad, by Oliver Optic.

3273. *Optic.* Break Up; or the Young Peace-Maker, by Oliver Optic.

2305. *Optic.* The Starry Flag; or the Young Fisherman of Cape Ann, by Oliver Optic.

2306. *Optic.* Breaking Away; or the Fortunes of a Student, by Oliver Optic.

2307. *Optic.* Seek and Find; or the Adventures of a Smart Boy, by Oliver Optic.

2308. *Optic.* Freaks of Fortune; or Half Around the World, by Oliver Optic.

2309. *Optic.* Make or Break; or the Rich Man's Daughter, by Oliver Optic.

2310. *Optic.* Down the River; or Buck Bradford and his Tyrants, by Oliver Optic.

2311. *Optic.* Shamrock and Thistle; or Young America in Ireland and Scotland.

2312. *Optic.* Cross and Crescent; or Young America in Turkey and Greece, a Story of Travel and Adventure, by Oliver Optic.

2313. *Optic.* Red Cross; or Young America in England and Wales, a Story of Travel and Adventure, by Oliver Optic.

2314. *Optic.* Outward Bound; or Young America Afloat, a Story of Travel and Adventure, by Oliver Optic.

2315. *Optic.* Down the Rhine; or Young America in Germany, a Story of Travel and Adventure, by Oliver Optic.

2316. *Optic.* Dykes and Ditches; or Young America in Holland and Belgium, a Story of Travel and Adventure, by Oliver Optic.

2317. *Optic.* Palace and Cottage; or Young America in France and Switzerland, a Story of Travel and Adventure, by Oliver Optic.

Optic. See W. T. Adams.

3185. *Ormerod.* British Social Wasps; an introduction to their Anatomy, Physiology, Architecture, and General Natural History, with Illustrations of the Different Species and their Nests, by E. L. Ormerod, M. D. 1868.

1040. *Orfila.* A Popular Treatise on the Remedies to be Employed in Cases of Poisoning and Apparent Death, including the Means of Detecting Poisons, of Distinguishing Real from Apparent Death, &c., &c., by M. P. Orfila. 1818.

Ornaments. See Wallis.

Ornithology. See Wilson, Cassin.

2341. *Orton.* Lightning Calculator, and Accountant's Calculator, by H. D. Orton.

4314. *Orton.* The Andes and the Amazon, or Across the Continent of South America, by James Orton.

1184. *Otis.* Life of James Otis, by Francis Bowen.

4390. *Osborn.* The Holy Land, past and present; Sketches of Travels in Palestine, by Henry S. Osborn.

Ottoman Empire. See Deans.

626. *Overman.* Mechanics for the Millwright, Machinist, Engineer, Civil Engineer, Architect, and Student; containing a clear Elementary Exposition of the Principles and Practice of Building Mechanics, by Frederick Overman, author of the Manufacture of Iron, and other Scientific Treatises. Illustrated by 154 fine wood engravings.

1417. *Owen.* Hints on Public Architecture, containing, among the Illustrations, Views and Plans of the Smithsonian Institution; together with an Appendix relative to Building Materials, by Robert Dale Owen. 1849.

868. *Owen.* The Wrong of Slavery, the Right of Emancipation, and the Future of the African Race in the United States, by Robert Dale Owen.

P.

1854. **Palmer.** The Desert of the Exodus; Journeys on Foot in the Wilderness of the Forty Years Wanderings, by E. H. Palmer.

79. **Pamphlets.** Report on Penal Code; Auditor's Report on Railroads.

80. **Pamphlets.** Memoir of Samuel Breck, Historical Society, Signers' Monument, State Library, Ways and Means, Condition of the Pennsylvania Railroad Company, Farmers' Market Company.

3799. **Pamphlets.** History of Camden, New Jersey, Gallatin on the Western Insurrection, Reply to Joseph Read.

2044. **Papworth.** Rural Residences, consisting of a Series of Designs for Cottages, Decorated Cottages, small Villas, and other Ornamental Buildings, accompanied by Hints, &c., by Papworth. 1832.

2910. **Paris.** Purple Tints of Paris, Character and Manners of the New Empire, by Bayle St. John.

658. **Paris.** Galignani's New Guide to Paris. *Gift of O. R. Knight.*

4608. **Paris.** Parisian Sights and French Principles, seen through American Spectacles. 1856.

854. **Parker.** Morning Stars of the New World, by H. F. Parker. 1854.

4267. **Parkman.** History of the Conspiracy of Pontiac and the War of the North American Tribes against the English Colonies after the Conquest of Canada, by F. Parkman. 1851.

2917. **Parkman.** Prairie and Rocky Mountain Life; or the California and Oregon Trail, by F. Parkman. 1854.

1082-3. **Parkyns.** Life in Abyssinia, being Notes collected during Three Years' Travel in that Country, by Mansfield Parkyns. 2 vols. 1854.

3140. **Parley.** Peter Parley's Thousand and One Stories of Fact and Fancy, Wit and Humor, Rhyme, Reason and Romance.

3141. **Parley.** Peter Parley's Merry Stories in Fact, Fancy and Fiction; a Collection of very Merry Stories, Anecdotes, &c., by Peter Parley.

2510. **Parnell.** The Poetical Works of Thomas Parnell, with a Life, by Oliver Goldsmith.

4700. **Parr.** Dorothea Fox, by the Author of "How It All Happened."

1136. **Parson.** Poems by Parson, inscribed to John C. Warren, M. D., Professor, &c., in the University of Cambridge. 1854.

4756. **Parton.** The Life of Horace Greeley, &c., &c., by John Parton.

64. **Parton.** Eminent Women of the Age; being a Narration of the Lives and Deeds of the Most Eminent Women of the Present Generation, by Parton and others.

3143. **Parton.** The Humorous Poetry of the English Language from Chaucer to Saxe; Narratives, Satires, Enigmas, Burlesques, &c., by James Parton.

316-1. **Patents.** Report of the Commissioner of Patents for the Years 1851, 1855, 1859. 6 vols.

1223. **Payne.** Rambles in Brazil; or, a Peep at the Aztecs, by one who has seen them, by A. R. M. Payne. 1854.

1921. **Pearson.** The Young Pioneers of the Northwest, by Dr. C. H. Pearson. 1871.

1922. *Pearson.* The Cabin on the Prairie, by Dr. C. H. Pearson.

2072–3. *Penn.* Correspondence of Wm. Penn and James Logan, Secretary of the Province, and others. 1872. 2 vols.

1027–8. *Penn.* Memorials of the Professional Life and Times of Sir William Penn, Knt., Admiral and General of the Fleet during the Interregnum, Admiral and Commissioner of the Admiralty and Navy after the Restoration, 1644 to 1670, by Granville Penn, Esq. 1853.

2920. *Penn.* No Cross, No Crown; a Discourse showing the Nature and Discipline of the Holy Cross of Christ, &c., &c., to which is added the Living and Dying Testimonies of many Persons of Fame and Learning, &c., by William Penn. 1853.

Penn. See Janney, Dixon, Ellis.

Pennsylvania. See Wood, Hazzard, Read, Purdon, Troubat and Haly, Day, Bowen, Watson, Arthur.

712–26. *Pennsylvania.* Minutes of the Provincial Council of Pennsylvania, from the Originating to the Termination of the Proprietary Government, published by the State, 15 vols. 1852. *Gift of Charles O'Neill.* See Hazzard.

1388–03. *Pennsylvania.* The Register of Pennsylvania, devoted to the Preservation of Facts and Documents, and every other kind of Useful Knowledge respecting the State. 16 volumes. 1828 to 1844.

297. *Pennsylvania.* Acts of the General Assembly of the Commonwealth of Pennsylvania, passed 1803.

4425. *Pennsylvania.* Catalogue of the Pennsylvania State Library.

27. *Pennsylvania.* Reports of the Heads of Departments, transmitted to the Government in pursuance of Law, for the Financial Year ending 1859, with the Report of the Superintendent of Common Schools.

415. *Pennsylvania.* Report of the several Railroad Companies of Pennsylvania, communicated to the Auditor-General. 1864.

302–11, 295. *Pennsylvania.* Laws of the Commonwealth of Pennsylvania, from 1700 to 1810. 15 vols.

1501-2. *Pennsylvania.* Annual Report of the Board of Public Charities of the State of Pennsylvania, for 1871 and 1872, with appendix, &c.

22. *Pennsylvania.* Annual Report of the Auditor General of the State of Pennsylvania, with Deductions from the Reports of Railroad, Canal and Telegraph Companies. 1868.

1374. *Pennsylvania.* Annual Report of the Superintendent of Common Schools.

343–4. *Pennsylvania.* Laws of the General Assembly of the State of Pennsylvania, passed 1834-6. *Gift of James Hutchinson.*

348–0. *Pennsylvania.* Journal of the House of Representatives of the Commonwealth of Pennsylvania, 1834-5. 3 vols. *Gift of James Hutchinson.*

245–7. *Pennsylvania.* Journal of the Senate of Pennsylvania, 1834-5. 3 vols. *Gift of James Hutchinson.*

4411–5. *Penny Magazine.* Magazine of the Society for the Diffusion of Useful Knowledge, a new series, complete in 5 vols.

4753. *Pepper.* Cyclopædia Science Simplified, by J. H. Pepper.

1857. *Pepper.* The Play Book of Metals; including Personal Narrative of Visits to Coal Lands, Copper and Tin Mines, with interesting experiments, by John Henry Pepper.

271–4. *Pepys.* Diary and Correspondence of Samuel Pepys, F.R.S., Secretary to the Admiralty in the Reigns of Charles II and James II, the Diary Description by the Rev. J. Smith, from the original Short-hand in the Pepysian Library, with a Life and Notes by Richard, Lord Braybrooke. 4 vols. 1855.

3991. *Perrault.* Les dix Livres d'Architecture de Vittruve, corriges et traduitz, par M. Perrault. 1784.

26. *Perry.* Narrative of the Expedition of an American Squadron to the China Sea and Japan, in 1852, '53, and '54, under the command of Commodore M. C. Perry, U. S. Navy, by order of the Government of the United States, compiled from the Notes, Journals, &c., by F. L. Hawks. 1856.

1860. *Perry.* Life Lessons from the Book of Proverbs, by W. S. Perry.

Perspective. See Wood.

Peru. See Hawks, Prescott.

4758. *Peterson.* Pemberton; or One Hundred Years Ago, by H. Peterson.

254. *Peterson.* History of Rhode Island and Newport, by Edward Peterson. 1853.

4045. *Pether.* Book of Tablets, by T. Pether.

1096. *Pfeiffer.* Visit to the Holy Land, Egypt, and Italy, by Madame Ida Pfeiffer. 1852.

1207. *Pfeiffer.* A Woman's Journey round the World, from Vienna to Brazil, Chili, Tahiti, China, Hindostan, Persia, and Asia Minor, by Ida Pfeiffer. 1852.

1208. *Pfeiffer.* A Lady's Second Journey round the World from London to the Cape of Good Hope, Borneo, Java, Sumatra, Celebes, Ceram, the Mallaccas, California, Panama, Peru, Ecuador, and the United States, by Ida Pfeiffer. 1856.

4325. *Phelps.* Reviews and Essays on Art, Literature, and Science, by A. L. Phelps.

426. *Philadelphia.* Address before the Centennial Meeting of the Philadelphia Contributionship for the Insurance of Houses from Loss by Fire.

2031. *Philadelphia.* Catalogue of Books added to the Library of the Library Company of Philadelphia, since the large Catalogue of 1835. 1844.

1000. *Philadelphia.* Philadelphia in 1830-1, or a Brief Account of the Various Institutions and Objects of Interest in the Metropolis, 1830.

261–96. *Philadelphia.* The Ordinances of the Corporation of the City of Philadelphia, to which is prefixed the Act of Incorporation and the several Supplements thereto. 1805.

351–76, 734–40. *Philadelphia.* Journal of the Select and Common Council of Philadelphia, 1835 to 1846, 1855 to 1857, and 1863. 25 vols.

1347. *Philadelphia.* History of the Philadelphia Society for the Establishment and Support of Charity Schools.

Philadelphia. See Watson, Simpson, Fairmount.

337–41. *Philadelphia.* Journal of Select Council, 1835 to 1840. 5 vols. *Gift of Jas. Hutchinson.*

342. *Philadelphia.* Journal of Select Council, 1848 to 1849.

1632–7. *Philadelphia.* Journal of Common Council, 1835 to 1838. 6 vols. *Gift of Jas. Hutchinson.*

278–81. *Philadelphia.* Annual Report of the Chief Engineer of the Water Department of the City of Philadelphia, 1868 to 1871.

234. *Philadelphia.* Ordinances and Joint Resolutions of Councils, 1855.

432. *Philadelphia.* Ordinances and Joint Resolutions of Councils of Philadelphia, 1864.

238. *Philadelphia.* Digest of Acts of Assembly, &c., &c., relating to the Northern Liberties of Philadelphia. 1838.

433. *Philadelphia.* Digest of the Acts of Assembly, &c., relating to Philadelphia. 1856.

236. *Philadelphia.* Digest of Ordinances of the City of Philadelphia. 1828.

1646. *Philadelphia.* Digest of the Acts of Assembly relating to Philadelphia. 1856.

4050. *Philadelphia.* Journal of Industry and American Engineer, devoted to Manufacturing Progress, &c. 1870.

Phillippines. See Gironiere.

Philosophy. See Cousin.

Phrenology. See Combe.

851. *Physiology.* A Popular Treatise on Vegetable Physiology, published under the Auspices of the Society for the Promotion of Popular Instruction. 1842. See Leuces, Draper.

3930. *Pictorial.* The Pictorial Museum of Animated Nature, Mammalia, Birds.

3929. *Pictorial.* The Pictorial Gallery of the Useful Arts. See Laud, Lossing.

1187. *Pike.* Life of Zebulon M. Pike, by Henry Whiting.

4335. *Pilkington.* The Artist's Guide and Mechanic's Own Book, embracing Chemistry, applicable to the Mechanic Arts, &c., &c., by James Pilkington.

3214. *Pilleur.* Wonders of the Human Body, from the French of A. Le Pilleur. 1871.

4426. *Plutarch.* Plutarch's Lives, translated from the original Greek, with Notes, Critical and Historical, and a Life of Plutarch, by J. Langhorne. 1854.

Poet. See Holmes.

Poisons. See Orfila.

Poland. See Saxton, Stephens.

Polar Seas. See Leslie.

3156. **Pollard.** The Virginia Tourist; Sketches of the Springs and Mountains of Virginia, &c., &c., by E. A. Pollard.

1855. **Pollock.** Life in the Exode, by A. D. Pollock. 1872.

Polynesia. See Russell.

Pompeii. See Gell.

Pontiac. See Parkman.

1756. **Pope.** A Treatise on Bridges' Architecture, in which the superior advantages of the Flying Pendant Lever Bridge is fully proved, with an Historical Account and Description of Different Bridges erected in Different Parts of the World, by Thomas Pope. 1811.

2507-9. **Pope.** The Poetical Works of Alexander Pope, with a Life, by A. Dyce, 3 vols. 1854.

1930. **Porter.** Summer Driftwood for the Winter Fire, by R. Porter.

4342. **Porter.** Thaddeus of Warsaw, by Jane Porter.

4343. **Porter.** The Scottish Chiefs; a Romance, by Jane Porter.

4312. **Porter.** Books and Reading; or What Books Shall I Read and How Shall I Read Them, by N. Porter.

Portugal. See Madeira.

1191. **Posey.** Memoir of Thomas Posey, by James Hall.

131. **Pouchet.** The Universe; or the Infinitely Great and the Infinitely Little, by M. A. Pouchet, M.D. 1872.

4375. **Powers.** Muskingum Legends, with other Sketches and Papers descriptive of the Young Men of Germany and the Old Boys of America, by Stephen Powers.

1194. **Preble.** Life of Edward Preble, by Lorenzo Sabine.

Presidents. See Messages.

3604-6. **Prescott.** History of the Reign of Ferdinand and Isabella the Catholic, by William H. Prescott. 3 vols. 1853. See Robertson.

3609-11. **Prescott.** History of the Conquest of Mexico, with a Preliminary View of the Ancient Mexican Civilization, and the Life of the Conqueror, Hernandez Cortez, by William H. Prescott. 3 vols. 1853.

4253. **Prescott.** Biographical and Critical Miscellanies, by William H Prescott. 1856.

233-5. **Prescott.** History of the Reign of Philip II, King of Spain, by William H. Prescott. 3 vols. 1855.

3607-8. **Prescott.** History of the Conquest of Peru, with a Preliminary View of the Civilization of the Incas, by William H. Prescott. 2 vols. 1847.

3804. **Prescott.** Life of William Hickling Prescott, illustrated with Steel Portraits and Wood Engravings.

1024-6. **Prescott.** Charles V. History of the Reign of the Emperor Charles V, by William Robertson, D. D., with an Account of the Emperor's Life after his Abdication, by William H. Prescott. 3 vols.

4597. **Prescott.** The History, Theory and Practice of the Electric Telegraph, with 100 Engravings, by George B. Prescott.

2249. **Preston.** Old Song and New, by M. J. Preston.

Preston. See Valmere.

261. **Price.** Limitation of Actions and of Liens against Real Estate in Pennsylvania, by Eli K. Price.

1404. **Price.** The British Carpenter, or a Treatise on Carpentry, containing the most concise and authentic Rules of that Art, &c., by Francis Price. 1765.

4349. **Price.** The History of Consolidation of the City of Philadelphia, by Eli K. Price.

4736. **Prime.** Around the World; Sketches of Travel through many Lands and over many Seas, by E. G. D. Prime.

2529-0. **Prior.** The Poetical Works of Matthew Prior, with a Life, by J. Mitford. 2 vols. 1853.

4261. **Pritchard.** The Natural History of Man, comprising Inquiries into the modifying Influence of Physical and Moral Agencies on the different Tribes of the Human Family, by James C. Pritchard. 1848.

2208. **Professor.** The Professor at the Breakfast Table, with the Story of Iris.

4315. **Proctor.** Light Science for Leisure Hours; a Series of Essays on Scientific Subjects—Natural Phenomena, by R. A. Proctor.

4742. **Proctor.** The Orbs About Us; a Series of Familiar Essays on the Moon, Planets, Meteors, Comets, &c., &c., by R. A. Proctor.

1856. **Proctor.** Other Worlds than Ours; the Plurality of Worlds studied under the Light of recent Scientific Research, by Richard A. Proctor. 1871.

4757. **Proctor.** The Russian Journey, by Edna Dean Proctor, with Illustrations.

3834. **Propertius.** Erotica. The Elegies of Propertius, Satyricon, of Pretonius Arbiter, Kisses of Johannes Secundus, and Love Epistles of Aristaenetus. Edited by W. H. Kelly. 1854.

2056-7. **Pugin.** Views of Paris and its Environs, displayed in a series of Picturesque Views, by A. Pugin. 2 vols.

4042. **Pugin.** An Apology for the Revival of Christian Architecture in England, by A. W. Pugin. 1843.

1419-0. **Pugin.** Specimens of Gothic Architecture, selected from various ancient edifices in England, in 2 vols., by A. Pugin. 1821.

1421. **Pugin.** Gothic ornaments, selected from various ancient Buildings in England and France, &c., by A. Pugin. 1844.

1426-8. **Pugin.** Examples of Gothic Architecture, selected from various ancient edifices in England, consisting of plans, sections, elevations, and parts at large, calculated to exemplify the various styles, practical construction, and accompanied by historical and descriptive accounts, by A. & A. W. Pugin. 3 vols. 1850.

1186. **Pulaski.** Life of Count Pulaski, by James Sparks.

4589. **Pulszky.** The Tricolor on the Atlas; or Algeria and the French Conquest, from the German of De Wagner and other Sources, by Francis Pulszky, Esq. 1855.

262. **Purdon.** Abridgment of the Laws of Pennsylvania, 1700 to 1811, by J. Purdon.

1387. *Pardon.* A Digest of all the Laws of Pennsylvania, 1700 to 1840, by Purdon and Story.
281. *Pardon.* Supplement to ditto.
1098. *Putnam.* The World's Progress; a Dictionary of Dates, with tabular views of general history, and an Historical Chart, by G. P. Putnam. 1853.

Q.

1761-82. *Quarterly Review.* American Quarterly Review; or papers by different Hands, embracing a critical Examination of a variety of Subjects, Review of new Works, &c. 22 vols.
Queens. See Hall, Strickland, Headley.
4601. *Quincy.* The Life of Josiah Quincy of Massachsuetts, by his son, Edmund Quincy. 1868.
869. *Quotations.* A new Dictionary of Quotations, from the Greek, Latin, and Modern Languages, with an extensive Index.

R.

3202. *Radau.* Wonders of Acoustics; or the Phenomena of Sound, from the French of Rudolphe Radau.
1189. *Rale.* Life of Sebastian Rale, Missionary to the Indians, by Convers Francis.
798. *Ramsey.* The Annals of Tennessee, to the end of Eighteenth Century, by J. C. M. Ramsey, A.M., M.D.
1928. *Ramsey.* Reminiscence of Scottish Life and Character, by E. B. Ramsey.
1519. *Randolph.* The Domestic Life of Thomas Jefferson, compiled from Family Letters and Reminiscences, by his Granddaughter, S. W. Randolph.
Randolph. See Garland, Thomas.
1861-3. *Ranke.* The History of the Popes; their Church and State, and especially of their conflicts with Protestantism, &c., by L. Ranke. 3 vols.
1706-7. *Ranlett.* The Architect, a Series of original Designs for decorative and ornamented Cottages and Villas, connected with Landscape Gardening, adapted to the United States, by W. H. Ranlett. 2 vols. 1853.
Ranlett. Same as 1706.
4345. *Ratcliffe.* The Romance of the Forest, by Annie Ratcliffe.
4302. *Ray.* Contributions to Mental Pathology, by I. Ray, M.D.
298-9. *Read.* An Abridgment of the Laws of Pennsylvania, &c., by C. Read, being a Complete Digest of all such Acts as concern the Commonwealth at large, by C. Read. 2 vols. 1801.

168   THE CARPENTERS' COMPANY.

632. **Read.** Precedents in the Office of a Justice of the Peace, to which
      is added a short system of Conveyancing, by C. Read. 1801.
2866. **Read.** The House by the Sea, a Poem, by Thos. B. Read. 1856.
3695. **Read.** Life and Correspondence of George Read, a Signer of the
      Declaration of Independence, with Notices of some of his Con-
      temporaries, by W. J. Read. 1870.
2294. **Reade.** It is Never Too Late; a matter of fact Romance, by
      Charles Reade.
1865. **Reason.** The Reason Why; Natural History, illustrating the Natu-
      ral History of Man and the Lower Animals, by the Author of
      "Inquire Into."
3721. **Reclus.** The Earth; a descriptive History of the Phenomena of the
      Life of the Globe, by Elesce Reclus, &c.
3694. **Reconstruction.** Report of the Joint Committee on Reconstruction
      to Congress. 1866.
2869-1. **Redhead.** The French Revolutions from 1789 to 1849, by T. W.
      Redhead. 3 vols. 1854.
4265-6. **Reed.** Life and Correspondence of Joseph Reed, Military Secre-
      tary of Washington, &c., by his Grandson, Wm. B. Reed. 2 vols.
      1847.
1590-1. **Reed.** Lectures on the British Poets, by Prof. Henry Reed.
      2 vols.
1190. **Reed.** Life of Joseph Reed, by his Grandson, Henry Reed.
629. **Reed.** Lectures on English History and Tragic Poetry, as illustrated
      by Shakspeare, by Prof. Henry Reed.
630. **Reed.** Lectures on English Literature, delivered in the University
      of Pennsylvania, by the late Prof Henry Reed.
4160-4206. **Rees.** Cyclopædia; or Universal Dictionary of Arts, Sciences,
      and Literature, by Abraham Rees; in 47 vols, with plates and
      Atlas.
3958. **Register.** Visitors' Register at Carpenters' Hall, 1857 to 1865.
3956. **Register.**   "   "   "   " 1865 to 1872.
525. **Reid.** Ventilation in American Dwellings, with a series of Dia-
      grams, presenting Examples in different classes of Habitations,
      by David Boswell Reid, to which is added an Introductory
      outline of the progress of Improvement in Ventilation, by E.
      Harris, M. D.
970. **Reid.** Quadrupeds; what They Are, and Where Found, a Book of
      Zoology for Boys, by Captain Mayne Reid. 1867.
3256. **Reid.** Bruin; The Great Bear Hunt, by Captain Mayne Reid. 1869.
3257. **Reid.** The Forest Exiles: or the Perils of a Peruvian Family amid
      the Wilds of the Amazon, by C. M. Reid. 1869.
3258. **Reid.** The Boy Tar; or, a Voyage in the Dark, by C. Mayne Reid.
3259. **Reid.** The Young Voyagers; or the Boy Hunters in the North, by
      C. M. Reid. 1869.
3260. **Reid.** The Cliff Climbers; or the Lone House in the Himalayas, a
      Sequel to the Plant Hunters, by C. Mayne Reid.
3249. **Reid.** The Desert Home; or the Adventures of a lost Family in the
      Wilderness, by C. M. Reid.

3250. **Reid.** The Bush-Boys; or the History and Adventures of a Cape Farmer in the Wild Karoos of Southern Africa, by C. M. Reid.

3251. **Reid.** Odd People; being a popular description of singular Races of Men, by C. M. Reid.

3252. **Reid.** Ran Away to Sea; an Autobiography for Boys, by C. Mayne Reid. 1860.

3253. **Reid.** The Boy Hunters; or Adventures in Search of a Wild Buffalo, by C. Mayne Reid.

3254. **Reid.** The Plant Hunters; or Adventures among the Himalaya Mountains, by C. M. Reid.

3255. **Reid.** The Young Yagers; or a Narrative of Hunting Adventures in South Africa, by C. M. Reid.

67. **Religions.** History of all the Religious Denominations in the United States, containing authentic accounts of the Rise and Progress, Faith and Practice, Localities and Statistics, of the different Persuasions, &c., &c. 1854.

1651-71. **Report.** Report of the Superintendent of the Coast Survey, showing the progress of the Survey, 1853 to 1860.

Report. Report of the Commissioner of Patents for 1851. *Gift of Wm. Linn Brown.*

423. **Report.** Report to Council of New York, on the Obsequies of Henry Clay.

1374. **Report.** Report of the Superintendent of Common Schools of Pennsylvania, for the year 1857.

80. **Report.** Report of the Committee on a Monument in Independence Square, to the Signers of the Declaration of Independence.

3600. **Report.** Election Frauds in New York.

3601 **Report.** On the Condition of the Indian Tribes.

3602-3. **Report.** Supplement to the Conduct of the War. 2 vols.

415. **Report.** Of Rail Road Companies of Pennsylvania.

2675-80. **Report.** Report of Committee on Agriculture. 6 vols.

2681. **Report.** Report on Civil Service, Retrenchment.

2682. **Report.** On the Physics and Hydraulics of the Mississippi.

2683. **Report.** On the Mineral Resources of the Western States.

2684. **Report.** On the New Orleans Riots.

2685-6. **Report.** On the Regents of the Smithsonian Institute, 1849-68.

3694. **Report.** Report of Committee on Reconstruction.

Repton. See London.

4097. **Republican.** The Republican Court, or American Society in the days of Washington, by Rufus Griswold. 1855.

3825. **Revere.** A Tour of Duty in California, Description of the Gold Region, Account of the Voyage around Cape Horn, Notes of Lower California, Gulf and Pacific Coasts, &c., by J. W. Revere, U. S. Navy. 1849.

1864. **Revere.** Keel and Saddle; a Retrospect of Forty Years of Military and Naval Service, by Jos. W. Revere. 1872.

4719. **Reuter.** Seed-Time and Harvest; or During My Apprenticeship, from the "nt Mine Stromtid" of Fritz Reuter.

2036-7. *Revolution.* The Pictorial Field Book of the Revolution; or Illustrations by Pen and Pencil of the History, Relics, Biography, Scenery, and Traditions of the War of Independence, by B. J. Lossing. 2 vols. 1851.

2823. *Reynolds.* Map of London and Visitors' Guide.

Rhode Island. See Peterson.

1189. *Ribault.* The Life of John Ribault, by Jared Sparks.

1866. *Richardson.* Wonders of the Yellow Stone. Edited by James Richardson. 1873.

4765. *Richardson.* House-building; from a Cottage to a Mansion, &c., &c., by C. J. Richardson.

279. *Richman.* An Attempt to discriminate the Styles of Architecture in England from the Conquest to the Reformation, by T. Richman. 1848.

3939. *Riddell.* The Scientific Stair Builder, by Robert Riddell, illustrated with forty engravings. 1854.

4001. *Riddell.* Architectural Designs for Model Country Residences. illustrated by Colored Drawings of elevations and ground plans, by John Riddell. 1861.

1416. *Riddell.* The Carpenter and Joiner, and elements of Hand-Ruling, by Robert Riddell.

228-9. *Ripley.* The War with Mexico, by R. S. Ripley. 2 vols. 1849.

1422-3. *Ritch.* Original Designs of Cheap Country and Village Residences, with Details, by John W. Ritch. 2 vols. 1848.

Roads. See Gillespie.

4465. *Robertson.* The History of the Discovery and Settlement of America, by Wm. Robertson. 1852.

4485-7. *Robertson.* The History of the Reign of the Emperor Charles the Fifth, by William Robertson, with an Account of the Emperor's Life after his abdication, by W. H. Prescott. 1857.

686-9. *Robinson.* Biblical Researches in Palestine, and in the adjacent Regions; a Journal of Travels in the Year 1838, by E. Robinson, add E. Smith; drawn from the original Diaries, with historical illustrations, by Edw. Robinson. 3 vols. With Map.

2284. *Robinson.* Helen Erskine, by M. H. Robinson.

2348. *Robinson.* The Swiss Robinson Family; or Adventures in a Desert Island.

3161-2. *Robinson.* Diary, Reminiscence, and Correspondence of Henry C. Robinson. 2 vols.

4752. *Roe.* Barriers Burnt Away, by the Rev. E. P. Roe.

4729. *Rodwell.* A Dictionary of Science, comprising Astronomy, Chemistry, Dynamics, Electricity, &c., by G. F. Rodwell.

4760. *Rogers.* Social Economy, by J. E. T. Rogers.

1338. *Rogers.* The Poetical Works of Rogers, Campbell, Montgomery, Lamb, and Kirke White. 1856.

1138. *Rogers.* Recollections of the Table-talk of Samuel Rogers, to which is added Porsoniana. 1856.

42 30-3. *Rollin.* The Ancient History of the Egyptians, Carthaginians Assyrians, Babylonians, Medes and Persians, Macedonians and Grecians, by Charles Rollin. 4 vols. 1854.

S.

77. *Sale.* The Koran, commonly called the Alkoran of Mahommed, translated from the original Arabic, with notes, &c., &c., by Geo. Sale. 1855.

1183. *Salle.* Life of Robert Cavalier de la Salle, by Jared Sparks.

3833. *Sallust.* Sallust, Florus, and Vellerius Paternellis, with Notes, and general Index, by Jas. Watson. 1852.

San Francisco. See Soule.

4213. *Santvoord.* Sketches of the Lives and Judicial Services of the Chief Justices of the Supreme Court of the United States, by G. V. Santvoord. 1854.

Saracens. See Taylor.

4613. *Sargent.* The Life and Career of Major John Andre, Adjutant-General of the British Army in America, with portrait, by Winthrop Sargent.

4388. *Saunders.* Israel Mort. Overman; a Story of the Muse, by John Saunders.

3216. *Sausay.* Wonders of Glass Making, br A. Sausay.

4376. *Saxe.* The Poems of John Godfrey Saxe.

4381. *Saxe.* Tables and Legends of many Countries, by John Godfrey Saxe.

4313. *Saxon.* Five Years Within the Golden Gate, by Isaboll Saxon.

4632-3. *Saxton.* Fall of Poland, containing an analytical and a philosophical account of the Causes which conspired to the Ruin of that Nation, together with a History of the Country from its Origin, by L. C. Saxton. 2 vols. 1852.

664. *Schiller.* History of the Revolt of the Netherlands, Trials and Executions of Counts Egmont and Horn, and the Siege of Antwerp, by Frederick Schiller; translated from the German.

1210. *Schlesinger.* Saunterings in and about London, by Max Schlesinger; the English edition, by Otto Wemkstern. 1853.

4500. *Schœdler.* The Wonders of Nature; an Elementary Introduction to the Sciences of Physics, Astronomy, Chemistry, Mineralogy, Geology, Botany, Zoology, and Physiology, by P. Schœdler; translated by H. Medlock, 1854.

4500. *Schœdler.* The Book of Nature, an Elementary Introduction to the Science of Physics, Astronomy, Chemistry, Mineralogy, Geology, Botany, Zoology, and Physiology, by F. Schœdler. 1854.

1925. *Schonberg.* Winifred Bertram and the World she Lived in, by the Author of the Schonberg Cotta Family.

1936. *Schonberg.* Chronicles of the Schonberg Cotta Family.

3159. *Schonberg.* The Early Dawn; or Sketches of Christian Life in England in the Olden Time, by the Author of the Schonberg Family.

3160. *Schonberg.* On both Sides of the Sea; a Story of the Commonwealth, and the Restoration, a Sequel to the Draytons and Devenants, by the Author of the Schonberg Family. See Drayton.

7-9, 3948-50. *Schoolcraft.* Information respecting the History, Condition, and Prospects of the Indian Tribes of the United States, Col-

CATALOGUE OF BOOKS.   173

lected and Prepared under the direction of the Bureau of Indian Affairs per Acts of Congress, &c., by II. R. Schoolcraft. 6 vols.

1331. **Schoolcraft.** Summary Narrative of an Exploring Expedition to the Source of the Mississippi River in 1820, resumed and Completed by the Discovery of its Origin in Itasca Lake in 1832, by Authority of the U. S., &c., by II. R. Schoolcraft. 1855.

4228. **Schoolcraft.** Personal Memoirs of a Residence of Thirty Years with the Indian Tribes on the American Frontiers, with Brief Notices of Passing Events, Facts, &c., 1812 to 1842, by II. R. Schoolcraft.

244. **Schoolcraft.** Notes on the Iroquois; or Contributions to American History, Antiquities, and general Ethnology, by II. R. Schoolcraft. 1847.

4451. **Schoolcraft.** Scenes and Adventures in the Semialpine Regions of the Ozark Mountains of Missouri and Arkansas, which were first traversed by De Soto in 1541, by II. R. Schoolcraft. 1853.

3870. **Schoolcraft.** The Myth of Hiawatha, and other oral legends, mythologic and allegoric, of the North American Indians, by Henry R. Schoolcraft.

3228. **Schooldays.** Schooldays at Rugby, by an Old Boy.

1374. **Schools.** Report of the Superintendent of Common Schools of Pennsylvania for 1857.

Schuyler. See Lossing.

2010-3, 4130-56. **Scientific American.** The Scientific American, an illustrated Journal of Art, Sciences, and Mechanics.

4462. **Sciography.** Sciography, or Examples of Shadows, with Rules for their Projection, &c., by Joseph Gwilt. 1833.

1336. **Scott.** The Poetical Works of Sir Walter Scott, with a Sketch of his Life, by J. W. Lake, complete in one vol.

Scott. See Mansfield.

1001-3. **Scott.** Infantry Tactics and Rules for the Exercise and Manoeuvre of the United States Light Infantry, by Major-General Scott. 2 vols.

3782. **Scott.** Waverly—Guy Mannering, by Sir Walter Scott.

3783. **Scott.** Antiquary—Black Dwarf–Old Mortality, by Sir Walter Scott.

3784. **Scott.** Rob Roy—The Heart of Midlothian, by Sir Walter Scott.

3785. **Scott.** Bride of Lammermoor—Legend of Montrose—Ivanhoe, by Sir Walter Scott.

3786. **Scott.** The Monastery—The Abbott, by Sir Sir Walter Scott.

3787. **Scott.** Kennelworth—The Pilot, by Sir Walter Scott.

3788. **Scott.** Fortunes of Nigel—Peveril of the Peak, by Sir Walter Scott.

3789. **Scott.** Quintin Durwood—St. Ronan's Well, by Sir Walter Scott.

3790. **Scott.** Red Gauntlet—The Betrothed—The Talisman, by Sir Walter Scott.

3791. **Scott.** Woodstock—Chronicles of the Canonsgate, by Sir Walter Scott.

3792. **Scott.** The Fair Maid of Perth—Anne of Geierstein, by Sir Walter Scott.

3793. **Scott.** Count Robert of Paris—Castle Dangerous—My Aunt Margaret's Mirror, by Sir Walter Scott.

Scotland. See Haslett.

Scrap Book. See Field, Lossing.

3126. *Seaton.* A Biographical Sketch of Wm. Winston Seaton of "The National Intelligencer," &c., with passing events of his Associ- tes and Friends. 1871.

2336. *Sedgwick.* The Poor Rich Man, and the Rich Poor Man, by M. Sedgwick. See Dewey.

1932. *Seeley.* Roman Imperialism, and other Lectures and Essays of J. R. Seeley. 1871.

4331. *Seiler.* The Voice in Singing, from the German of Emma Seiler.

Selbourne. See White.

4020. *Semple.* A Treatise on Building in Water, in 2 parts, principally addressed and peculiarly adapted to young and inexperienced readers, by George Semple. 1776.

999. *Senneff.* The Bible Advocate, or an Answer to Elias Hick's Doctrines and others, by George Senneff. 1836. 2 copies.

Sevigne. See Hale.

Sewers. See Dempsey.

624. *Sewell.* The Ordeal of Free Labor in the British West Indies, by Wm. G. Sewell.

Shadows. See Nicholson, Gwilt.

3176. *Shackleford.* The Knight's Armor, a History of the early origin of the Knights of Pythias, and review of its Principles, by H. K. Shackleford.

4269. *Shakspeare.* The Works of William Shakspeare complete, accu- rately printed from the Text of the corrected Copy left by the late George Stephens, Esq., with a Memoir by A. Chambers, 1856.

3921. *Shallus.* Chronological Table for every day in the Year, compiled from the most authentic documents, by F. Shallus. 1807.

1948. *Shatemuc.* The Hills of the Shatemuc, by the Author of "The Wide, Wide World."

4014. *Shaw.* Civil Architecture, being a complete Theoretical and Prac- tical System of Building, &c., by Edward Shaw. 1852.

4259. *Shea.* Discovery and Exploration of the Mississippi Valley, with the Original Narrative of Marquette and others, by J. G. Shea. 1852.

2562-4. *Shelley.* The Poetical Works of Percy Bysshe Shelley, edited by Mrs. Shelley, with a Memoir by James Russell Lowell. 3 vols. See Trelawny.

2060. *Shepherd.* Metropolitan Improvements, or London in the 19th Century, being a Series of Views of the new and most interesting Objects in the British Metropolis and its Vicinity, by T. H. Shepherd.

2907-8. *Sheridan.* Memoir of the Rt. Hon. Richard Brinsley Sheridan, by Thomas Moore. 2 vols. 1858.

444-8. *Shobert.* The History of the French Revolution, by M. A. Thiers, late Prime Minister of France, translated, with Notes and Illustrations, from the most authentic Sources, by Frederick Shoberl 2 vols. 1851.

Siam. See Neale.

Siberia. See Atkinson.

1843. **Sibree.** Madagascar and Its People; Notes of a Four Years' Residence, Sketches of History, &c., &c., by James Sibree.

4323-4. **Silliman.** Life of Benjamin Silliman, Professor of Chemistry, Geology and Mineralogy in Yale College, by G. P. Fisher. 2 vs.

2862-3. **Silliman.** A Visit to Europe in 1851, by Prof. B. Silliman, of Yale College. In 2 vols. 1854.

2710-34. **Silliman.** American Journal of Science and Art.

38. **Simpson.** The Lives of Eminent Philadelphians, now deceased, from authentic sources, by H. Simpson. 1860.

665. **Sismondi.** History of the Italian Republics, being a View of the Rise, Progress and Fall of Italian Freedom, by J. C. L. Sismonde de Sismondi.

2559-1. **Skelton.** The Poetical Works of John Skelton, with Memoir by the Rev. A. Dyce. 3 vols.

4046. **Sloan.** Constructive Architecture; a guide for the builder and carpenter; exhibiting the construction of a series of designs for roofs, domes, spires, and the five orders of architecture, selected from the best specimens of Grecian and Roman Art, with the figured dimensions of their height, projection, and profile. To which is added a treatise on practical geometry. The whole illustrated by 62 plates, and accompanied by explanatory text, by Samuel Sloan, Architect, author of the "Model Architect," "City and Suburban Architecture," &c., &c.

3936. **Sloan.** City and Suburban Architecture; in which are exhibited numerous designs and details for public edifices, private residences, and mercantile buildings. Illustrated with 136 folio engravings, accompanied by specifications and historical and explanatory text, by Samuel Sloan, author of the "Model Architect," "Sloan's Constructive Architecture," &c.

788. **Sloan.** Homestead Architecture; containing forty designs for villas, cottages and farm-houses, with essays on style, construction, landscape gardening, furniture, &c. Illustrated with upwards of 200 engravings, by Samuel Sloan, Architect.

1437. **Sloan.** The Carpenter's New Guide, a complete Book of Lines for Carpentry and Joinery, treating fully on Practical Geometry, Soffits, Groins, Niches, Roofs and Domes, containing a great Variety of original Designs; also a full Exemplification of the Theory and Practice of Stair-building, Cornices, Mouldings, and Dressings of every Description, by Samuel Sloan. 1854.

1708-9. **Sloan.** The Model Architect; a series of Original Designs for Cottages, Villas, Suburban Residences, &c., accompanied by explanatory, perspective and elaborate Details; prepared expressly for the use of Projectors and Artisans throughout the United States, by Samuel Sloan. 2 vols. 1852.

176   THE CARPENTERS' COMPANY.

4010. *Sloan.* The Carpenter's New Guide, a complete Book of Lines for Carpentry and Joinery. Treating fully on Practical Geometry, Soffits, Niches, Roofs, and Domes, and containing a great variety of original designs. Also a full exemplification of the theory and practice of stair building, cornices, mouldings, and dressings of every description. Including also some observations and calculations on the strength of timber, by Peter Nicholson, author of the "Carpenter's and Joiner's Assistant," the "Student's Instructor to the Five Orders," &c. The whole being carefully and thoroughly revised by N. K. Davis, and containing new, improved, and original designs for roofs, domes. &c., by Samuel Sloan, Architect, author of the "Model Architect."

2047-9. *Smeaton.* Reports of the late John Smeaton, made on various occasions in the course of his employment as a Civil Engineer. 3 vols.

2068. *Smeaton.* Miscellaneous Papers, by John Smeaton.

Smedley. Atlas of the City of Philadelphia, prepared from official records in the survey department of Philadelphia, &c., &c., by Samuel L. Smedley. 1862.

1523. *Smiles.* The Huguenots; their Settlement, Character, and Industries in England and Ireland, by S. Smiles. 1868.

1844. *Smiles.* Character, by S. Smiles.

1845. *Smiles.* Round the World; including a Residence in Victoria, and a Journey by Rail Across North America by a Boy, edited by Samuel Smiles.

4610. *Smiles.* Industrial Biography, Iron-workers and Tool-makers, by Samuel Smiles.

4611. *Smiles.* Self-Help: with Illustrations of Character and Conduct, by Samuel Smiles, Author of "The Life of George Stephenson," "Lives of the Engineers."

2290. *Smith.* The Married Belle; or, Our Red Cottage at Merry Bank, by John P. Smith.

4295. *Smith.* A Dictionary of the Bible; comprising its Antiquities, Biography, Geography, and Natural History, &c., by William Smith.

4728. *Smith.* An Inquiry into the Nature and Causes of Wealth of Nations, by Adam Smith, LL. D.

Smith and Founder's Director. See Cottingham.

1017. *Smith.* The Poetical Works of Horace Smith and James Smith, with Portraits and Biographical Sketch. 1857.

3977. *Smith.* American Historical and Literary Curiosities, consisting of fac similes of original documents relating to events of the Revolution, with a variety of Relics, Antiquities and Modern Autographs, by Smith and Watson. 1852.

2853-4. *Smith.* A Memoir of the Rev. Sidney Smith, by his Daughter, Lady Holland, with a Selection from his Letters, edited by Mrs. Austin. 2 vols. 1856.

2852. *Smith.* Wit and Wisdom of the Rev. Sidney Smith, being Selections from his Writings and Passages of his Letters, and Table-talk, with a Biographical Memoir and Notes, by E. A. Duyckinck. 1856.

1733–4. *Smith.* The Panorama of Science and Arts, embracing the science of Aerostation, Agriculture, Gardening, Architecture, Electricity, Galvanism, Hydrostatics and Hydraulics; the Arts of Building, Brewing, Inkmaking, Casting in Plaster, Varnishing, &c. The Method of Working in Wood and Metal, by James Smith. 2 vols. 1824.

1749. *Smith.* A Synopsis of the Origin and Progress of Architecture, to which is added a Dictionary of General Terms, by William Smith. 1821.

4480. *Smith.* Essay on the Construction of Cottages, suited to the Dwellings of the Laboring Classes, illustrated by Working Plans, &c., by George Smith. 1834.

4454. *Smith.* The Works of the Rev. Sidney Smith, complete in one volume. 1853.

1219. *Smith.* The Story of Mont Blanc, by Albert Smith. 1853.

1128. *Smith.* The Natural History of the Human Species, its typical Forms, primeval Distribution, Filiations and Migrations, by Charles H. Smith. 1852.

257–9. *Smith.* Dictionary of Greek and Roman Biography and Mythology, edited by William Smith; in three vols. 1849.

2685–95. *Smithsonian.* Annual Reports of the Regents of the Smithsonian Institute. 1847 to 1868. 12 vols.

4234–7. *Smollett.* The History of England from the Invasion of Julius Cæsar to the Death of George the Second, by D. Hume and T. Smollett. 4 vols. 1835.

3963. *Snowden.* A Description of the Medals of Washington, of National and Miscellaneous Medals, and of other objects of interest in the Museum of the Mint. Illustrated by 7–9 fac-simile engravings. To which are added Biographical Notices of the Directors of the Mint, from 1792 to the year 1851, by James Ross Snowden, Director of the Mint.

4274. *Snowden.* A Description of Ancient and Modern Coins in the Cabinet Collection of the Mint of the United States. Illustrated with 27 Plates of nearly 200 fac-similes of coins, executed in silver, gold, and bronze. Prepared under the direction of James Ross Snowden, Director of the Mint.

3845. *Socrates.* The Ecclesiastical History of Socrates, surnamed Scholasticus, or the Advocate, comprising a History of the Church, in seven books, from the Accession of Constantine, A.D. 305, to the 38th Year of Theodosius the Second, a Period of 140 years. 1853.

2005. *Soane.* Plans, Elevations, and Sections of Buildings erected in the Counties of Norfolk, &c., &c., by John Soane. 1787.

3976. *Soane.* Designs for Public and Private Buildings, by John Soane. 1829.

3201. *Sonrel.* The Bottom of the Sea, by L. Sonrel.

2923. *Sophocles.* The Tragedies of Sophocles, in English Prose, the Oxford Translation. 1855.

177. *Soule.* The Annals of San Francisco, containing a Summary of the History of the first Discovery, Settlement, Progress, and present Condition of California, and a complete History of all the important Events connected with its great City ; to which is added Biographical Memoirs, &c., by Frank Soule. Gihon and Nisbet. 1855.

2573-82. *Southey.* The Poetical Works of Robert Southey, with Memoir by Henry T. Tuckerman. 10 vols.

661. *Spain.* The Martyrs of Spain and the Liberators of Holland.

Spain. See Gautier, Prescott, Taylor, Helps, Mackenzie.

4294. *Sparks.* The Life of Benjamin Franklin, containing the autobiography, with Notes and a Continuation, by Jared Sparks. 1856.

4424. *Sparks.* The Life of George Washington, by Jared Sparks. 1854.

Sparks. Library of American Biography, edited by Jared Sparks, LL.D. Portraits, &c. 15 vols.

1183. Vol. I.—Life of Robert Cavalier de la Salle, by Jared Sparks. Life of Patrick Henry, by Alexander H. Everett.

1184. Vol. II.—Life of James Otis, by Francis Bowen. Life of James Oglethorpe, by William O. B. Peabody.

1185. Vol. III.—Life of John Sullivan, by Oliver W. B. Peabody. Administration of Jacob Leisler, by Charles F. Hoffman. Memoir of Nathaniel Bacon, by William Ware. Life of John Mason, by George E. Ellis.

1186. Vol. IV.—Life of Roger Williams, by William Gammell. Life of Timothy Dwight, by William B. Sprague. Life of Count Pulaski, by Jared Sparks.

1187. Vol. V.—Life of Count Rumford, by James Renwick. Life of Zebulon Montgomery Pike, by Henry Whiting. Life of Samuel Gorton, by John M. Mackie.

1188. Vol. VI.—Life of Ezra Stiles, by James L. Kingsley. Life of John Fitch, by Charles Whittlesey. Life of Annie Hutchinson, by George E. Ellis.

1189. Vol. VII.—Life of John Ribault, by Jared Sparks. Life of Sebastian Rale, by Convers Francis. Life of William Palfrey, by John Gorham Palfrey.

1190. Vol. VIII.—Life of Charles Lee, by Jared Sparks. Life of Joseph Reed, by Henry Reed.

1191. Vol. IX.—Life of Leonard Calvert, by George W. Burnap. Life of Samuel Ward, by William Gammell. Memoir of Thomas Posey, by James Hall.

1192. Vol. X.—Life of Nathaniel Greene, by George W. Greene.

1193. Vol. XI.—Life of Stephen Decatur, by Alexander Slidell Mackenzie.

1194. Vol. XII.—Life of Edward Preble, by Lorenzo Sabine. Life of William Penn, by George E. Ellis.

1195. Vol. XIII.—Life of Daniel Boone, by John M. Peck. Life of Benjamin Lincoln, by Francis Bowen.

1196. Vol. XIV.—Life of John Ledyard, by Jared Sparks.
Vol. XV.—Life of William R. Davie, by Fordyce M. Hubbard.
Life of Samuel Kirkland, by Samuel K. Lothrop.
Specifications. See Bartholomew.
230-1. *Spectator.* The Spectator, by Joseph Addison, complete in 2 vols. 1851.
3130-1. *Spencer.* The Principles of Biology, by Herbert Spencer. 2 vols.
3132. *Spencer.* Illustrations of Universal Progress, a Series of Discussions, by Herbert Spencer.
3136. *Spencer.* First Principles of Philosophy, by Herbert Spencer.
1846. *Spencer.* Recent Discussions in Science, Philosophy, and Morals, by Herbert Spencer.
4603. *Spencer.* Social Statics; or the Conditions essential to Human Happiness specified, and the first of them developed, by Hubert Spencer.
2554-8. *Spenser.* The Poetical Works of Edward Spenser, with Memoir by Francis J. Child; carefully revised and illustrated; with Notes, original and selected, by F. Child. 2 vols.
651-3. *Spooner.* Anecdotes of Painters, Engravers, Sculptors and Architects, and Curiosities of Art, by S. Spooner. 3 vols. 1853.
2237. *Springer.* Beechwood, by R. R. Springer.
3951. *Squier.* Ancient Monuments in the Mississippi Valley, by E. G. Squier and E. H. Davis. 1848.
4467-8. *Squier.* Nicaragua—its People, Scenery, Monuments, and the Proposed Interoceanic Canal, with numerous Original Maps and Illustrations, by E. G. Squier. 2 vols. 1852.
1012-3. *Stansbury,.* An Expedition to the Valley of the Great Salt Lake of Utah, including a description of its Geography, Natural History, and Minerals, and an analysis of its Waters, with an authentic account of the Mormon Settlement, illustrated by numerous beautiful plates from drawings taken on the spot; also a reconnoissance of a new route through the Rocky Mountains, and two large and accurate maps of that region, by Howard Stansbury, Captain Corps of Topographical Engineers, U. S. A. 2 vols.
Stair Builder. See Riddell.
4730. *Stanley.* How I Found Livingstone—Travels, Adventures, and Discoveries in Central Africa, including an account of a four months' residence with Dr. Livingstone, by Henry M. Stanley.
Statesmen. See Brougham.
St. Domingo. See Kimball, Hasard.
4372. *Stephens.* Off to the Geysers; or, the Young Yachters of Iceland, as recorded by "Wade," by C. A. Stephens.
1521. *Stephens.* A Review of Alexander Stephens' "War between the States," by a Constitutionalist.
1931. *Stephens.* Camping Out, as recorded by "Kit," by C. A. Stephens.
4558. *Stephens.* Critical and Miscellaneous Essays, by James Stephens 1853.

1320-1. *Stephens.* Incidents of Travel in Egypt, Arabia Petræa, and the Holy Land, by John L. Stephens, with Map, &c. 2 vols.

1322-3. *Stephens.* Incidents of Travel in Greece, Turkey, Russia and Poland. In 2 vols. 1854.

1339-0. *Stephens.* Incidents of Travel in Yucatan, by John L. Stephens, illustrated by 120 engravings. In 2 vols. 1848.

601. *Stephenson.* The Life of George Stephenson, Railway Engineer. With a copy of Lucas's Portrait, on steel, by Schoff.

1180. *Stewart.* Brazil and La Plata, the personal Record of a Cruise, by C. S. Stewart, A.M., U.S.N. 1856.

1933. *Stewart.* Physics, by Balfour Stewart. 1873.

1188. *Stiles.* The Life of Ezra Stiles, by Jas. L. Kingsley.

3727. *Still.* The Underground Rail Road; a Record of Fact, Authentic Narrative, Letters, &c., the Hardships, Hair-Breadth Escapes and Death Struggles of the Slaves in their efforts for Freedom, by Wm. Still.

1522. *Stocton.* Round-about Rambles in Lands of Fact and Fancy, by F. R. Stocton.

1934. *Storer.* Why Not? a Book for Every Woman—the Prize Essay awarded the Gold Medal of 1865, by H. R. Storer.

398-9. *Story.* Life and Letters of Joseph Story, Associate Justice of the Supreme Court of the United States, and Professor of Law at Harvard University, edited by his son, W. W. Story. 2 vols. 1851.

1115-6. *Stowe.* Sunny Memories of Foreign Lands, by Harriet Beecher Stowe. 2 vols. 1854.

63. *Stowe.* Men of Our Time, or the Leading Patriots of the Day; Lives and Deeds of Statesmen, Generals and Orators, with Sketches, Anecdotes, &c.

2829. *Stowe.* The Chimney Corner, by C. Crossin. Edited by Stowe.

3145-2. *Strickland.* Lives of the Queens of Scotland, and English Princes connected with the regal succession of Great Britain, by Agnes Strickland. 4 vols. 1854.

1050-5. *Strickland.* Lives of the Queens of England, from the Norman Conquest, with Anecdotes of their Courts; from official records and other authentic documents, private as well as public, by Agnes Strickland. 6 vols.

3987. *Strickland.* Reports on Canals and Railways, Roads, and other Subjects, made to the Pennsylvania Society for the Promotion of Internal Improvements, by Wm. Strickland. 1826.

4002-5. *Stuart.* The Antiquities of Athens, measured and delineated, by Stuart & Revett. 4 vols. 1825.

791-3. *Stuart.* A Dictionary of Architecture, historical, descriptive, topographical, decorative, theoretical and mechanical, alphabetically arranged, by Robert Stuart. 3 vols.

1185. *Sullivan.* Life of John Sullivan, by O. W. B. Peabody.

Surgery See Cooper.

2516. *Surry.* The Poetical Works of Henry Howard, Earl of Surry, with a Memoir.

3990. **Swan.** A Collection of Designs in Architecture, containing new Plans and Elevations of Houses for General use, with a great Variety of Sections of Rooms, from a common room to the most grand and magnificent, by Abraham Swan. *Gift of James Hutchinson.*

3992. **Swan.** Same.

3993. **Swan.** Same.

2006. **Swan.** The British Architect, or the Builder's Treasury of Stair cases, containing an easier, more intelligible and expeditious Mode of drawing the Five Orders, by Wm. Swan. 1750.

2007. **Swan.** Same.

3944. **Swan.** Same.

2008. **Swan.** Same.

3988. **Swan.** Same. *Gift of James Hutchinson.*

3994. **Swan.** Same.

2536-8. **Swift.** The Poetical Works of Jonathan Swift, with a Life, by J. Mitford. 3 vols. 1853.

T.

4045. **Tablets.** A Book of Tablets, by T. Pether.

3846-7. **Tacitus.** The Works of Tacitus, the Oxford Edition revised, with Notes. 2 vols. 1854.

4731. **Taine.** Italy, Rome, and Naples; from the French of H. Taine.

4351. **Taine.** Notes on England, by H. Taine.

4458. **Talfourd.** Critical and Miscellaneous Writings of T. N. Talfourd. 1853.

1135. **Talleyrand.** Life of Prince Talleyrand, with Extracts from his Speeches and Writings, by Charles K. McHarg.

3169. **Tappan.** The Life of Arthur Tappan. 1870.

3922-5. **Tatler.** The British Essayist, with Preface, Historical and Biographical, complete in 4 vols.

2247. **Tautphœus.** At Odds; by the Baroness Tautphœus.

1220. **Taylor.** Japan in Our Day; compiled and arranged by Bayard Taylor.

2827. **Taylor.** Colorado; A Summer Trip, by Bayard Taylor. 1867.

1851. **Taylor.** Travels in South Africa, compiled and arranged by Bayard Taylor. 1872.

1852. **Taylor.** Travels in Arabia, compiled and arranged by Bayard Taylor. 1872.

1224. **Taylor.** Poems of Home and Travel, by Bayard Taylor. 1856.

1225. **Taylor.** Poems of the Orient, by Bayard Taylor. 1856.

1108. **Taylor.** History of the State of Ohio, by James W. Taylor, First Period, 1650 to 1787.

691. **Taylor.** Statistics of Coal, including mineral bituminous Substances employed in Arts and Manufactures, with their geographical, geological and commercial Distribution and Amount of

Production and Consumption on the American Continent, with incidental Statistics of the Iron Manufactures, by R. C. Taylor. 1855.

1232. *Taylor.* Travels in Sweden, Denmark, and Lapland, by Bayard Taylor.

1231. *Taylor.* Travels in Greece, Rome and Crete, by B. Taylor.

1229. *Taylor.* Visit to India, China, and Japan, by B. Taylor.

1230. *Taylor.* At Home and Abroad, a Sketch of Life, Scenery, and Men, by B. Taylor.

1226. *Taylor.* A Journey to Central Africa, or Life and Landscapes from Egypt to the Negro Kingdoms of the White Nile, by Bayard Taylor, with Maps and Illustrations.

1097. *Taylor.* Views Afoot, or Europe Seen with Knapsack and Staff, by B. Taylor. 1854.

1228. *Taylor.* The Lands of the Saracen; or Pictures of Palestine, Asia Minor, Sicily, and Spain, by Bayard Taylor. 1855.

3932. *Taylor.* Designs for Shop Fronts and Door Cases, by L. and J. Taylor.

3933. *Taylor.* Same.

4039. *Taylor.* Designs for Chimney Pieces, with Mouldings and Bases at length, by L. and J. Taylor.

1227. *Taylor.* Eldorado, or Adventures in the Path of Empire, comprising a Voyage to California, via Panama, Life in San Francisco and Monterey, Pictures of the Gold Region and Experiences of Mexican Travel, by Bayard Taylor. 1855.

4029-30. *Technologist.* The Technologist, especially devoted to Engineering, Manufacturing and Building, 1870 and 1871. 2 vols. (Continued under title of Industrial Monthly, which see.)

2934-5. *Tennyson.* Poems by Alfred Tennyson, Poet Laureate. 2 vols.

Tennessee. See Carpenter.

Texas. See Braman.

2337. *Theed.* What She Did With Her Life, by Marion F. Theed.

4447-8. *Thiers.* The History of the French Revolution, by M. A. Thiers, late Prime Minister, &c., translated by Frederick Shoberl. 2 vs. 1852.

4227. *Thiers.* History of the Consulate and Empire of France under Napoleon, forming a sequel to the French Revolution, by M. A. Thiers. 1847.

4615. *Thomas.* John Randolph of Roanoke, and other Sketches of Character, including William Wirt, together with Tales of Real Life, by B. F. Thomas. 1853.

526. *Thomas.* Pronouncing Medical Dictionary. A Comprehensive Medical Dictionary, containing the Pronunciation, Etymology, and Signification of the Terms made use of in Medicine and the Kindred Sciences, with an Appendix comprising a complete list of all the more important articles of the Materia Medica, arranged according to their medicinal properties; also, an explanation of the Latin terms and phrases occurring in Anatomy, Pharmacy, &c., together with the necessary directions for writ-

ing Latin Prescriptions, &c., &c., by J. Thomas, M. D., author of the system of Pronunciation in "Lippincott's Pronouncing Gazetteer of the World."

1233. *Thomas.* Travels in Europe, Egypt, and Palestine, by Mrs. S. B. Thomas.

133-4. *Thomas.* Universal Pronouncing Dictionary of Biography and Mythology, by J. Thomas. 1870. 2 vols.

1847. *Thomas.* Life in the East Indies, by W. H. Thomas. 1873.

4469. *Thomson.* History of the Wars of the United States, from the earliest Colonial times to the close of the Mexican War, by J. L. Thomson.

4017. *Thompson.* Retreats, a series of Designs, consisting of Plans and Elevations for Cottages, Villas, and Ornamental Buildings. 1827.

2539-0. *Thompson.* The Poetical Works of James Thompson, in 2 vols. 1854.

770. *Thrilling.* Thrilling Incidents of the Wars of the United States, comprising the most striking and remarkable Events of the Revolution, the French Wars, the Tripolitan War, the Second War with Great Britian, and the Mexican War. 1848.

3836-7. *Thucydides.* The History of the Peloponnesian War, by Thucydides, translated by H. Dale, M. A. 2 vols. 1852.

2510. *Tickell.* The Poetical Works of Thomas Tickell, with a Life, by Dr. Johnson. 1854.

3794-6. *Ticknor.* History of Spanish Literature, by George Ticknor. 3 vols.

1853. *Timbs.* Wonderful Inventions, from the Mariner's Compass to the Telegraph Cable, by John Timbs. 1872.

Titcomb. See Holland.

4614. *Titcomb.* Letters to the Joneses, by Timothy Titcomb, Esq.

4609. *Titcomb.* Letters to Young People, Single and Married, by Timothy Titcomb.

1937. *Trading.* Trading; finishing the Story of the House in Town, by the Author of "Wide, Wide World."

4387. *Trafton.* The American Girl Abroad, by Adeline Trafton.

4702. *Treadwell.* A Manual of Pottery and Porcelain for American Collectors, by J. H. Treadwell.

1433. *Tredgold.* Elementary Principles of Carpentry; a treatise on the Pressure and Equilibrium of Timber Framing, the Resistance of Timber, and the Construction of Floors, Centres, Bridges, Roofs, and uniting Stone with Timber, &c., &c., by Thomas Tredgold. 1840.

4021. *Tredgold.* Elementary Principles of Carpentry; a treatise on the Pressure and Equilibrium of Beams and Timber Frames, the Resistance of Timber, and the Construction of Floors, Roofs, &c., by Thomas Tredgold. 1820.

2066. *Tredgold.* The Steam Engine; comprising an Account of its Invention and Progressive Improvement, with an Investigation of its Principles, and the proportion of its parts for sufficiency and Strength, by Thomas Tredgold. 1827.

620. *Trelawney.* Recollections of the Last Days of Shelley and Byron, by E. I. Trelawney.

3163. *Triumph.* Complete Triumph of Moral Good over Evil. 1870.

865. *Trollope.* North America, by Anthony Trollope.

265. *Troubat.* A Digest of the Acts of the Assembly of Pennsylvania, from 1824 to 1829, by Troubat and Halp.

1858. *Trowbridge.* A Chance for Himself; or Jack Hazard and his Treasure, by J. T. Trowbridge.

4369. *Trowbridge.* Jack Hazard and his Fortunes, by J. T. Trowbridge.

419-2. *Tucker.* The History of the United States, from their Colonization to the end of the 26th Congress in 1841, by George Tucker; in 4 vols.

1048. *Tuckerman.* Essays, Biographical and Critical, or Studies of Character, by Henry T. Tuckerman. 1853.

3224. *Tuckerman.* The Criterion; or the Test of Talk about Familiar Things: a series of Essays, by H. T. Tuckerman.

245. *Tuckerman.* Book of the Artist—American Artist Life—Comprising Sketches of American Artists; Rise and Progress of the Arts in America, by H. T. Tuckerman. 1867.

1859. *Tuckerman.* The Greeks of To-Day, by Charles K. Tuckerman. 1872.

1382-3. Turner. Some account of Domestic Architecture in England, from the Conquest to Richard the Second, with numerous Illustrations of Existing Remains, by T. H. Turner. 2 vols. 1853.

1935. *Tuttle.* The Boy's Book about Indians; being what I saw and heard for Three Years on the Plains, by E. B. Tuttle.

387. *Tuthill.* History of Architecture, from the Earliest Times; its present Condition in Europe and the United States; with a Biography of Eminent Architects, &c., by Mrs. L. C. Tuthill. 1848.

400. *Twain.* The Innocents Abroad; or the New Pilgrim's Progress—Account of the Steamship Quaker City—Pleasure Excursion to Europe, Holy Land, &c., &c., by Mark Twain. 1870.

4720. *Twain.* Roughing It; by Mark Twain (Samuel L. Clemens). Fully Illustrated.

Tyler. See Ware.

4502. *Tyndall.* Heat, considered as a mode of Motion; being a Course of Twelve Lectures, delivered at the Royal Institution of Great Britain, in the summer of 1862, by John Tyndall, F. R. S.

1850. *Tyndall.* The Forms of Water in Clouds and Rivers, Ice and Glaciers, by John Tyndall. 1872.

1848. *Tyndall.* Fragments of Science for Unscientific People; a series of Essays, Lectures, Reviews, &c., by John Tyndall.

1849. *Tyndall.* Hours of Exercise in the Alps, by John Tyndall.

4330. *Tyrwhitt.* Christian Art and Symbolism, by St. John Tyrwhitt.

U.

United States. See Constitution, Cooper, Bancroft, De Tocqueville, Thrilling Incidents, Curtis, Religious Denominations, Frost, Wilkes, Ingersoll, Kane, Thomson, Burke, Gazetteer, Lanman, Tucker.

96. *United States.* Journal of the Proceedings of the United States Centennial Commission at Philadelphia, in 1872.

654. *Upham.* Life of Madame Catharine Adorna; including some Leading Facts and Traits in her Religious Experience; together with Explanations and Remarks tending to Illustrate the Doctrine of Holiness, by T. C. Upham.

68. *Upland.* Records of the Court at Upland, 1676 to 1681.

268–9. *Ure.* A Dictionary of Arts, Manufacture, and Mines, containing a clear Exposition of their Principles and Practice, by Andrew Ure. 1853. 2 vols.

Urns. See Designs.

Utah. See Ferris.

V.

4367. *Valmore.* Memoirs of Madame Desbordes Valmore, &c., with a Selection from her Poems, translated by H. W. Preston.

4481. *Valentine.* History of the City of New York, by D. T. Valentine, Clerk of Common Council. 1853.

4178. *Vambery.* Sketches of Central Asia; additional chapters of my Adventures, and on the Ethnology of Central Asia, by Arminius Vambery.

2511. *Vaughan.* The Sacred Poems and Private Ejaculations of Henry Vaughan, with a Memoir, by H. F. Lyte.

771. *Vaux.* Villas and Cottages; A series of Designs Prepared for Execution in the United States, by Calvert Vaux, Architect (late Downing & Vaux). New edition, revised and enlarged. Illustrated by nearly five hundred Engravings.

Venice. See Flagg.

Ventilation. See Harris, Reid, Warming.

Vere. See De Vere.

Vermont. See Arthur.

3199. *Viardot.* Wonders of Italian Art, by Louis Viardot.

1945. *Viardot.* Wonders of European Art, by Louis Viardot. 1871.

Views. See Pugin, Shepherd, Bartlett, Lancashire, Fisher, Jones.

3835. *Virgil.* The Works of Virgil, literally translated into English Prose, with Notes by Davidson, &c. 1853.

Virginia. See Arthur.

2069.   *Virtue.* Picturesque Beauties of Great Britian, in a Series of Views,
comprising the Principal Cities and Towns, Public Edifices, and
Dock Yards.

Vittruvius. See Campbell.

621.   *Vogdes.* An Elementary Treatise on Mensuration.

3885.   *Vogdes.* Mensuration, by H. Vogdes.

614.   *Voltaire.* History of Charles XII, King of Sweden, by M. D. Voltaire. New edition.

W.

4746.   *Walker.* The Source of Wealth; a Manual of Political Economy,
&c., &c., by Amasa Walker.

1870.   *Wallace.* A Woman's Experience in Europe; including England,
France, Germany and Italy, by Mrs. E. D. Wallace.

4045.   *Wallis.* Book of Ornaments, by N. Wallis.

1191.   *Ward.* Life of Samuel Ward, Governor of Rhode Island, by W.
Gemmell.

3943.   *Ware.* The Four Books of Andrea Palladio, wherein, after a short
Treatise of the Five Orders, those Observations that are most
necessary in Building Private Houses, Streets, Bridges, Piazzas,
Xisti, and Temples, are treated of, by Isaac Ware. 1738.

2309.   *Ware.* Same.

Wagner. See Crookes.

4495.   *Warming.* The Theory and Practice of Warming and Ventilating
Public Buildings, Dwelling Houses, and Conservatories, inclu-
ding a General View of the Changes Produced in Atmospheric
Air by Respiration, by an Engineer. 1825.

677.   *Warner.* New Theorems, Tables, and Diagrams for the Compu-
tation of Earth-work; designed for the use of Engineers in
preliminary and final estimates, of Students in Engineering,
and of Contractors and other non-professional Computers. In
two parts, with an Appendix.
Part I. A Practical Treatise.
Part II. A Theoretical Treatise, and the Appendix.
Containing notes to the rules and examples of Part I; explanations of the construction of scales, tables, and diagrams, and a
treatise upon equivalent square bases and equivalent level
heights. The whole illustrated by numerous original engravings, comprising explanatory cuts for definitions and problems,
stereometric scales and diagrams, and a series of lithographic
drawings from models; showing all the combinations of solid
forms which occur in railroad excavations and embankments,
by John Warner, A.M., Mining and Mechanical Engineer,
author of "Studies in Organic Morphology."

1941.   *Warner.* Saunterings, by Charles D. Warner. 1872.

1939.   *Warner.* Gardening by Myself, by Anne Warner.

3221. *Warner.* My Summer in a Garden, by Charles Dudley Warner. 1871.

4317. *Warren.* Adventures of an Attorney in Search of Practice, by Samuel Warren.

3186-7. ' *Washington.* Washington and the Generals of the Revolution, complete in 2 vols., with 16 portraits on steel.

2065. *Washington.* Maps to Life of Washington.

3946. *Washington.* Accounts of George Washington with the United States, 1775 to 1783.

3947. *Washington.* Monuments of Washington's Patriotism, containing a Fac-simile of his Public Accounts, kept during the Revolutionary War, and some of the most interesting Documents connected with his Military Command and Civil Administration. 1841.

Washington. See Marshall, Sparks, Griswold, Headley, Republican.

4482. *Watson.* Annals and Occurrences of New York City and State in the Olden Time; being a Collection of numerous Anecdotes and Incidents concerning the City, Country, and Inhabitants, from the Days of the Founder, &c., by J. F. Watson.

3977. *Watson.* Historical and Literary Curiosities, consisting of Fac-similes of original Documents relating to Events of the Revolution, with a variety of Relics, Antiquities, and Modern Autographs, by Smith & Watson. 1852.

864. *Watson.* Men and Times of the Revolution, or Memoir of Elkanah Watson, including his Journal of Travel in Europe and America, from 1778 to 1842, &c., &c., by his son, W. C. Watson. 1857.

3808. *Watson.* The Camp Fires of Napoleon, comprising the most brilliant Achievements of the Emperor and his Marshals, by H. C. Watson. 1850.

93-4. *Watson.* Annals of Philadelphia; being a Collection of Memoirs, Anecdotes, and Incidents of the City and its Inhabitants, from the Days of the Pilgrim Founders, by John F. Watson. 1830.

4483-4. *Watson.* Annals of Philadelphia and Pennsylvania in the Olden Time; being a Collection of numerous Anecdotes and Incidents of the City and its Inhabitants, and of the Earliest Settlements of the Inland Parts of Pennsylvania, from the Days of the Founders, intended to preserve the Recollection of the Olden Time, &c., by J. F. Watson. 2 vols.

3139. *Watson.* Camp Fires of the Revolution; or the War of Independence, illustrated by Thrilling Events and Stories, by the Old Continental Soldiers, by H. C. Watson. 1870.

2989. *Watts.* Horæ Lyricæ of Isaac Watts, to which are added the Divine Songs, and Moral Songs for Children, with a Life of the Author.

1942. *Weaver.* Hopes and Helps for the Young of Both Sexes, relating to the Formation of Character, Choice of Avocations, &c., &c., by G. S. Weaver.

4476-7. *Webster.* The Private Correspondence of Daniel Webster, edited by Fletcher Webster. 2 vols. 1857.

4214–9. *Webster.* The Works of Daniel Webster, in 6 vols. 1853.

1356. *Webster.* An American Dictionary of the English Language, by Noah Webster.

1181. *Westcott.* Life of John Fitch, the Inventor of the Steamboat, by T. Westcott.

1938. *Wetherill.* The Wide, Wide World, by Elizabeth Wetherill. 1872.

2253–4. *Wetherill.* Say and Seal, by Elizabeth Wetherill. 2 vols.

2925. *Wheeler.* An Analysis and Summary of Herodotus, with a Synchronistical Table of Principal Events, by J. T. Wheeler.

226. *Wheeler.* Historical Sketches of North Carolina, from 1584 to 1851, compiled from Original Records, Official Documents, and Traditional Statements, with Biographical Sketches of her Distinguished Statesmen, Jurists, &c., by John Wheeler. 1851.

3860. *Whewell.* Astronomy and General Physics, considered with reference to Natural Theology, by William Whewell.

4370. *Whipple.* Literature and Life, by E. P. Whipple.

4371. *Whipple.* Success and its Conditions, by E. P. Whipple.

3219. *Whipple.* The Literature of the Age of Elizabeth, by Edwin P. Whipple. 1869.

1943. *Whiteing.* Wonderful Escapes: from the French of E. Barnard, with original chapters added by Richard Whiteing. 1873.

2515. *White.* The Poetical Works of Henry Kirke White, with a Memoir, by Sir Harris Nicolas. 1854.

1213. *White.* The Natural History and Antiquities of Selbourne, with Observations on Various Parts of Nature, and the Naturalist's Calendar, by the late Gilbert White. 1853.

1538. *White.* The Poetical Works of Rogers, Campbell, J. Montgomery, Lamb, and Kirk White. 1856.

* 4602. *White.* The Massacre of St. Bartholomew, preceded by a History of the Religious Wars in the Reign of Charles IX, by Henry White. 1868.

3877. *White.* Words and their Uses, Past and Present, a Study of the English Language, by R. Grant White. 1870.

872. *Whitecar.* Four Years aboard the Whale-ship, embracing cruises in the Pacific, Atlantic, Indian, and Antarctic Oceans, by William B. Whitecar, Jr.

1009. *Whitney.* The Metallic Wealth of the United States, described and compared with that of other Countries, by J. D. Whitney.

649–0. *Whittier.* The Poetical Works of John Greenleaf Whittier. Complete in 2 vols.

3227. *Whittier.* Miriam and other Poems, by J. G. Whittier. 1871.

2288. *Whittier.* Snow Bound; a Winter Idyl, by J. G. Whittier.

3724. *Whymper.* Scrambles Among the Alps in the Years 1860 to 1869, by Edward Whymper. 1873.

870–1. *Wight.* Germany, by Madame, the Baroness de Stael Holstein, with Notes and Appendix, by C. W. Wight, A.M. 2 vols.

1014. *Wight.* Course of the History of Modern Philosophy, by M. V. Cousin, translated by O. W. Wight.

1113-4. **Williams.** The Middle Kingdom, a Survey of the Geography of the Chinese Empire and its Inhabitants, by S. Wells Williams. 2 vols. 1851.

4586. **Williams.** A Year in China, and a Narrative of Capture and Imprisonment, when homeward bound, on board the Rebel Pirate Florida, by Mrs. H. Dwight Williams, with an Introductory Note by William Cullen Bryant.

1186. **Williams.** Life of Roger Williams, by William Gammill.

4296. **Williams.** Window Gardening; the Culture of Flowers and Ornamental Plants for Indoor Use and Parlor Decoration, by H. J. Williams.

1-6. **Wilkes.** Narrative of the United States Exploring Expedition, during the years 1838 to 1842, by Charles Wilkes, U. S. N., Commander of the Expedition. 1845.

1119-0. **Wilkinson.** A Popular Account of the ancient Egyptians, revised and abridged from his larger work, by Sir J. Gardner Wilkinson. 2 vols. 1854.

4455. **Wilson.** The Recreations of Christopher North, by John Wilson. 1854.

2911. **Wilson.** Hufeland's Art of Prolonging Life, edited by Erasmus Wilson. 1854.

2939. **Wilson.** The African Continent; a Narrative of Discovery and Adventure, by Hugh Murray, with an account of recent Exploring Expeditions, by John M. Wilson.

535. **Wilson.** Mexico and its Religion, with Incidents of Travel in that Country during part of the years 1851, '52, '53, and '54, and Historical Notices of Events connected with places visited, by Robert A. Wilson.

253. **Wilson.** American Ornithology, or the Natural History of the Birds of the United States, by Alexander Wilson, with notes by Jardine, to which is added a Synopsis of American Birds, including those described by Bonaparte, Audubon, Nuttall, Richardson, &c. 1854.

3935. **Wilson.** American Ornithology, or the Natural History of the Birds of the United States, with plates, by Alexander Wilson.

4626. **Wilson.** Western Africa; its History, Condition, and Prospects, by Rev. J. Leighton Wilson, eighteen years a Missionary in Africa, and now one of the Secretaries of the Presbyterian Board of Foreign Missions; with numerous Engravings.

769. **Wilson.** A New History of the Conquest of Mexico, in which Las Casas' denunciation of the popular Histories of that war are fully vindicated, by Robert Anderson Wilson.

2213. **Wilson.** Caliban; the Missing Link, by Daniel Wilson, LL. D.

3722. **Wilson.** The Recovery of Jerusalem; a Narrative of Exploration and Discovery in the City and the Holy Land, by Captain Wilson and others.

Witterveden. See Gibson.

1871. **Winchell.** Sketches of Creation; a popular View of some of the grand conclusions of the Sciences in reference to the History of Matter and of Life, &c., &c., by Alexander Winchell, LL. D. 1872.

10-1.   *Winkles.* Architectural and Picturesque Illustrations of the Cathedral Churches of England and Wales, &c. 2 vols. 1836.

773-4.   *Winthrop.* The History of New England, from 1630 to 1649, by John Winthrop, First Governor of the Colony of Massachusetts Bay. From his Original Manuscript. With Notes by James Savage. New edition. 2 vols.

1142.   *Winthrop.* The Canoe and the Saddle: Adventures among the Northwestern Rivers, and Forests, and Isthmania, by Theodore Winthrop.

1331.   *Wirt.* The Life of Patrick Henry, by William Wirt. 1831. See Thomas.

2915.   *Wirt.* The Letters of the British Spy, by William Wirt, Esq., to which is prefixed a Biographical Sketch of the Author.

1092-3.   *Wirt.* Memoir of the Life of William Wirt, Attorney-General of the United States, by J. P. Kennedy. 2 vols. 1851.

3725.   *Winslow.* Force and Nature; Attraction and Repulsion, the radical principle of Energy, discussed in relation to Physical and Morphological Developments, by C. F. Winslow. 1869.

4380.   *Wise.* The Young Man's Counsellor, or Sketches and Illustrations of the Duties and Dangers of Young Men, by Daniel Wise, M.A.

1520.   *Wise.* Seven Decades of the Union; the Humanitarian and Materialism Illustrated by a Memoir of John Tyler, with reminiscence of some of his great contemporaries, the Transition state of the Nation—its Dangers and their Remedy, by Henry A. Wise. 1872.

2207.   *Wister.* Countess Gazela, from the German of E. Marmlitt, by Mrs. L. Wister.

2303.   *Wister.* The Old Mam'selle's Secret, after the German of E. Marmlitt, by A. L. Wister.

2304.   *Wister.* Gold Elsie; from the German of E. Marmlitt, by A. L. Wister.

2233.   *Wister.* Why did he not Die; or the Child from the Ebraergang, after the German of A. Von Volckhausen, by A. L. Wister.

2289.   *Wister.* Only a Girl; or a Physician for the Soul; a Romance from the German, by A. L. Wister.

2257.   *Wister.* The Little Marland Princess; from the German of E. Marmlitt, by A. L. Wister.

2248.   *Witt.* Maria Derville; a Story of a French Boarding School; from the French of M. Guizotte De Witt, by M. G. Wells.

Women. See Crossland.

1483.   *Women.* Women of Worth; a Book for Girls.

Wonders. See Schodler.

1872.   *Wood.* Strange Dwellings, being a Description of the Habitations of Animals, by J. G. Wood.

1151.   *Wood.* Wandering Sketches of People and Things in South America, Polynesia, California, and other places visited during a Cruise on board the U. S. Ship Levant, &c., by W. M. Wood.

1757. *Wood.* The Mosaic History of the Creation of the World, illustrated by Discoveries and Experiments deduced from the present enlightened state of science, by Thomas Wood. 1831.

4018. *Wood.* Lectures on the Principles and Practice of Perspective, as delivered at the Royal Institution, illustrated by engravings, by J. G. Wood. 1844.

1345. *Wood.* Address at the Centennial Celebration of the Founding of the Pennsylvania Hospital, by G. B. Wood.

3805. *Wood.* Fankwei, or the San Jacinto in the Seas of India, China, and Japan, by William Maxwell Wood, M. D., U. S. N., late Surgeon of the Fleet to the United States East India Squadron, author of "Wandering Sketches in South America, Polynesia," &c., &c.

3723. *Wood.* Historical and Biographical Memoirs, Essays, Addresses, &c., written at various Times during the last Fifty Years, by G. B. Wood. 1872.

3719. *Wood.* A Dispensatory of the United States of America, by G. B. Wood and Franklin Bache. 1873.

3728. *Wood.* Homes without Hands, being a Description of Animals Classed according to their Principles of Construction, by J. G. Wood.

1940. *Wood.* Thermic Fever, or Sun Stroke, by H. C. Wood. The Boylston Prize Essay. 1872.

3718. *Wood.* Insects at Home, being a popular account of Insects, their Structure, Habits, and Transformation, by J. G. Wood. 1872.

2263. *Woodville.* Left to Herself, by J. Woodville.

607. *Woodward.* Graperies and Horticultural Buildings, by George E. & F. W. Woodward, Architects, &c.

534. *Woodward.* Country Homes, by G. E. & F. W. Woodward, Architects.

1944. *World.* The Old World seen with Young Eyes. 1871.

2513. *Wyatt.* The Poetical Works of Sir Thomas Wyatt, with a Memoir. 1854.

1869. *Wythe.* The Agreement of Science and Revelation, by Joseph H. Wythe, M. D. 1872.

Y.

239-0. *Yoakum.* History of Texas, from its first Settlement, in 1681, to its Annexation to the United States, in 1846, by H. Yoakum. 2 vols. 1856.

1868. *Yonge.* Three Centuries of English Literature, by Charles D. Yonge. 1872.

4582. *Youmans.* The Correlation and Conservation of Forces; a series of Exposition, by Professors Grove, Helmholtz, Mayer, Faraday, Liebig, and Carpenter, with an introduction and brief biographical notices of the chief promoters of new views, by E. L. Youmans.

4328.   *Youmans.* The Culture demanded by Modern Life, a Series of Addresses and Arguments on the Claims of Scientific Education, by E. L. Youmans.

4215.   *Young.* Chronicles of the First Planters of the Colony of Massachusetts Bay, from 1623 to 1646, now first collected from Original Records and Contemporaneous Manuscripts, and illustrated with Notes, by Alex. Young. 1846.

2919–0.   *Young.* The Poetical Works of Edward Young, in 2 vols. 1854.

Yucatan. See Stephens.

Z.

1431-2.   *Zell.* Zell's Popular Encyclopædia, a Universal Dictionary of the English Language, Science, Literature, and Art, by L. Colange. 1870. 2 vols.

Zoology. See Agassiz.

www.ingramcontent.com/pod-product-compliance
Lightning Source LLC
Chambersburg PA
CBHW030839270326
41928CB00007B/1132